W9-AUM-946

novel VOICES

Edited by Jennifer Levasseur & Kevin Rabalais

WRITER'S DIGEST BOOKS
CINCINNATI, OHIO
www.writersdigestbooks.com

Earlier versions of these interviews originally appeared in the following: *Brick* (Charles Johnson); *Five Points* (Melanie Rae Thon); *Glimmer Train Stories* (Richard Bausch, Andre Dubus, Stuart Dybek, Siri Hustvedt); *Hogtown Creek Review* (Elizabeth McCracken); *The Kenyon Review* (Richard Ford, William H. Gass); *Mississippi Review* (Tim Gautreaux); *The Missouri Review* (Ernest J. Gaines, Antonya Nelson); and *Sonora Review* (Valerie Martin). Ha Jin and Charles Baxter were originally published in *Tin House Magazine* in fall 2000 and spring 2001, respectively.

Photographs of Richard Bausch on page 4 and Andre Dubus on page 45 © Marion Ettlinger; Charles Baxter on page 19 © Paul Thacker / Ann Arbor, MI; Carrie Brown on page 36 © Jerry Bauer; Richard Ford on page 72 © Alain Mercier of Radio France; Ernest J. Gaines on page 91 © David G. Spielman 1997; Tim Gautreaux on page 114 © Winborne Gautreaux; William Gass on page 104 © Joe Angeles / Washington University in St. Louis; Siri Hustvedt on page 127 © Ben Watkins; Ha Jin on page 143 and Elizabeth McCracken on page 195 © Boston University Photo Services; Charles Johnson on page 157 © Inye Wokoma / *Colors NW Magazine*; Antonya Nelson on page 215 © Jack Parsons; Ann Patchett on page 231 © Carol Sternkopf; Melanie Rae Thon on page 245 © Karen Nichols; authors Jennifer Levasseur and Kevin Rabalais by Edward K. Newman

Novel Voices. Copyright © 2003 by Jennifer Levasseur and Kevin Rabalais. Manufactured in the United States of America. All rights reserved. No part of this book may be reproduced in any form or by any electronic or mechanical means including information storage and retrieval systems without permission in writing from the publisher, except by a reviewer, who may quote brief passages in a review. Published by Writer's Digest Books, an imprint of F&W Publications, Inc., 4700 East Galbraith Road, Cincinnati, OH 45236. (800) 289-0963. First edition.

Visit our Web site at www.writersdigest.com for information on more resources for writers.

To receive a free weekly e-mail newsletter delivering tips and updates about writing and about Writer's Digest products, register directly at our Web site at http://newsletters.fwpublications.com.

07 06 05 04 03 5 4 3 2 1

Library of Congress Cataloging-in-Publication Data

Levasseur, Jennifer and Rabalais, Kevin
Novel voices: 17 award winning novelists on how to write, edit, and get published / edited by Jennifer Levasseur & Kevin Rabalais.—1st ed.
p. cm.
Includes Index
ISBN 1-58297-247-8 (alk. paper) ISBN 1-58297-245-1 (pbk.: alk. paper)
1. Fiction—Authorship. 2. American fiction—20th century—History and criticism—Theory, etc. 3. Novelists, American—20th century—Interviews. I. Levasseur, Jennifer. II. Rabalais, Kevin.

PN3355.N688 2003
808.3—dc21 2003041190
CIP

Edited by Donya Dickerson, Rachel Vater
Cover design by Lisa Buchanan
Interior design by Sandy Conopeotis Kent
Production coordinated by Michelle Ruberg

Acknowledgments

We would like to thank the following people for their support: Rhoda Faust and everyone at Maple Street Book Shop in New Orleans, Raymond Schroth, S.J., John Biguenet, Chris Wiltz, Ralph Adamo, J. Michael Kenny, Joseph Cohen, Tom Piazza, Michael Martin and Elisa Maranzana, Linda Swanson-Davies and Susan Burmeister-Brown, Holly MacArthur, Evelyn Somers, David H. Lynn, Thomas Bigelow, Michael Redhill, Andrew Horton, R.C. Davis-Undiano, David Clark, Richard Lawrence and the Eaton Literary Agency, Donya Dickerson, Rachel Vater, Kelly Nickell, and our parents, Terry and Susan Levasseur, and Rodney and Wanda Rabalais. Most importantly, many thanks to the authors included in this collection.

About the Authors

Jennifer Levasseur graduated from Loyola University New Orleans and completed an M.A. in creative writing from the International Institute of Modern Letters at Victoria University of Wellington, New Zealand. She is at work on a novel.

Kevin Rabalais was born in Bunkie, Louisiana. He received an M.A. in literature from Victoria University and teaches English in New Orleans.

Table of Contents

introduction

When we visited Andre Dubus in his home in the summer of 1998, he answered the door with only a hand towel covering his lap, having just completed an afternoon swim. He welcomed us inside, wheeled himself to another room to throw on some clothes, then returned to us so we could begin our conversation while he snacked on a shrimp cocktail.

As we look back over our experiences with the writers interviewed in this collection, this image of Andre Dubus sparsely clothed in his wheelchair, unashamed to expose himself, is the one that resonates. Not all the authors met us at the door this way—in fact, no one else did—but when we met them in restaurants, hotels, offices, or their homes, they all opened themselves to us in surprising ways. In the middle of an Oklahoma thunderstorm, Ha Jin expressed his feelings of camaraderie with the long-dead masters of literature. Richard Bausch and Charles Baxter took us on car tours of the places that inspire their fictional settings. Tim Gautreaux joined us for po'boys at one of his hangouts, a place that seemed to spring from the pages of his fiction. Elizabeth McCracken took us along to pick up her dry cleaning. We drove to the airport with Ann Patchett's dog perched on our laps.

When we decided to approach some of our favorite writers for interviews, we anticipated these moments of disclosure. Not only did we expect writers to agree to the interviews, we also had no doubt that they would tell us everything. Our naïveté paid off. They told us about their failures (abandoned novels, bad reviews, poor sales) and successes (book deals, respect from their peers, prizes and recognition). Only now do we truly realize how generous these writers were to have allowed us to briefly enter their personal lives.

The responses we received from writers were almost unfailingly encouraging, even from the ones who declined meetings. It didn't take long before we realized that successful, published writers are people who are more like us than they are different. Though they create magic on the page, theirs is a job like many others.

Before we accepted this fact, we wanted writers to tell us firsthand how they read, commit themselves to their work, find their ideas, edit their writing, teach this craft to others, find agents and publishers for their work. We wanted them to slip us all the secrets. Through the course of these conversations, we learned that there are no tricks—no easy formulas that will work for each person, no simple right or wrong answers—and each voice in this collection is a testament that the creative process must be individually mapped.

The writers in this collection often have more differences than they have similarities. They range from William H. Gass, one of the elder statesmen of metafiction, and Ernest J. Gaines, a founding member of the Fellowship of Southern Writers, to Melanie Rae Thon and Elizabeth McCracken, both chosen by *Granta* as Best Young American Novelists.

To prepare for the interviews, we read each writer's body of work, researched, and prepared questions. We then spent several hours with the writer, except for Stuart Dybek and Carrie Brown, with whom we corresponded by phone, mail, and e-mail. We transcribed our conversations and invited the writers to view the transcripts to add or clarify any points. Some changed a word or two; others methodically expanded their comments. Some, notably

Melanie Rae Thon, became so involved in this stage that we continued to correspond and add to the interview for many months.

We traveled from our home in New Orleans to Washington, DC; Seattle; Las Cruces, New Mexico; Norman, Oklahoma; Columbus, Ohio; Haverhill and Boston, Massachusetts; Lafayette and Hammond, Louisiana; Brooklyn; Nashville, Tennessee; and Ann Arbor, Michigan. After our first few meetings, we quickly discovered the key point of a book of interviews with American novelists: Each has his own working methods, and a collection of these thoughts provides an opportunity for writers and readers to learn more about the craft of fiction and getting published. Each time we met with a writer, he or she told us something different, often in opposition to what the last writer said. These juxtapositions became liberating and reminded us that there are no secrets to writing fiction. However, in these seventeen talented authors, we found experienced guides who can help writers find their own styles and develop their own methods.

Now, instead of looking at these writers as phenomena, we can take them for what they really are: talented, driven people who took risks, profited from them, and are now willing to share everything they learned the hard way. Their mistakes don't have to be ours. Their failures can be a comfort; their successes, something concrete to aspire to.

In the introduction to John Gardner's *On Becoming a Novelist*, Raymond Carver wrote, "A young writer certainly needs as much, I would even say more, encouragement than young people trying to enter other professions." In that same book, Gardner reminds us that his thoughts on craft are only "one writer's opinion." *Novel Voices* offers seventeen diverse views. These conversations have the same effect as a good creative writing workshop: They make us want to stop whatever we're doing and write.

We hope that these interviews are an inspiration to writers, that they are useful to teachers of creative writing, and that readers will enjoy the ideas presented by this selection of America's great novelists.

walking the path

RICHARD BAUSCH

The late, celebrated story writer Andre Dubus once said of Richard Bausch's fiction, "If only I could write a story *that* good." The story he spoke of—"What Feels Like the World"—explores a man's relationship with his overweight granddaughter who struggles to perform gymnastics for an audience.

Domestic issues like this recur in Bausch's work. His fiction illuminates everyday human relationships—a husband and wife talking on a typical afternoon, a father and daughter arguing on the phone. When asked about his fiction, Bausch says that he takes characters whom he loves and visits trouble upon them.

Born in Fort Benning, Georgia, on April 18, 1945, Bausch worked several jobs before becoming a full-time writer and teacher. He served in the Air Force and spent time as a stand-up comedian and songwriter. He attended Northern Virginia Community College and George Mason University (where he now teaches), and he received an M.F.A. from the Iowa Writers' Workshop.

His fiction has earned many awards, including an American Academy of Arts and Letters Award in Literature, a Guggenheim Fellowship, and PEN/Faulkner nominations for *Take Me Back* and *Spirits and Other Stories*. The Modern Library's editorial board chose him as one of the most important writers of the twentieth century. He is a member of the Fellowship of Southern Writers, which was founded in 1987 by twenty-six distinguished Southern authors, including Robert Penn Warren, Eudora Welty, Ernest J. Gaines, and Walker Percy.

Aside from publishing nine novels and numerous stories, Bausch has contributed to the compilation novel *The Putt at the End of the World* and edited *The Cry of an Occasion: Stories From the Fellowship of Southern Writers*. His novel *The Last Good Time* was adapted for film in 1995.

The father of five children, Bausch lives with his wife, Karen, and their family in Virginia.

Books by Richard Bausch

Real Presence (novel), The Dial Press, 1980

Take Me Back (novel), The Dial Press, 1981

The Last Good Time (novel), The Dial Press/Doubleday, 1984

Spirits and Other Stories (stories), Simon & Schuster, 1987

Mr. Field's Daughter (novel), Simon & Schuster, 1989

The Fireman's Wife and Other Stories (stories), Simon & Schuster, 1990

Violence (novel), Houghton Mifflin/Seymour Lawrence, 1992

Rebel Powers (novel), Houghton Mifflin/Seymour Lawrence, 1993

Rare and Endangered Species (stories), Houghton Mifflin/Seymour Lawrence, 1994

Aren't You Happy for Me? (stories), Macmillan Paperback First, 1995

The Selected Stories of Richard Bausch, Modern Library, 1996

Good Evening Mr. and Mrs. America, and All the Ships at Sea (novel), HarperCollins, 1996

In the Night Season (novel), HarperFlamingo, 1998

Someone to Watch Over Me (stories), HarperFlamingo, 1999

Hello to the Cannibals (novel), HarperCollins, 2002

You've written many novels and collections of stories. In which form do you feel more comfortable?

I always feel, as the writer William Maxwell said, that there must be somebody better able, more prepared to do this. Whatever I happen to be writing at the time feels like what I should be working on. Sometimes I say that stories are more fun because I happen to be working on a novel that's killing me. When I wrote *Rebel Powers*, every aspect was fun. I never had to use an alarm clock. There was a big shadow of the house on the lawn, and I knew that by the time I was through with that day's work, the shadow would be on the other side of the house. I would go sit on the porch after having worked all morning and play guitar. It felt so good that I didn't want to finish the book. But I always feel like I'm not good enough for whatever story I'm trying to write.

Which novel troubled you?

Mr. Field's Daughter about killed me. It had nothing to do with the darks, the depths I was exploring. It was just intractable work, and I couldn't figure out the structure. At times, the real battle had to do with my attitude toward it. It has to be, to me, more than the cold application of skill. And that's all it was for the longest time—craftily putting this novel together. My heart wasn't engaged. It wasn't until I started writing the chapters where the characters address the reader in present time that I became interested.

How do you feel about it now?

I'm rather proud of it. I'm especially happy with the complicated structure and use of time that none of the critics noticed. I was still reading reviews back then.

You don't read reviews anymore?

Right before *Violence* came out, I decided not to read them. I wish I could say that integrity caused me to stop, but it was mortal fear. I had written a book about domestic violence, and I was afraid the critics would derail me. That book was line-by-line awfully scary. I said, "I'll wait until it's all over and then read the reviews." The book came out in January, and I toured all over the country with it. I remember, that summer, thinking, "Well, it's July. I can read the reviews now." The book's history was mostly over by that time, and it didn't matter anymore. I knew it would feel like reading old news.

What are your expectations for your work?

I want to write. I would like the market to be good enough, the sales good enough, that I could just keep doing what I'm doing. I don't want to buy a yacht. As long as I'm allowed to write, I'll be happy. You work with the knowledge and expectation that whatever you do will probably disappear with you. But it's a dignified way of spending your time. I don't think anybody has a right to expect anything more than that. When I'm tempted to, I think about aeons and stars. When the sun dies, it's all going away no matter what we wrote or how long we're remembered. You provide something now to make your life meaningful and to feel like you've done your job. You showed up for work in the mornings, as Norman Mailer [*The Armies of the Night*] put it.

How do you distinguish ideas for novels from those of short stories?

Sometimes that's hard. I thought *Rebel Powers* was a ten-page story, but it ended up as a novel. I thought *Real Presence* was a novella, but it also became a novel. I was pretty sure *Take Me Back, The Last Good Time,* and *Good Evening Mr. and Mrs. America, and All the Ships at Sea* were all novels from the start, and they stayed that way. My new novel, *Hello to the Cannibals*, is about friendship that takes place across time and the grave. This friendship—a spiritual relation, call it—between two women is separated by a century: my made-up character, Lily Austin, who is graduating from college at the end of this century, and a historical person, the British explorer Mary Kingsley, who died in 1900. I didn't know how it was all going to work out. I found it out by writing. I don't know much about a story when I start, and I am usually surprised by where it goes. In fact, if it doesn't surprise me, I'm suspicious of it.

I don't know much about a story when I start, and I am usually surprised by where it goes. In fact, if it doesn't surprise me, I'm suspicious of it.

Do you become close to your characters?

Oh, yeah, all of them. I understand perfectly that they are made-up constructions, but it's like when you were a kid and had imaginary friends. You see with their eyes, and you have some of their memories, which is a wonderful thing. Mary Lee Settle [*The Killing Ground*] talks about her characters like it's gossip. I picked some of that up from her. But I really don't know how it works. It just comes with the character, thinking about it, dreaming it up.

Is there a particular character who has stuck with you?

The characters who stay with me the longest are the ones I write about again. The couple in "The Fireman's Wife" appear again—although they're not quite identifiable—in the novella "Rare and Endangered Species," and they also show up in "Evening" as a fractious couple. I always want to put another face or another name on them because I don't want readers to think they're reading about the same characters all the time.

It's been said that your writing—especially your characterization—blends the best of women's and men's writing.

I'm proud of that. I have women come up to me all the time and ask me how I know things. The answer is simple. What you do is think, first, of a *person,* and then write. I learned that with my first novel when I was writing about a priest. I was trying to figure out what a priest would do or say. You have to be honest and open to the experience and be whoever this person is and feel whatever he feels. Fiction is empathy. It is trying to feel like somebody else. It is getting into other people's minds without regard to sex, ethnic makeup, race, or color. It upsets me when people deny this real and occasional—by that I mean *casual, common*—operation of the writer's task. That shows how little they have read in the world's literature. Either they haven't read it, or they haven't been up to it.

You are Southern by birth, but your work hasn't been received as traditional Southern fiction.

You would get arguments from a lot of people about that. Other Southern writers spend a lot of time writing about place. My landscape is interior. I find terrain less interesting than psychology. There are writers who can do the terrain and the psychology. I'm not shortchanging those writers. For me, it's not all that interesting. I've traveled all over, and it's just land, rocks, and mountains. I like the appellation "Southern" mostly because of who else is Southern: George Garrett, Mary Lee Settle, Allen Wier, Richard Ford, Barry Hannah, Josephine Humphreys, Ellen Douglas, Lee Smith, Jill McCorkle, Madison Smartt Bell, my brother Robert, Shelby Foote, Ernest Gaines, Eudora Welty. Richard Ford has said he doesn't want to be known as a "Southern" writer, but he's really talking about being regionalized as a writer, and I don't want to be regionalized, either. As he put it once, "I'm writing for everybody who can read, but I don't mind being from the South."

My concerns are in some respects traditionally Southern. With *In the Night Season*, I deal with race. I'm exhausted with the way this country obsesses about race. And, of course, every day, people make it matter more than it should, on both sides.

Is Bishop from *In the Night Season* your ideal American? He doesn't really think of himself as a black man. He tries to avoid issues of race all his life.

Bishop's feelings are a lot like mine. I've known folks who've felt this way a long time. You and I can walk out on the street and be anybody. A black person walks out on the street, and he is a black person. If you go to Harlem, you get some feeling of how that is. You're a white person, and you can feel it. You can feel what it's like to be looked at that way, and it ain't fun. Bishop's idea is what I hope for. It's too bad he had to die.

His death early in the novel throws out the reader's expectations.

It's ironic because the death of Bishop is not a race crime. "We're equal opportunity criminals," one of the killers says. When you write a plot-heavy book like that, the events can't be arbitrary. But I had no idea how the book was going to end. It took me three days to figure out whether the boy in the novel lives. And when he did live, it wasn't resonant enough. I went away from it for a while and wrote a couple of stories. When I went back, I realized the sheriff had to have lost a child, too. So I had to go through and re-earn the whole novel. It took about two months of going through and rewriting everything just to make that one moment resonate. I like to tell new writers about that experience because you have to be willing to take great pain to make it work, to make it work better.

There is a lot of violence in your work. Is this what you, as a social observer, see in our society?

Fiction is about trouble. I make up characters who are decent or who are trying to be decent, and I add trouble. The more the better. There are plenty of good villains in fiction, and if you hold yourself to making everybody right, you end up writing a mushy California-everybody-is-sweet sort of thing. The older I get, the more inclined I am to explore some of that evil. Another side of me wants to write about light as wonderfully as William Maxwell has, to write a story in which you feel suffused in light—to say, "My God, this light has just been turned on in my soul, and I'll never be the same." Maxwell's story "The Thistles in Sweden" is like that. At the end, he says, "I think if it is true that we are all in the hands of God, what a capacious hand it must be." It's just beautiful.

How important is the sentence?

It's everything. Many new writers have trouble understanding that. If you can't make the sentence, forget it. If you can write one good sentence, then you can write another one, then another one. I hate it when people say, "In poetry, you have to pay attention to every word, and in short stories you have to pay attention to every sentence, and in novels, you can ramble." A novel is written word by word, sentence by sentence, if you are any good at all. Some mornings I don't write any more than a page. Today I got about a page and a half. That's fine, a day's work.

Who are some of the writers you continue to learn from?

Tolstoy, Chekhov, the Russians. You can learn how to write everything you'll ever write by reading Tolstoy's novels. I believe Shakespeare was the greatest dramatist and poet, and Tolstoy was the greatest fiction writer. And you know, Tolstoy hated Shakespeare, thought he was too dirty minded. I would love to know what Shakespeare would have thought of Tolstoy. He probably would have found him too prissy.

Are you an avid reader?

You can't do this and *not* be. I don't think anybody who writes books isn't an obsessive reader. I read some books every year. I've read *The Great Gatsby* about thirty-five times. I've read *War and Peace* four times. Consequently, I'm not as up on what's contemporary. I keep up with my friends, which is a large and productive group of writers.

In 1997, you were inducted into the Fellowship of Southern Writers. What is the importance of a community of writers?

It's absolutely the best. It's crucial. I like writing programs because they form that kind of community early. Allan Gurganus [*Oldest Living Confederate Widow Tells All*] and I were at Iowa together, and we have had a blessed friendship that I wouldn't trade for anything. I know he is out there doing it. I don't talk as often to Jane Smiley [*Horse Heaven*],

Richard Bausch on Editing

Does anyone read your work before it's complete?

I read every day's work to my wife, Karen. She sits behind me in a chair. Her response is visceral. It's either involved or it isn't, and if it isn't, I have to be attentive to that. People say my prose is spare. I have a listener who wants the story; she doesn't want anything in the way. As a writer I like to be effaced. I'd like the words themselves to disappear so that it's just the reader and my characters. But, as a reader, I sometimes like to feel the presence of the author. I like Dickens and the overblown, lush passages of Faulkner. I just don't want to do it myself.

From there, what is your editing process?

I read from the beginning of a book or story to where I am each day. I read it and read it and read it. That's why I don't read reviews anymore. I've written these books so many thousands of times that by the time a review comes out, there is nothing the reviewer knows about it after one reading that I don't know about it in spades.

What is your favorite part of the editing process?

Going over the galleys for the last time. Tinkering with phrases, catching tics and unconscious repetitions that one simply never sees until one is looking at print.

How do you handle editorial suggestions that you don't agree with?

I have always been extremely fortunate where editors are concerned: Larry Michelotti; Alan Peacock; Fran McCullough; Camille Hykes (Sam Lawrence's literary editor—a beautiful woman with perfect pitch); the late and beloved Robert Jones, who happened also to be a wondrously good writer; and presently Dan Conaway, who inherited my large manuscript for *Hello to the Cannibals* and had a whole lot to do with the final shape and form of the book. He's a sharp and sympathetic reader, and as understanding a friend as I have ever worked with. With all these fine people, I have either agreed (roughly 80 percent of the time) or disagreed, in which case I've either insisted on it as it is or found a third way that everybody could live with.

When did you get your first publishing break?

I sold *Real Presence,* luckily, nine days after I sent it to my agent, Harriet Wasserman.

How did you find your agent?

Gordon Lish, when he was running *Esquire* magazine, liked a story of mine and sent it to her. He said in a note to me that he "trusted" I would not feel abused by that. I didn't, and I still owe him for it.

but she was a classmate and over the years I've kept up with her. Some days, I wake up and feel like slumping off, and then I say, "No. Jane's working. Allan's working."

How did you start writing "All the Way in Flagstaff, Arizona"?

That story was a later chapter in a failed novel. It started the whole ball rolling in selling stories to the magazines. I wouldn't have even sent it out except I had to have something to give a reading. I thought, well, if I'm going to give a reading, I'm going to put some laughs in. So I created the picnic scene. Originally, the story was in the form of a letter the father writes to his sister and says, "I knew I had trouble with drinking when I was playing with the kids and realized they were afraid of me."

Richard Bausch on Generating Story Ideas

How do you find subjects for your work?

Most of the time they find me. They *occur* to me in the flow of experience. "Aren't You Happy for Me?" came about when I was watching the Steve Martin remake of *Father of the Bride.* In the movie, the groom is going to be a world-class geophysicist or something. But what if there was something really hard? What if the girl was calling her father to tell him she's marrying someone old enough to be his father? And then she's pregnant—the whole thing of adding trouble. What if the father's splitting up with her mother? It sort of wrote itself. It took about three days to write from beginning to end.

What kind of exercise was it to write your story, "Nobody in Hollywood," which was chosen for *The Best American Short Stories 1997*? You said that you and a former student came up with a first sentence, "I was pummeled as a teenager," and then bet on who would finish the story first.

The "pummeled" thing was fun. Peter Taylor [*A Summons to Memphis*] had received a student's story with the opening line, "He would have no more of her drunken palaver." Someone said to him, "Even you, as talented as you are, couldn't write a story with that as an opening line." So he took the bet and wrote "The Fancy Woman," the opening line of which is "He would have no more of her drunken palaver."

Later, Steve Amick said something funny and I said, "You were beat up as a teenager," and he said, "Yeah, I was pummeled." We started laughing. I think he was the one who said, "We ought to do that Taylor thing; we ought to try to write a story from that line." So we did. As I say in that note in *The Best American Short Stories,* he finished first. He wrote a funny story called "Fat Tracy."

What are some other idea generators you've used?

I sometimes tell students "Here is an opening line; write a story about it: 'I kicked him in the stomach; it was like being in church.' " And they love it. I steal some from John Gardner [*The Art of Fiction*], who was good at this. One exercise is to describe a field of flowers from the point of view of somebody who is about to kill a child. Or try to deliver a situation through dialogue only.

Like your story "Aren't You Happy for Me?"

And I have another story called "The Murmur From the Other Room." It's two voices in a motel room. There's not one line of description. When one of the people doesn't speak, there's an ellipsis on the line where that person would have spoken. It's as if you've got your ear against the wall. There are other exercises: Create a town, give it a social history. I have my students imitate a Hemingway passage, for instance, "What if she should die?" They have to write the passage, but they can't use the word "die."

Have you ever abandoned a novel or story?

I've written four novels—and God knows how many stories—that I never let out of the house. But I'm stubborn. There's a story called "Where Is John Wayne?" that never worked. I wrote it forty-seven times with a flare pen, and I don't know how many times I typed it.

As I wrote that, I realized the reader has to see that scene. So I wrote it and put some comedy in it.

You've talked about how many good short stories there are today. Why do you think the audience for them is small?

The population of active readers has traditionally been relatively small.

And the story requires *plenty* of attention, a deeper kind of attention, I think. Especially good stories. The real matter of the short story requires attention some people aren't willing to give. Sometimes, too, life is stressful and there's so much going on. So the average person—hell, anybody, everybody—says, "I want it done *for* me; I want my emotional responses to be passive, and I don't want to have to invest anything of myself in order to be entertained." This is true especially now that we have this sense-drug, television, blaring at us. I think television is one of the great mistakes in the history of human civilization. It has harmed our ability to concentrate and our ability to be empathetic.

What do you think you've learned most about your own writing through teaching writing?

To be shrewd in decisions. Whatever vision you have at first will not change. Your ability to tap into it can be increased. That involves work and keeping regular work habits, especially in the beginning. I think the most important thing I've learned is to be open to all the different ways of doing things, to try not to tell someone what he should do in a story. I try to treat students like real writers, encourage them, take them seriously. That's what Vance Bourjaily did for me at Iowa.

Everybody always has to contend with doubt. If you learn how to use that doubt to make yourself more careful, to help you revise, then that can lead to good things. The other thing is not to think about publishing, not to worry about it. Try just to write; good things will come.

Every time I sit down, I have to learn all over again. I make the same mistakes I made when I first started.

Because of that, do you find yourself unwilling to criticize new writers?

I always try to tell them things that will keep them going, to find ways to encourage, even when what is given to me is terrible, because I remember that I was terrible. For everything I've published, there are twenty pieces that never worked. I tell them I'm never talking about their talent; I'm only talking about this one piece of work. I understand how doubt feels.

There's something that feels selfish about this arduous occupation. But you have to understand that it's not an indulgence. If you have any gift for it, it is an obligation. Indulgences are what you give up to do it. You don't give up your family. You don't give up being kind. You don't give up being a person in the world. You give up the party, television, or whatever. I know every corner of how that feels. I tell them, "This is normal. If you're not scared, there's something wrong with you. Your talent will be tested, and you have to be willing to accept failure as a part of this." You say, "I accept failure as my destiny" the same way you say, "I accept death as my destiny."

You wait to hear that voice say, "You are a writer." And it has to be another writer saying it. It can't be a family member, although that's good, too. I remember my sister saying, "I can't believe it. My own brother's a poet." It felt so good. I was eighteen years old. I walked around for days thinking, "I'm a poet."

How does the time-consuming and often solitary occupation of writing affect your relationship with your family?

I made up my mind when I was young and starting out that living came first. I was never going to go to a colony and write, and I never have. I believed that I should be up to my elbows in life if I was going to write about it. I wasn't going to deny myself any of that. We didn't have any money, and I didn't have a job, and we still wanted to have children. I trained myself early to work in confusing circumstances with lots of things happening. I've written with babies sleeping on my chest. Once, I was typing something and I had my daughter Maggie on my lap. I felt this cold something, and I realized she had fallen asleep and was drooling. So I laid her down and went back to work. I leave the door open so the kids can come in any time they want.

I don't believe that when I think of something to say, I have to get it down or it'll escape into oblivion. If it's really good and if it matters enough, it'll surface again, maybe in a better way than I originally thought of it. I used to write from about midnight to two or three in the morning. I would read for an hour or two before drifting off to sleep. Now I try to work in the mornings and then forget about it, do whatever it is I do all day.

You've shown real stamina in your career—nine novels, five collections of stories. Do you see yourself ever concentrating on one form?

I hope it will always be both. I'd like to write twenty novels and books of stories. I don't think of writing as hauling things out of myself, like drilling oil from a well. It's a path I walk. In fact, I'm convinced that's the secret. If you think of yourself as *containing* the material, then everything becomes limited by what you can hold. But if it's a path you're taking—hell, you can go *anywhere*, right? So, when I sit down to write, I'm thinking about going somewhere, walking around and seeing what I find. And there's never a time when I sit down and it isn't there. You just walk the path. I never worry about whether it's good. I'm walking the path. I know that if I can bring enough attention to it and be honest and open to it and not cheat it, it'll be fine.

I love the writer William Stafford's advice. Someone asked him, "What do you do about writer's block?" Stafford said, "Lower my standards and keep on going." That's such beautiful advice. What you get done doesn't have to do with how gifted you are or how much ability you have; it has to do with *your own attitude toward it.* If your attitude is "This is my work; this is what I do every day, and I don't have any expectations except that I will have worked today," then you will get a tremendous amount done. Some of it will be good. Some of it won't be so good. But you're showing up for work, putting in the hours. And, anyway, perfection is an illusion. I don't teach writing. I teach patience and toughness, stubbornness and willingness to make the mistakes and go on. And the willingness to look like an idiot sometimes. That's the only way any good thing ever gets done.

recognizing the ordinary

CHARLES BAXTER

Charles Baxter is a master of the mundane. His writing explores the everyday events that ordinary people face: the emotional consequences a man experiences throughout his life because of a childhood promise; the inability of a person to feel at home or at peace in a new setting; the daily struggle of a single mother.

Though Baxter is best known for his short stories, novels, and essays on fiction, he began his writing career as a poet. Born in Minneapolis in 1947, he published his first book of poetry, *Chameleon*, in 1970. Another collection, *The South Dakota Guidebook*, quickly followed. From the first appearances of his fiction, Baxter received praise for his eloquent voice and wise, truthful rendering of characters.

His first collection of fiction, *Harmony of the World*, received the Associated Writing Programs Award for Short Fiction judged by Donald Barthelme. Baxter prepared *Burning Down the House*, essays on fiction, as a series of lectures for his M.F.A. students at Warren Wilson College. *The Feast of Love* is his ambitious novel that chronicles the love lives of several connected first-person narrators. It was a finalist for the 2000 National

Book Award. He is a recipient of a fellowship from the National Endowment for the Arts and has been honored with an American Academy of Arts and Letters Award in Literature.

Baxter teaches creative writing at the University of Michigan in Ann Arbor, where he lives with his wife, Martha.

Books by Charles Baxter

Chameleon (poems), New Rivers Press, 1970

The South Dakota Guidebook (poems), New Rivers Press, 1974

Harmony of the World (stories), University of Missouri Press, 1984

Through the Safety Net (stories), Viking Press, 1985

First Light (novel), Viking Press, 1987

Imaginary Paintings and Other Poems (poems), Paris Review Editions, 1989

A Relative Stranger (stories), Norton, 1990

Shadow Play (novel), Norton, 1993

Believers (stories), Pantheon Books, 1997

Burning Down the House (essays), Graywolf Press, 1997

The Feast of Love (novel), Pantheon Books, 2000

You've said that you began to write fiction when you lost the knowledge of how to write poetry. What were you not able to do in verse that you thought you could achieve in prose?

When I started to write fiction, I wasn't interested in character or characterization the way I was in verbal textures. As a graduate student, I studied modernist novels, like Djuna Barnes's *Nightwood* and Malcolm Lowry's *Under the Volcano,* which are sentence-driven at least as much as they are character-driven. I emulated those books, but the fiction I wrote as a result didn't do what I wanted, and I couldn't figure out why. It may seem as if I moved from poetry to fiction because there wasn't room for the expansion of characterization in poetry, but that's not true because I wasn't working with characterization in fiction in those days, either. Between 1974 and 1984, when *Harmony of the World* appeared, I discovered that I couldn't write fiction without learning some basic rules of characterization. Purely language-driven fiction did not work for me. I thought the fiction I first wrote had characters in it, but when I look at it now—on those days when I can bear to look at it—the first thing I see is that there are none.

What do you find in your early fiction?

There's a visionary world powered by great anxiety and a manic exuberance. There are nightmarish features. Pasteboard figures wander through a world of excluded middles in cartoonish ways. When I wrote those stories, I thought I had many wonderful sentences that stood on their own.

What moved you from language-driven to character-driven fiction?

My first ambition in this regard was to be less ambitious. I thought that since these grand schemes I had for brilliant visionary writing had turned out to be neither brilliant nor visionary, I had better do something else. The stories that I wrote as a consequence, those collected in *Harmony of the World*, are closely observed stories of the sort of characters whom I knew, people I had met in my twenties and early thirties in Minnesota, Michigan, and western New York. When I sat down at the typewriter, I thought, "I'm not going to try to storm the heavens with this." I tried to put recognizable people onto the page: old Polish-American piano teachers; young women with unhappy love lives. I set myself a goal of what I call "recognizability," and that means simply that I paid more attention to visual detail and the actions a character takes under conditions of stress. I also was attentive to the ways people talked, which I had never spent a minute on before. I tried to write prose that was not grand but serviceable.

I tried to put recognizable people onto the page: old Polish-American piano teachers; young women with unhappy love lives.

Do the stories and novels now begin for you with character?

All of it is character-driven now. I start with the characters and have some fairly clear intuitions about what the plot will be, but that's secondary.

Before you begin to write, how long do you spend getting to know your characters?

I spend months on that, mostly daydreaming my way through it. It varies, depending on who shows up in the story. For instance, when I started writing *The Feast of Love*, I thought Chloé would be comic relief, that she would serve as a minor character who brightens things up when the reader has gotten tired of Bradley, Diana, Harry Ginsberg, and the rest of that crew. But she had so much energy that, almost from the moment she came in, she hijacked the novel. Her voice caught me completely by surprise. It was a happy occasion for me. The first sentence of her first chapter came into my head, and I thought, "Who is this person?"

All the first-person voices in *The Feast of Love* are distinct and immediately recognizable. How did you manage the multiple first-person voices?

I thought that if I did my job, the reader would know almost immediately who is speaking, just the way that if the phone rings late at night and you answer it and it's someone you know, you recognize the person's voice usually within the first few words. I didn't want to head each chapter with the narrator's name. That would be a failure of craft.

I thought that if I did my job, the reader would know almost immediately who is speaking, just the way that if the phone rings late at night and you answer it and it's someone you know, you recognize the person's voice usually within the first few words.

And when I'm in the dreamworld of the book, these people are as real to me as people in my own life. When I finished one chapter, let's say a chapter with Chloé, and I was moving over to Harry or Bradley, I thought, "OK, what's Harry saying today? What's Bradley worrying about this time?" I can't explain exactly how I kept them distinct, but I never forgot them or how they talked. If I needed a reminder, I would go back and read an earlier chapter. That was all I had to do, except in the early parts of the book when I first started to write in Bradley's voice. I had made him too acidic, too gruff. As I wrote more of him, I looked back at earlier material and thought, "That's not Bradley; he wouldn't say that." I toned him down in the revisions.

Did writing *The Feast of Love* seem like you were writing several first-person novels? Was it more difficult than writing a book with a single narrator?

The book was not more difficult to write because of all the first-person narrators. It is the first novel I wrote using first person, and I loved—just loved—doing that. It felt like a great liberation. From a technical point of view, it was not any more difficult to write than *First Light* or *Shadow Play*. The only difficulty I had was getting the voices and the tone of the novel right in the first place. I thought Diana and David would be the main characters. What I assembled with those two was something dark, obsessive, erotic, and serious. But that was not the novel I wanted to write. And so I got stuck, and I didn't get free of that until one Saturday morning when I was reading a magazine. Bradley's voice came to me in this phrase, which now serves as the opening of chapter nine of the novel: "Sometimes I feel as if my life is a murder mystery, only I haven't been murdered yet, and I don't plan on being murdered at all, of course." That's what the novel needed, something that was comic and serious at the same time. The novel was never easy—it took five years to write—but once I had that, I could write it.

Was the Charlie Baxter character, who ties all the narratives together in *The Feast of Love*, always part of the novel?

Including that character was not always part of the plan. I had all these first-person accounts of happy or unhappy love lives, and I needed a structure to hold the accounts into some kind of shape and solution. If I didn't explain where these voices were coming from and how we could hear them, the book would seem even more episodic than it is. That is when I decided to use a metafictional device of a narrator, Charlie Baxter, who goes out into the streets of Ann Arbor to collect stories. I didn't think it was particularly wild or experimental. It's actually an ancient way to structure a story. You can find a lot of precedent for this device. Some of the reviewers seemed quite shocked that there is a character named Charlie Baxter, but it is incredibly naive to think that this character is me. It testifies to a certain lack of sophistication among readers to believe that just because I say there is a mirror at the bottom of the stairs in his house that doesn't reflect anymore, that in my house there is such a mirror.

The problem in that book that had to be solved was that people don't just talk about their love lives to anybody; it's private. Even though there's a rupture between the public and private now—particularly with TV shows that make entertainment of the intimate details of regular people's lives—I still had to explain the origin of these voices. I needed a character people would trust enough in order to reveal themselves. Once the reader gets used to the openness and honesty of the characters, I could eliminate Charlie from the mixture and let the story tell itself.

It has surprised me how taken aback some reviewers are by the Charlie Baxter character. They think I've radically broken some rules. They're quite shocked, and I'm shocked that they're shocked.

Do you think readers react this way because they want to locate the author in the novel?

Readers are fascinated by autobiography, and it may be because mass media encourage a culture of scandal and personal revelation. It seems increasingly common that the readership in this country—maybe because of the rise of confusion between public and private—look at a text and say, "The writer must be here." We're trained to go after the personal. For me, one of the great pleasures of reading fiction is getting out of the writer and into a different world. I'm not in the business of self-expression anymore, if I ever was. I try to get onto the page people who are not really like me but whom I can imagine into life. I'm bored with myself. Chloé and Harry are both much more interesting than I am.

In many ways, *The Feast of Love* is about breaking the rules of fiction. The character Bradley even tells Charlie that he can't start his novel, also titled *The Feast of Love*, with a character waking up, which is how your novel begins.

Some reviewers have taken me to task for breaking that rule. Some creative writing teachers tell students, "Don't start a story with a character waking up in bed," but it's by no means a universal rule.

In *First Light*, you also break narrative rules by telling the story backward, beginning with a brother and sister at middle age and following them to the sister's birth. What prompted you to explore this structure?

I was reading a book on twentieth-century British literature, and there was a reference to a novel by C.H. Sisson called *Christopher Homm*, which was written in backward chronology. That idea stuck in my head. I had been focused on a book about a brother and sister for some time before that. I saw a little girl pasting stars on the ceiling of her bedroom and thought, "Maybe she grows up to be a physicist, an astrophysicist." At that point, it occurred to me that I could write this book as a backward chronology because if she were an astrophysicist, a cosmologist, she would be interested in the origins of things. I wanted to go back to the origins of this particular family, not because there is any one point of origination—there isn't—but because it would give the reader a feeling of simultaneous dramatic moments, all of them in the present tense. *First Light* is a mosaic novel. You start at the beginning and read forward, which is to say move backward in time. The last chapters feel like a silent movie. I wanted them to be mostly visual because that is how almost everybody's first memories seem.

How did you research the scientific element of Dorsey's character? Did you know much about astrophysics?

I knew nothing about it. I don't like research much, but I couldn't put a character in a book and say that she's an astrophysicist or a cosmologist and not show that she has any idea what these things are. I did a lot of reading, mostly popularizations of contemporary physics. I took some physicists out to lunch and talked to them. I read accounts of Oppenheimer and the Los Alamos atomic bomb project. The physics is cobbled together from what I read and what I thought Dorsey might think. There are places where she is too ambitious, where an actual, practical physicist is not likely to have thought what she thought. The novel does take some liberties with that material, but I think it's reasonably close to the sensibilities of a young and fairly gifted physicist. The physics—missing mass, for example—gives, I hope, a metaphorical dimension to her life.

In *Burning Down the House*, you write about the importance of not "overparenting" a character. What do you mean by this?

You have to give characters sufficient desires to get them to move in a particular direction or sufficient fears to have them moving away from something they are not eager to confront. Richard Bausch likes to say, "I think up characters whom I love and then I visit trouble upon them." In order to do that, you have to give them something to do, and you can't give them something to do unless they want something.

If you have "counterpointed characterization," you can usually give a character something to want. As long as you have one or two other people or circumstances on the stage as counterpoints, you'll have a story. I still

Charles Baxter on Revisiting Setting and Characters

Much of your work is set in the fictional town of Five Oaks, Michigan. What does this setting—and the cast of characters you weave in and out of your stories—provide you?

It's the joy of creating a model-train layout. I know where everything is in that town. My son once made a map of it so that I wouldn't get confused about the location of various businesses in relation to the river that goes through it.

As a Midwesterner I don't have the advantage, or the disadvantage, of calling upon areas that everybody knows about, such as New York, San Francisco, Los Angeles—instantly recognizable places with certain rules that lots of people know. I also don't have some of the more recognizable features of Southern or Southwestern writing. As a young man, thinking of myself as quite an experimentalist, I decided to do something absolutely conventional and characteristic of Midwestern writers, which was to create a community and stay with it, in the way that writer Sherwood Anderson did. I hadn't expected to stay in Five Oaks as long as I have. It has as many disadvantages to me as it has advantages. But I do have this cast of characters, and I know where everything is. This is my world. I couldn't set *The Feast of Love* there because I needed a community where everybody talks all the time, and Ann Arbor is full of people who give lectures, go to therapy, and sit around talking all day and evening.

We even get glimpses of Five Oaks in *The Feast of Love*, when Bradley visits the town to retrieve his dog from his sister who lives there.

continued

It's the economy of character. Once you've created a character, you don't throw him away. You just save him or her for the next available opportunity, as Philip Roth [*American Pastoral*] does with Nathan Zuckerman. It saves wear and tear on the brain cells. I have a handful of people, including Saul and Patsy, whom I've written stories about. The truth is that you can say most of what you want to say about human beings and their behavior with a relatively limited number of characters if you send them through enough fiery hoops.

Saul and Patsy are two of your recurring characters. What are other advantages to revisiting characters?

I don't know that there is an advantage, really. I've lately been working on a book about Saul and Patsy, and the first three chapters are the three stories that I've written about them: "Saul and Patsy Are Getting Comfortable in Michigan," "Saul and Patsy Are Pregnant," and "Saul and Patsy Are in Labor." I've discovered that what I thought worked to my benefit in the past—the fact that I reused characters—has turned out to be not so lucky. The Saul and Patsy of the second story, "Saul and Patsy Are Pregnant," don't seem to be the same characters that are in "Saul and Patsy Are Getting Comfortable in Michigan." Saul has assimilated himself to Five Oaks in the first story, and in the second story he hasn't. It turns out that he has more difficulties than I thought he had. The rather large amount of time between the writing of the first and second story—seven years, more or less—has proved to be unfortunate. So now I'm retyping these stories, making fairly subtle revisions to make sure that they line up properly.

What makes characters like Saul and Patsy stick with you?

They stay in my mind because I love them. Why I love them is something of a mystery, I guess. Sometimes I identify with my characters, and sometimes I find them funny or amusing. There's something telling about characters whom you go on caring about. Saul never feels at home in the world, or when he does, it's brief and he's always thrown into a repeated sense of alienation. And Patsy always feels pretty good no matter where she is. The fact that they love each other and help each other gives those stories a certain amount of energy. But I can maintain that contrast for only two or three chapters, and then have to introduce another element into it.

think that's true, but what I've thought about lately is what I call "congested subtext." What people want on the surface is often not particularly interesting. What's more telling is the congested subtext, which is what they really want underneath what they say they want. It's congested in the sense that the more you unpack it, the less clear it gets. This can be both comic and tragic: You wanted love, but you got fame; you wanted fame, but you got money. In *The Feast of Love*, Harry wants his son back, but instead he gets Chloé. People don't always get what they want, but what they do get creates the story.

I'm still trying to formulate this set of ideas. I see it in relation to a Parker Brothers board game from my youth called Careers. In that game, you had to get sixty points, and you had to decide ahead of time what you wanted and in what proportion. The points could be in fame, money, or love. You could go for broke and say, "All I want is sixty points in love." The first person to get sixty points in the proportion he or she asks for wins. If you say at the beginning that you want sixty points in love and you get sixty points in fame, you don't win because you've gotten something you didn't want. This is a pretty good metaphor not only for life, but for narrative, as well. J.F. Powers's stories are good examples of this. His priest characters are often in a state of lifelong dramatic irony. They want spiritual lives, but they get worldly lives as priests—raising money, managing the parish day to day. Powers has little interest in the spiritual lives of these characters. He's interested in priests who've gotten something they didn't expect.

This day-to-day management of affairs goes back to what you said about wanting to create a place for the mundane in *First Light.* Why have you chosen to focus on everyday events in your fiction?

One of the blessings and curses of being a late twentieth century, early twenty-first century white, middle-class American is that I'm not privy to a historical calamity unless I go somewhere and observe it. For better or worse, the lives that many Americans experience are incredibly blessed and privileged. As a writer, I have to come to terms with what that means. I can go to Bosnia and write a book about calamity, but then I would have to deal with "historical tourism." I can search out metaphysical and historical disasters in the way that, say, Robert Stone [*Dog Soldiers*] does. Or I can try to make a smaller dramatic compass come alive through the attention that I pay to it, which is more or less what I do. My challenge as a writer is to turn the elements of fortune, blessedness, and privilege into interesting fictional material.

How do you balance the seemingly simple desire to discover characters and the more complex issues of craft to complete a novel?

I don't think about structure and form when I write. I don't think, "Now I've got to avoid an epiphany, and I've got to bring in a counter-pointed character." Nothing that I've thought abstractly, as far as craft is concerned, is much help in the first drafts. I try to see the characters, hear them, and get them into some kind of interesting trouble. It's only in the revisions and the rewriting that those techniques help. Paul Auster [*The New York Trilogy*] has said that in his first drafts he just feels his way. In many cases, the writer's eye is almost entirely on the character, on what that person is moving toward, and he tries to find suitable language and feeling for the story. Writing first drafts is the experience of not knowing how to do something and persisting at it until it begins to feel right.

Before any of your novels were published, you wrote three "apprentice" novels. Since then, have you had to abandon a project?

I haven't had to ditch anything since then because it didn't work. I thought for a while that I would have to abandon *The Feast of Love.* That was as close as I've come. I wrote four chapters of that book, and it wasn't going well. Every time I start a book, there is always the possibility that it won't work, that it's not going to please anyone. There are no guarantees in writing, and I'm not particularly a confident writer. It's not in my makeup to write a book and then send it out if I'm not absolutely sure that it's okay. I'd rather pulp it than have it published.

It's not in my makeup to write a book and then send it out if I'm not absolutely sure that it's okay. I'd rather pulp it than have it published.

Do you read fiction while you write, and who are some of the writers you enjoy reading?

I used to say that I couldn't, but it's not true any more. It is true, though, that I'm susceptible to adapting or stealing something if I can turn it to my own use. When I was younger, I couldn't read other fiction because the voice would infect me. I would go to the desk to write and it would suddenly sound like Jim Harrison, Ann Beattie, or, God help us, Henry James. Now it doesn't affect me as much. When I was working on one of the stories in *Believers,* I read Deborah Eisenberg's stories. I was first filled with despair because the stories are good, and then I realized, "No. This is exhilarating." Reading can spur me on. If I'm having a dull, flat day, I can read Deborah Eisenberg's stories. If fiction can be that good, I should keep at it.

William Maxwell has been a great model for me. I can't hope to emulate the purity and clarity of his work, but he's a great figure in American literature. I couldn't have written *First Light* without the books of Evan S. Connell, particularly his *Mrs. Bridge* and *Mr. Bridge* novels. I reread Katherine Anne Porter's stories all the time. Those three writers have made a great difference in my writing life.

When you were in school, you had the opportunity to study with John Barth [*The Floating Opera*] and Donald Barthelme [*Snow White*], but you decided not to.

That was lunacy on my part. I'd heard that Don Barthelme sometimes said, while holding up a story in class, "This is amateur night." If he'd said that about my work, I would have been crushed, utterly defeated. I had great ambitions and a fragile ego. I wanted desperately to be a writer. I didn't have the nerve to enroll in a class with either Barth or Barthelme, so I made all these bonehead mistakes as a young writer that I think they would have cured me of in two weeks. But who knows? You only know where the trolley you got on took you.

What are some exercises you suggest to beginning writers?

It depends on what the writer needs. I've asked students to write scenes in which the subjective experience of time for the characters is different from clock time; dialogue in which no one is listening to anybody and dialogue in which characters are picking up cues from one another; scenes in which something is obvious to the reader but not to the character; scenes in which the writer tries the reader's patience a little. You need to be a fairly practiced hand at this to make these exercises work. In lower-level classes, I give exercises like "Ten things I know about her," and one of them has to be a secret. At the more advanced level, we deal with questions of communication, of time sense and maybe subtext: Put a character on the page who constantly says one thing but means something else; congest the subtext. It depends on what a particular writer needs. If

I gave everybody the same exercises, I would be like a doctor who gives the same prescription to all of his patients.

You've dealt with unreliable characters in "Gryphon" and in *The Feast of Love.* What are your views on the unreliable narrator?

Far, far too much has been made of the unreliable character. Some readers have said, "There's nobody we can depend on. Everything is just a point of view." Well, it's true that everybody has a point of view, but this doesn't mean that everybody is unreliable. It simply means you have to take a point of view into account. The famous case of the unreliable narrator is Ford Madox Ford's *The Good Soldier*, where the narrator is, it becomes clear, obtuse. But I think an obsession with unreliable narrators suggests that there is no true value and no account on which we can depend. You have to believe that this character's way of seeing things is reliable enough to want to go on the ride she's going on. That's the pleasure of reading. If you have a first-person narrator, of course she will miss or misinterpret some things. That doesn't mean that she is unreliable. Deconstruction has encouraged people to practice a universal skepticism that is, finally, anti-narrative. Claims of total unreliability are themselves unreliable. If you say you can rely on no one, what kind of life will you have? That turns into a practical rather than a metaphysical position. This decision can lead to a life of incredible solitude.

What about the writing life itself, especially for short story writers? How do you view the state of the American short story?

I think the short story continues to be a diminished thing in our culture. Stories don't seem to have the same impact that they did twenty or thirty years ago. The last time that I heard a lot of people say, "Did you read that story?" it was in reference to Lorrie Moore's "People Like That Are the Only People Here" when it appeared in *The New Yorker.* That hadn't happened in a long time, and it hasn't happened much since. At the same time, it seems to me that the form itself is quite healthy. There are a number of very good story writers—Jhumpa Lahiri [*Interpreter of Maladies*] is one of them—who are doing wonderful things with stories. So is Richard Bausch. The form is alive; it's just a matter of whether anybody pays attention to it.

The real energy in short stories now may be moving to under-represented minorities. Sherman Alexie's stories [*The Lone Ranger and Tonto Fistfight in Heaven*] are notable. Junot Diaz's *Drown* had a real impact, partly because you feel as if you're reading about a world you don't know, and Diaz introduces you to it bit by bit.

Why do you think many American readers prefer the novel?

As a friend of mine once said, "When I buy a book, I want a long-term relationship. I don't want a one-night stand." But I would rather read a book of stories than a novel. I enjoy the concentration that stories require. I like to pick up characters and then drop them after twenty or twenty-five pages.

Writer Frank O'Connor says that the genius of American writing is the short story. We have a good tradition in this country of short stories—Ernest Hemingway, F. Scott Fitzgerald, Katherine Anne Porter, Richard Wright, Flannery O'Connor, and J.F. Powers—a lot of absolutely wonderful stories that can stand up against anybody's. Americans are particularly good at short stories because the form tends to emphasize impulsive behavior. American culture has been impulsive, and the short story, at its best, often shows that.

You've been an advocate of slowness, especially in regard to reading.

The issue of slowness is becoming serious because data processing is used as a model, even for experiences that are personal and have an element of love, caring, or attention in them. These things can't be improved by adding speed. Fiction that tries to increase its velocity as a function of intensity will work only for the short term. Literary fiction may become somewhat marginal if the attention spans we bring to it are so conditioned by the features of modern life that we can't slow down our consciousness enough to pay attention to the way fiction works, which is much slower than movies and TV. The model of speed is applied to a lot of places where it shouldn't be, which is why I'm getting fanatical about slowness. For instance, you don't want to rush certain features of courtship.

I think it's interesting that you can ask someone about a movie and that person will say, "It was slow," and that is criticism. You can say, "It was slow, *but* I liked it anyway." You have to justify why you thought slowness was synonymous with quality. The ideology of this culture is for efficiency, and efficiency means speed. What may be good for business is not good for art. It's not good for literary art, anyway. Most people spend all day at an office, rushing and being distracted all the time. When they sit down to read a book, will they want that same rhythm, or will they want something else? That's what concerns me, whether we can adjust our sense of time anymore. I buy or am given more books than I can possibly read. It's hard to keep up, and I fall behind. Look at all these books.

bringing empathy to fiction

CARRIE BROWN

Carrie Brown's characters are unlike her; that's why she finds them fascinating. She chooses people with different backgrounds, problems, and situations to contemplate how others live. In her first novel, *Rose's Garden*, an elderly man must re-create his life after his wife dies and an apparition appears in her garden. In *Lamb in Love*, a man and woman discover they might have a last chance at romance. Her third novel, *The Hatbox Baby*, follows participants of the 1933 Chicago World's Fair, including an exotic dancer, her wily and devoted cousin, and a doctor who experiments with baby incubators.

Brown grew up in New England and also spent time in England and Hong Kong. She received a B.A. in English from Brown University, then moved to Maryland to work for a newspaper as a general assignment reporter. She later worked as a writer and editor.

In 1994, she and her husband, writer John Gregory Brown [*Decorations in a Ruined Cemetery*], moved to Sweet Briar, Virginia, where she began to write fiction. She received an M.F.A. from the University of Virginia, where she held a Henry Hoyns teaching fellowship.

Rose's Garden won the 1998 Barnes and Noble Discover Award. *The Hatbox Baby* received the 2001 Library of Virginia Award.

She lives with her husband and their three children.

Books by Carrie Brown

Rose's Garden (novel), Algonquin Books, 1998

Lamb in Love (novel), Algonquin Books, 1999

The Hatbox Baby (novel), Algonquin Books, 2000

The House on Belle Isle (stories), Algonquin Books, 2002

Confinement (novel), Algonquin Books, 2003

You turned to novel writing after moving to Virginia and leaving your job as a reporter and editor. How did journalism prepare you to write creatively?

Despite having been a voracious reader as a child and as a young person, it was through journalism that I learned how to structure a story. Before I started deliberately listening to people's stories and trying to retell them for a new audience, I understood the notion of structure only in the most abstract or academic way. I was drawn to writing first through language, not plot, and like a lot of young writers I was enchanted by words but had no ideas to speak of, and no sense of how to tell a story, so in that sense my years as a journalist were very instructive. I also learned empathy as a journalist (I grew up a lot as a reporter), and it has seemed to me since that empathy is what controls and shapes a story, structurally and in terms of tone or mood. Empathy is also, for me, that route to understanding and creating character. I don't necessarily have to like a character, but I have to know him; I have to know what it feels like to be him.

Empathy is also, for me, that route to understanding and creating character. I don't necessarily have to like a character, but I have to know him.

Is there any connection between the kind of research you did for your newspaper stories and for your historical novel, *The Hatbox Baby?*

I do research in the most embarrassingly ad hoc way, on an as-needed basis, periodically stopping writing and reading something instead, based on some instinct that tells me I'm floundering. Research can be a real siren song, however. It's much easier to research than to write, and eventually one has to abandon the learning curve, resign oneself to everything one will never know, and go back to writing.

Do you ever think of going back to journalism?

I often feel tempted by returning to journalism, in fact, and hope one day to go back to it even if only for a sabbatical from fiction. I've used my years in newspapers very heavily as a fiction writer. It's all great material, a ringside seat, as it were.

What is your writing process?

The best description of my writing process would be that it is like moving in a dark room after leaving a brightly lit space. I've no idea where I'm going, the way might be dangerous, and all I can see are these blazing images imprinted on the retina and fading fast.

Have you abandoned any novels or stories that never seemed to work?

I've tried three times now to write a novel based on the life of Caroline Herschel, the eighteenth-century astronomer and sister to Sir William Herschel, the astronomer who discovered Uranus. I've been stalled each time, a hundred or so pages in, by my failure to sufficiently understand the science behind the Herschels' work. I've concluded that I'm just too stupid for the subject. If I can't understand what they do, I don't understand them as human beings, and then, of course, I can't do the work of making the characters feel fully alive. Absent that necessary vitality, I've got nothing. *Que sera.*

Carrie Brown on the Publishing Process

What is the most difficult part of the editing process for you?

I once had to kill off a character that my editor, quite rightly, said was too whiny to be likable. That was a difficult thing to do—to wipe someone off the page entirely, like wiping her off the face of the earth. However, once I'd done it, the novel improved almost instantly. I quite like the editing process—after all, you're nearly done then, aren't you?

How many rejections did you receive before your first book was accepted for publication?

Very few, as my agent put my first novel quite quickly into the hands of a brilliant and sensitive editor at Algonquin Books, Shannon Ravenel, who saw potential in it and made an offer on faith, as the novel needed a lot of work.

You appear to have produced a large body of work in a short period of time. Did you have a backlog of novels, or are you able to write and polish quickly?

I try to write five days a week, a few hours a day, whatever I can manage along with my other responsibilities—teaching part-time, raising a family. We have three children and an old farmhouse with a couple of old cars, and so we're constantly aware of needing money. I try to regard the act of writing as I would any job, meaning I have to get up and do it. I try not to be too romantic about it.

That said, writing—like any art—is not something over which one has complete control. Some days, everyone in the novel seems to cooperate with you in moving the thing forward. Other days, they refuse to even get out of bed. Those are miserable times. But then, every job has its miserable times. Then you just have to show up and punch the clock and do your best. The notion of a backlog of novels is a lovely dream from which I would never wish to awake.

Are you able to read fiction while you write it?

I can't imagine a life without reading; actually, I can't imagine a day without reading (something), and there would be long stretches when I'd have to do without it if I couldn't do the two together. What I read doesn't seem to get mixed up with what I write, thank God. How would I fall asleep at night if I couldn't read?

Are there particular authors or books you read that help with your own writing?

Not in a directly tutorial sense, but there is no question that the writers I love—an ever-expanding list, but one that always begins with Chekhov, Alice Munro, William Trevor, Penelope Fitzgerald, Eudora Welty, Jane Austen—have served as inspiration. I worship at their shrine, as it were, and their stories—and my gratitude for their stories—always remind me, when the going gets tough, of why I write in the first place, of what it is I'm hoping somehow to apprehend and set forth for a reader.

In *Rose's Garden,* Conrad sees an angel in his wife's garden. Were you concerned about the risk of writing about the paranormal?

I've had people ask me if I was worried about such a risk, particularly writing about angels because they've become such a cheap commodity in mass culture. I was interested in finding out what would happen to a character who is skeptical by nature if he was confronted with something that caused him to question what the world is really made of. It was a way of examining how we come by faith in general, and that seems to me an absolutely universal kind of search.

Your novels often focus on the lives of men. Is there a reason the male

characters have taken the foreground in your books? Are you more interested in writing characters who are different from you?

I've written almost nothing that feels autobiographical to me except for one story, and in that case I changed the point of view from my own to that of another character (a male character, in fact). William Trevor once explained his interest in writing fiction to nosiness about other people's lives. This seems like a good and honest (and funny) answer. But I also think that imagination is born out of empathy. Indeed, I think empathy is, for me, necessary to imagination. I am not very much interested in myself, at least as far as my writing is concerned, because it requires no act of empathy to consider my own life, and therefore nothing interesting or imaginative arises for me out of pondering it. I already know what it feels like to be me. I'm interested in—I'm nosy about—what it feels like to be somebody else.

Are there certain themes or types of characters you find yourself revisiting in your fiction?

A reviewer once commented that I love an underdog, and I suppose that's true. I'm interested in what seems to me the harrowing ordinariness of an ordinary life, and maybe the underdog is the archetypal ordinary man. Many Russian writers—Gogol, Tolstoy, Chekhov—see the "ordinary man" in that light: pervasively oppressed, suffering in a way that feels hauntingly familiar. I am a great admirer of Iris Murdoch, who took her philosophical training at Oxford and then went on to write some thirty or so novels, a remarkable achievement. I like her work because I like her characters' preoccupations with the state of their souls and the nature of goodness—their own, other people's, the world's.

I'm interested in goodness the way some writers are interested in evil, perhaps, although maybe they're just two sides of the same coin. I'm interested in how we grapple with the ethical, moral questions in our lives, and I see the conflicts of our lives in those terms, as questions of right and wrong, good and bad. I'm interested in the emotional and psychological

Carrie Brown on Characters

You've said you often remain close to a character, even after the book is completed. Do your books begin with a character?

They seem to begin with a moment—a particular person in a particular place at a particular moment. The novel I'm working on now began with a man being driven in the backseat of a car down a long lane toward a house at night. It has been snowing heavily. The time period seems to be the late 1940s, post-World War II. At first I didn't know who he was, nor who was driving him, nor where he was going, nor why he was going there, but eventually I began to discover these things. These moments don't seem to become the beginnings of the stories, necessarily—I work both forward and back from them—but they are the seeds from which the stories spring, and I can locate them in most of my novels.

What kind of relationships do you have with your characters?

I have different relationships with different characters, which makes sense, I suppose, because they're all different people; presumably our relationships in life are the same way. Some characters have to be coaxed out from among the shadows, because that's the sort of people they are, and some characters lean over my shoulder and breathe heavily in my ear and try to tell me what to do, because that's the kind of people they are.

dimension of the struggle to be good, to live an ethically responsible life. I'm interested in how shockingly difficult it is to be good. And of course I'm interested in our failures in that regard—exactly how we fail and why, how we console ourselves and others, how we forgive ourselves and others, how we fail to forgive. . . .

This all sounds very abstract, perhaps, but it feels very ordinary. To me, these issues feel present in the most ordinary life, under the most ordinary circumstances. The challenge is to render those lives, those ordinary lives, as dramatically as I feel they are lived, so that the characters' engagement with questions of moral goodness—their heroism, as it were—can be felt by the reader, and can be as gripping and unforgettable and important as a life lived on much more conventionally dramatic terms. William Trevor is an absolute master at this, I think. So is Alice Munro, Flannery O'Connor, and many others.

The challenge is to render those lives, those ordinary lives, as dramatically as I feel they are lived.

In terms of other consistencies throughout my work, it seems to be true that I like to write about older men. Maybe I just like older men in general, although that might be a dangerous confession. It also seems to be true that I often write about characters, even if they're not the main characters in a story, who are flawed physically or emotionally and psychologically in some way—people with mental illness or mental retardation, people who are blind or deaf, people who are "crippled" in some way. I have a disabled child, and her life has made me aware of the enormous complexities of a life lived on those terms, but I don't set about deliberately trying to elucidate those issues.

What kind of writing relationship do you have with your husband, writer John Gregory Brown?

My husband and I serve as first readers for each other, though I secretly feel that he is much more useful to me than I am to him. Being a fiction writer does not necessarily make one a good editor, but John is gifted in that regard, and I'm always grateful for his wise and careful eye. Also, don't fiction writers always want to push their pages under somebody's nose? It's very convenient, having that nose in bed beside you.

What is your advice to beginning writers?

To write the best book they can. I hate giving advice, because it seems so superior and dreary, and it certainly doesn't promise a quick fix. But I believe that good books eventually find publishers—no matter who your agent is, no matter who you know (or don't know) in the business, no matter how much experience you have marketing yourself and your work. That said, there are ways to get noticed, if you don't have, or can't seem to get, an agent who can do the selling for you. Summer writers conferences are one good way to form a relationship with a successful writer who might be of some assistance, putting material he or she admires into the right hands, for instance, or even offering useful criticism of a work in progress. But still, my first advice stands. Write the best book you can. Then pray.

a limited, beautiful effort

ANDRE DUBUS

Andre Dubus, the beloved short story writer, was born August 11, 1936, in Lake Charles, Louisiana, and died in Haverhill, Massachusetts, on February 24, 1999.

As a retired Marine Corps captain, Dubus wrote his only novel, *The Lieutenant.* Between writing it and a proposed second novel, he discovered the short fiction of Chekhov. Through his reading, particularly the story "Peasants," Dubus decided to learn the art of the short story.

Dubus went on to write seven collections of short fiction, including *The Times Are Never So Bad, We Don't Live Here Anymore,* and *Dancing After Hours,* which was a finalist for the National Book Critics Circle Award. For his achievement in the short story, he received the PEN/Malamud Award, the Rea Award for excellence in the form, the Boston Globe's first annual Lawrence L. Winship Award, and the Jean Stein Award from the American Academy of Arts and Letters.

Dubus is also the author of *Voices From the Moon,* a novella, and two collections of essays. *Broken Vessels,* in which he recounts the injury he suffered while assisting with a traffic accident in 1986 that confined him to a wheelchair, was a finalist for the Pulitzer Prize. *Meditations From a Movable Chair*, his last published book, explores family, faith, and writing.

After receiving his M.F.A. from the Iowa Writers' Workshop and teaching fiction and creative writing for many years at Bradford College, Dubus started a fiction workshop in his home in Haverhill, Massachusetts, where he interacted with people of all ages and occupations interested in the craft of fiction. This interview was conducted seven months before his death.

Dubus is survived by his six children.

Books by Andre Dubus

The Lieutenant (novel), The Dial Press, 1967
Separate Flights (stories), David R. Godine, 1975
Adultery and Other Choices (stories), David R. Godine, 1977
Finding a Girl in America (stories), David R. Godine, 1980
The Times Are Never So Bad (stories), David R. Godine, 1983
Voices From the Moon (novella), David R. Godine, 1984
We Don't Live Here Anymore (stories), Crown, 1984
The Last Worthless Evening (stories), David R. Godine, 1986
Selected Stories, David R. Godine, 1988
Broken Vessels (essays), David R. Godine, 1991
Dancing After Hours (stories), Knopf, 1996
Meditations From a Movable Chair (essays), Knopf, 1998

For more than thirty years, you've published short stories almost exclusively. Your first published book, however, *The Lieutenant*, was a novel. You've said that book would have been better as a novella. What would you have changed?

I looked at *The Lieutenant* in the 1980s because a small press reprinted it and I had to read the galleys. I wouldn't have cut it then because they wanted to print it as it was and because I couldn't figure how to change it. I don't remember that novel, but I suspect I could have compressed some of it. I could not have compressed more at twenty-nine, though. If I had written it twelve years later, maybe I could have. I was learning while writing that novel.

You began a second novel, which was later abandoned, after the publication of *The Lieutenant.* Did any stories grow from that?

I had actually written a novel before *The Lieutenant.* I finally burned it after eighteen drafts because I had outgrown it. After *The Lieutenant* was published, I started one, and I think I was on the second chapter when I read a story by Chekhov called "Peasants." It covers one family, one village, and one year in thirty pages. I went for a drive, and when I came back, I read it again and thought, "I have to learn how to compress." I never looked back again. No, I didn't get any stories out of that novel.

Several of your characters reappear throughout the stories. What are the advantages of reusing characters in stories rather than writing a novel about them?

I do sometimes plan to have several stories with the same character, but I have never thought of the advantages. It could be a limitation; I don't know. Francois Mauriac said, "I don't know why anybody writes long novels. You could always write another novel about the same people."

How do you know when a character will stay with you for more than one story?

Well, I wrote a series about a boy, Paul Clement, in Louisiana, and I knew I would write those stories about him and his family. When I got older and looked back at those stories, I realized the characters in those stories weren't my parents; they were my memories of how I saw my parents when I was ten. The stories always changed anyway. There were also those three novellas—"We Don't Live Here Anymore," "Adultery," and "Finding a Girl in America"—and I didn't think there would be three. I wrote "We Don't Live Here Anymore," and I started worrying about the character Edith. I think she's the only one in those stories I liked. Then I wrote "Adultery." I was writing "Finding a Girl in America," a story about a man whose girlfriend aborts his child, and I decided to put Hank Allison in there. There are several LuAnn Arceneaux stories in *Dancing After Hours.* Those were a mess to get going. I used her when I decided to write a story about how two people meet because that always fascinates me. I knew I would try "Out of the Snow" with LuAnn. The idea for that one came from an experience I had when I was picking up my youngest daughters one day. I was in my wheelchair, and I saw a boy pushing a smaller boy around. I started to drive away, but then I thought, "I can't just let this happen." I said, "You stop that or I'll call the police." What else could I do? Another guy came up and said, "It's okay, mister. Don't call the police. That guy said something about his sister." I said, "That guy's too big. He shouldn't be doing that." I then thought I shouldn't disturb the police over something so foolish. But a woman came up behind me and spoke before dispersing them. And then I thought, "Why not write a story about a woman dealing with violence?"

You've said your characters often control the fate of the story.

In my story "Miranda Over the Valley," the character gets so bitter, and I kept rewriting the ending, but she kept doing the same thing.

So you think your characters hold the ultimate responsibility?

Yes. I wrote only nineteen words today, and I don't even know what the characters are doing in this story I'm writing. I've got to take a couple days off until they show me something. If I had finished that section today, I would have been screwed. It's a new section and I don't know what's going on, so I'll take a few days off and then see what happens.

Do you know more about your characters than what ultimately appears in the printed version?

I want to know about my characters' religion, their sensual habits, how they feel about death, life, where they are from, whom they are kin to. But that's not always what I get to know. I'm thinking about my story "Dancing After Hours." All I knew about the female character was her age and that she thought she was not pretty. I don't know where she's from, and I don't know anything about her family. Since she doesn't mention much about religion, I assume that is not part of her life.

I want to know about my characters' religion, their sensual habits, how they feel about death, life, where they are from, whom they are kin to.

I try to see the characters, to know some of their history. I think about characters for a long time rather than just starting the story and seeing what they do. I like to feel that I can get inside of a character. I used to tell students to write sketches. I told them they should know if their character prefers a bath or a shower.

Dialect is rarely used in your stories.

I don't use it, and I don't care much to read it. I have no dialect in this Western I'm working on now. I decided before I started that the black man was going to speak normally; he would not have any kind of accent that would denote slavery or anything else; he's educated, and everybody in the story would just speak normally as they do in Chekhov. I like dialect in the right hands. Faulkner did beautiful things with language. Sometimes he wrote a line that sounded more like dialogue than read like it. There was a voice he developed that made this so, I think. No good writer's dialogue ever sounds good in a tape recorder.

When did you begin reading drafts into a tape recorder?

I was at Iowa, and I don't know who told me about this wonderful idea. Reading aloud allows me to get physical and use my body so I can see mistakes more clearly. I cut a lot this way. It helps to check dialogue: Is this the wrong rhythm? Are these repetitions? I hear things that I don't see. I read it in a dull way. When I listen to it, it's even less interesting. If you heard the tapes, you would say, "This man's working."

After more than thirty years of publishing, how have your ideas changed about what fiction should accomplish?

I want to use physical details and spiritual light and darkness in such a way that a reader experiences them and becomes the character, goes through what the character goes through. When I'm writing, I always become the character. I go through the story with the character to see what happens.

You left the Marine Corps in 1964 as a captain. Were there similarities between the community of men on the ship and the community of writers at the Iowa Writers' Workshop?

There was some immediate shock. In the Marine Corps, I didn't talk about writing. Teaching was a lateral move. There were similarities between that and the Marine Corps. To be in a room full of writers and not hide that you were writing was an exciting thing for me, and I hadn't experienced that until Iowa.

Did you hide your writing?

Well, I didn't go around telling everybody. I had my first story published when I was in the Marine Corps, and there was nobody to tell. I couldn't just go knock on the major's door and say, "I wanted to tell you. . . ."

Would that have been looked down upon?

No. Actually, that was some kind of narcissism in my head from school days. My son Andre III, who is a writer, and I were talking about this. We were the ones who believed guys thought writing wasn't a guy thing to do. The guys didn't think that. I told him, "Good athletes used to ask me to help them with their school work. All I had to do was ask them to help me throw a football, and they would have been happy to." And he agreed.

Many of your stories are written in third person. Is this a conscious choice you've made in your body of work?

It is a conscious choice. When I write in first person, I tend to be too wordy. My first-person narrators tend to tell everything. I don't even know the last time I've tried using first-person narrators in stories, but I've written many first-person essays.

Do you approach the writing of essays differently than you do fiction?

I really bear down with the essays. I saw a nice review of *Meditations From a Movable Chair* in *The Philadelphia Inquirer*. The reviewer said, "Hemingway is an influence more than ever before in these personal essays." I said, "He may be right." They are hard to write, and it's hard to keep from launching into a monologue about my life.

I've got to squeeze it to make sure it doesn't wander all over the place. There's not the same kind of excitement with an essay. I always know what is going to happen because it happened to me, whereas with the stories, there is an element of suspense. When I'm writing the sentences it feels about the same. No, that's not true. If you write about a black cowboy beating up a white racist, it's a whole lot different from writing a sentence about something that happened to you and your children, as far as the rush is concerned.

Where do your characters come from?

They come from their actions and what they are thinking and feeling. My job is to figure out what they're feeling. I will have a physical description and some history in my head before I start a story. I'm writing this Western now, and I know this character is a black cowboy in southern California. I know his family went from Chicago to California during the gold rush, and his father set up a church in Los Angeles. That's not the story, but I know that.

Judging by similarities between some of your personal essays and short stories, you use material from your life in your fiction. One example is the essay "Giving Up the Gun" and a story from *Dancing After Hours* called "The Intruder."

That's an interesting observation. I wrote "The Intruder" aboard ship in 1961, and that's the story the *Sewanee Review* took while I was in the Marine Corps. Richard Yates [*Revolutionary Road*] read the story, and he liked it. Through the years when my collections were being published, he would always say, "Why don't you put 'The Intruder' in there?" A year after he died, I started thinking about "The Intruder" again. I was working on *Dancing After Hours*, so I took it out and read it, and it was like looking at a picture of myself when I was seven. I sent it to my editor, and I said, "This may look like I'm trying to fill up the book, but the truth is I think Yates is talking to me." Sure, I take raw material from my life, but that story was all made up.

You recently switched to publishing with Knopf after many years with Godine.

I was in my last year of a MacArthur Foundation grant, and I wasn't going to be able to afford my mortgage. The accountant said, "This is real. You will lose the house." I was feeling low, and then I realized I had to stop waiting for guys with suits to do something, that I needed to call my agent. I called and said, "I can't be loyal to anybody. I'm going to lose my damn house." My agent said, "This will be fun." So I got a two-year contract, and my house is paid for.

What do you think about the market for stories now?

I think it's great. There are all these quarterlies. I keep telling writers,

Andre Dubus on the Role of Editors and Writing Workshops

You've been critical of some fiction editors of magazines. You've also said, half-jokingly, that the two worst things for a young writer are literature professors and *The New Yorker*. What do you think is the role of an editor of a magazine?

I think their role is to say "yes" or "no" and not try to change the story. Finding mistakes, maybe suggesting a line be cut, that's all right. I've gotten weird letters from editors. One place wanted "The Timing of Sin," but the editors wanted the whole story to take place somewhere else, cutting the story in half. They wanted the story they thought they saw. It's a bad thing to tempt a young writer because young writers want recognition, and the magazine is waving the check, which won't do anybody any good in the long run.

I had a friend who told me a buddy of his had just sold his first story to *The New Yorker*. He said they made him change it from a Southern voice in first person to a neutral voice. I said, "Why did he change it?" He said, "Thirty-five hundred dollars." I said, "He's a graduate student. He can't go to Mexico for a year. He can't even buy a car. You know why he did that? Because nobody cares what anybody writes. You'd like to be able to walk into a bar in Akron, Ohio, and have the guy next to you say, 'What do you do?' and you say, 'I write.' He says, 'You been published?' and you say, 'Yeah, *The New Yorker*.' " It's not the money that's a bad influence; it's their need to rewrite the story.

And regarding literature professors, some of them go nuts on reading into things and, in turn, they ruin the purity and spontaneity of readers. They make literature some removed thing.

continued

Do you take advice from colleagues or members of your workshop?

I do if I respect the person. Gary Fisketjon at Knopf had some suggestions for *Dancing After Hours.* I sent "Andromache" to *The New Yorker,* and the editor sent back a good letter. I showed it to a wonderful writer named Thomas Williams who said, "I haven't read the story, but this is an interesting letter; maybe you should read it again." He was right. I had been reading too much William Styron. There were flashbacks inside flashbacks and vortexes. I wrote that story again, and it was better. I said to Tom Williams, "I wrote part of that story for myself. Some of it has nothing to do with anything, but what do I do?" He said, "Well, you just put it in the drawer and cry until you can use it somewhere else."

"If you keep it in the mail, somebody will take it." You just have to persist. I don't believe a good story will go unpublished.

How has your own sense of pacing evolved since you wrote *The Lieutenant*?

I'm not sure if I knew how to bear down then. I'm not sure if full concentration came to me during the writing of *The Lieutenant.* I was writing what I call horizontally, making scenes go. In my forties, I switched to writing vertically, trying to get inside a world and inside a character. Of course, the book was based on a story that actually happened. I changed the events a little to make the novel. That piece started in first person, too, but then realized I was writing everything as I remembered it, every detail from the ship. I started over in third person. To me, first person feels like talking.

How do you edit your work?

I write slowly, and I try to edit as much as I can while I'm writing.

The next day, I'll read from the beginning, so I'm doing it all over again. I don't read it when I'm finished that day. I put it aside and don't think about it until the next day.

In a review of *The Times Are Never So Bad,* Joyce Carol Oates said, "The stories read more like excerpts from longer works than stories complete in themselves." What is your definition of a story?

I stopped having them. My system for students was that every other week, they had to come in with five longhand pages and read them. I told them they could go both semesters without completing a story as long as they were working. I feel anybody who assigns three stories in a semester doesn't respect the form because a story may take three years to write, and you can't hurry it. I told students to keep working.

The finished stories started coming in, and every other week, one student, Michael Bussey, read a complete story. At first, I thought of them as sketches. By the end of the year, I saw he had written nine beautiful stories about a little boy and his brother, and he followed the boy until age nineteen. I said, "Michael, I'm never going to call a story a sketch again. Now I think a story is what feels like a story."

Themes run throughout your work, and some of the same ideas recur. Do you revisit scenes because you've reached a new understanding?

It's not intentional. I knew I had written about abortion, for instance, in "Finding a Girl in America," and I didn't look at it again. I didn't want to go back in that direction in "Falling in Love." I told a priest who is in the workshop about my situation. I said, "I've got another abortion story, and I've already gone there twice in stories. Do I have to go back again?" He said, "Yes." So I did. That doesn't bother me. There's a lot of repetition in a lot of writers I love, probably because of their passions, fears, what we love as humans.

How did you compress the novella "Adultery" from its original four hundred pages?

The first draft was a short novel, and it was terrible, embarrassing. Nobody ever saw that one. The idea came from two articles in the newspaper. One was about a guy traveling on the highway with his wife at night in Massachusetts. He stopped to get gasoline, and while the tank was getting filled, he went into the bathroom. His wife decided to go to the bathroom, too. He came out and drove away without her because he didn't realize she was gone. The other story was about a young guy who hitchhiked from Washington state to Boston. A trucker who was dying of cancer picked him up. The trucker was driving around drinking and smoking and talking into a microphone to his family, but he didn't have it connected because he didn't want them to hear him die.

So I thought, let's put Hank and Edith in this story. I had them go to Mexico. He drives off the road to go to the bathroom, and she crosses the highway and hitchhikes back with a trucker who dies in Maine. There was a funeral scene, and the whole thing was just awful. And then I got to work.

It was a long process. I thought I had a draft finished in the early stages, and then I realized it wasn't done. One time it was much shorter, and it almost worked on several occasions.

There's a lot of repetition in a lot of writers I love, probably because of their passions, fears, what we love as humans.

In your essay "Selling Stories," you write, "There is no one to sell out to as a story writer." Has this been one of the reasons you've continued to write stories?

I just don't see novels. I still think *The Lieutenant* is an idea for a short novella. I've written shorter pieces about more complicated matters. I don't get ideas for novels, and that's why I don't write them. I don't know how anybody does. My son Andre does, and he goes off for five years and then comes up with a new world he's made.

How do you feel about your son's decision to become a writer?

I love it.

How do your children respond to your writing?

They tell me they like it. The young girls haven't read it yet. They think it's just something Dad does. My oldest daughter, when I published *The Lieutenant*, was nine years old. She was very happy that her dad didn't go to work every morning but that he went to classes three days a week and then came home and wrote, and I felt the same way.

Every Thursday night since the fall of 1987, a writers' workshop has met at your house. How did this come about?

In the fall of 1987, a woman from south of Boston called. She said she had eight writers who wanted to pay a couple hundred dollars each for four nights of a workshop. Ten writers had given a benefit for me that winter. I thought, well all those writers gave me that, so I'm not going to charge writers until I have to. I said, "Come up and I'll see what you are doing." So that's how it began. There's been a major rotation over ten years.

Bradford was a women's college when you taught there. You've said in the past that women are better writers than men. Do you still feel this way?

Did I say that? I do read a lot of women writers. Women are the ones who read books. But I don't think women are better writers than men. They're different. I said in a class at Bradford, "Updike writes like a woman," and the women got upset. I said, "It's not an insult. A man goes into a room in a strange house he's never been to, and when he comes out he doesn't know what he saw. His wife will go in, and she will know the wallpaper, the curtains, the furniture, and every detail of the house. But the guy will come out and say, 'Well, they were nice people.' " I didn't know what was in my house until I got confined to it. I couldn't tell you what color the walls were.

Women are very sensuous. I have a group of abused teenagers I meet with every Monday night, and one of them asked to read some women writers. She said, "Let's read some Virginia Woolf." I said, "All the women writers I read are too complicated and lyrical and too sexy. I'm just not going to read them in here." In that group, we mostly read Tobias Wolff and Hemingway, stuff like that with sentences that are approachable. When a woman writer gets on a roll, boy, you get lost.

What have you been reading lately?

In line yesterday while I was getting my driver's license renewed, I started reading Dennis Lehane's novel *Gone, Baby, Gone.* I was reading *Cousin Bette* and loving it, but something interrupted me. I hope it was something like swimming or baseball. I finally gave it up and put it back on the shelf. I got a little burned out reading. When I was teaching at the University of Alabama, I bought Marguerite Duras's *The Lover.* When I began reading it, all of a sudden it felt like it weighed two hundred pounds, and I had to put it down. I was going to reread *War and Peace* for the third time last fall. Then I thought, "It will be the World Series. You are only going to read twelve pages a day."

I read a novel in manuscript by my middle sister last week. So the truth is that if I can keep up with family and friends, that's about all I can do.

Do any of your other family members write?

My oldest daughter is working on a screenplay. She can write well. My fourth child, who is a therapist in Santa Cruz, has written two novels, but neither one has been published. They can all write. My sixteen-year-old came over with my eleven-year-old, and we were all in the pool. I looked up and the older one was gone. I said, "Where's Cadence?" Madeline said, "She's writing a story." I said, "That's a serious sixteen-year-old."

Are there any stories you are most proud of?

They are mostly gone when I finish them. I remember the ones that were hardest to write. "Adultery" was hard, and I almost quit writing it a few times. "Dancing After Hours" was very hard, as well. I am fond of many of the stories in *The Last Worthless Evening.* I like "Molly" and "Deaths at Sea."

"Deaths at Sea" is one of your few stories that deals with racism. Did you make a decision to stay away from the topic?

There should be more. This Western I wrote last summer deals with it, and the sequel I'm working on now deals with it because the main character is black. But I don't know the answer. In the 1960s and 1970s, I shied away from writing about this topic because of the turmoil in our country. It probably just hasn't come up in the stories. I guess I haven't been writing about characters who are racist.

You just mentioned "Molly," which is a powerful story of a girl moving into adulthood and confronting her own sexuality. How did that story come to you?

That story was hard. It started from the point of view of a fishing captain who first sees the mother, Claire. It started on his fishing boat off the New Hampshire coast. Claire invites him over to her house for dinner. He's the first one who sees Molly. I didn't know how to finish it, and then a couple days later I realized it was finished, and that I just needed an epilogue. I wrote that epilogue with my daughter Cadence, who was three years old at the time, on my lap.

In your essay "After Twenty Years," you say you've "always known that writing fiction had little effect on the world; that if it did, young men would not have gone to war after *The Iliad.*" What do you feel a writer's role is in society?

I hate to tell you. Somebody wrote me about that essay, and she said, "It helps those of us who do read to help those who don't." And I think that's what reading does, but it doesn't get things done. Caesar Chavez did more than six John Steinbecks could have done. Workers don't own their own lives yet. It must have helped in communist countries, but it doesn't help in capitalistic societies. Have you ever seen any good come because somebody wrote a book of fiction? Individual good, yes. I think it's a limited effort, a beautiful effort that is a gift from God. I think people should do it and make music and paintings. I just wish the world would get better for everybody, and there would be true democracy.

Literature touches individual lives. It comforts, soothes, and delights. It turns us on, enrages us. When the day comes that a politician picks up a novel and sees the light, I'm just going to walk straight to heaven. I think art is for the individual soul. I never read Thomas More's *Utopia.* A woman I know read it, and she said, "There are no artists in there." I was educated by Christian Brothers, and a wise Jesuit once told me, "If there were no sins, there wouldn't be art." At the least, stories are fun to read.

magic in craft

STUART DYBEK

When we asked the novelists in this series about writers they read as exemplars of craft and technique, Stuart Dybek's name came up again and again.

Dybek, born April 10, 1942, in Chicago, published his first book, *Brass Knuckles*, a collection of poetry, six years after graduating from the Iowa Writers' Workshop. His first collection of stories, *Childhood and Other Neighborhoods*, won a Whiting Writers' Award and was followed ten years later by *The Coast of Chicago*, another story collection. Legendary for his seemingly relentless approach to editing and rewriting, Dybek often waits years before his fiction is published, which has led some writers and critics to label him a perfectionist.

Because of his beautiful language and control of the form, Dybek has been called a modern master of the short story. *Childhood and Other Neighborhoods* tells stories of children and adolescents in their attempts to understand customs of their elders, the mysteries of sex, and the process of assimilation. *The Coast of Chicago* contains long stories that alternate with very short "shorts," some just a few paragraphs long. In "Blight," a group of boys grows up in the years between the Korean and Vietnam wars in an "Official Blight Area" of Chicago.

Dybek, like some of his characters, has a long-standing interest in music. He plays the saxophone and worked in a record store.

Some of Dybek's most well-known work, such as the stories "We Didn't" and "Paper Lantern," both published in *The Best American Short Stories*, and his novella, "Orchids," are not yet available in book form.

Dybek has received many prestigious awards, including the PEN/Malamud Award, the Nelson Algren Award, a first-prize O. Henry Award for his story "Hot Ice," and another O. Henry Award for "Blight," both published in *The Coast of Chicago*.

Dybek has taught at the Warren Wilson M.F.A. program, Princeton University, the University of Iowa, and Western Michigan University in Kalamazoo, Michigan, where he has been a professor since 1973.

Books by Stuart Dybek

Brass Knuckles (poems), University of Pittsburgh Press, 1979
Childhood and Other Neighborhoods (stories), Viking Press, 1980
The Coast of Chicago (stories), Knopf, 1990
The Story of Mist (a chapbook of prose poems and short, short stories), State Street Press, 1993
I Sailed with Magellan (novel), Farrar, Straus and Giroux, 2003
Streets in Their Own Ink (poems), 2004

What is your hope for a phrase, sentence, or paragraph—from the first draft to its final form?

It depends on the phrase, I guess. Is it a phrase of strategic importance? Is it a central, formative image for the piece as a whole, for instance, or a sentence that establishes or varies the underlying prose rhythm of the piece as a whole? Or is it one that makes a necessary transition, a transition that perhaps launches a digression or eases the return from a digression or that might be a leap or an essential link? Is it a sentence of revelation or a paragraph of closure, one that gathers the momentum of all the other phrases through which a character steps into another reality, summoning the reader to follow? My ultimate hope is that these individual units—phrases, sentences, paragraphs—are knit into seamless relation to one another and contribute to the coherence of the piece as a whole. That's what makes for durable work.

What works demonstrate this?

A writer who exemplifies this quality for me—but then this particular writer exemplifies all that I love about literature—is Isaac Babel. But I could just as well have named Eudora Welty, Alice Munro, Milan Kundera, Jorge Luis Borges, Gabriel Garcia Marquez, Paul Bowles. . . .

The quality of coherence comes from a variety of factors in a piece of writing: a deeply resonant, formative image, for instance. The ingenuity of the transitions, for another. Early Hemingway and the hybrid he struck upon out of Sherwood Anderson and Gertrude Stein is instructive regarding the interplay between repetition and development. Then, to further the discussion, look at what Raymond Carver did a half-century later in his take of those 1920s writers. Citing a list of works that illustrates coherence makes for too broad an answer. Besides, what's more necessary in this age of hype and disposable art is that the student of writing recognizes the importance of coherence and comes to be able to sense it. Once that discernment is present, each student can seek out models and absorb or unriddle his or her designs.

You've spoken about the importance of making something rather than trying to say something in your writing. What is the relationship, for you, between music and prose?

Music has long been one of the organizing principles of my life. When I was a kid growing up in an inner-city neighborhood, it was music, jazz in particular, that served as the doorway to a wider world. I pursue music incessantly, obsessively, listen to music constantly, read about it, collect it, spend too much money on it, spend not enough money on it—you get the idea.

Music has taught me at least as much about writing as reading has; it's taught me things about a verbal art form in a nonverbal way. Sometimes while generating a new piece of writing, I use the heightened state music can put one in, almost as one might use a drug. I have a collection in my studio that I think of as "writing music," stuff that I don't usually listen to otherwise so as to not wear it out. But it's necessary to return to silence when it's time for the latter-stage rewrites because music can make one's words sound better than they are. Music can, I think, help transport one past the censors of the imagination, but, in the polishing stage of writing, it's necessary to turn off the soundtrack and to try for the impossible: to make the piece of writing itself have its own interior soundtrack, one that a reader who listens might almost detect.

There's a lot more I could say, especially on the underappreciated, seldom addressed subject of prose rhythm. After all, there are no metrics, no system of scansion by which to discuss the music of prose. John Gardner in *The Art of Fiction* writes wonderfully about the subtle effect of prose rhythm at the end of Joyce's "The Dead." He says something about Joyce finding a sentence rhythm more subtle than one possible in verse. Hemingway talks about the need for a writer to hear his way through a story, a fact missed terribly by his many tone-deaf imitators who manage to re-create his mannerisms but miss the underlying rhythmic coherence of his best stories. One aspect of prose rhythm that is usually wholly ignored is that a writer attentive to it, even if simply operating instinctively, often hears the rhythm before he writes the words. There is a rhythmic ebb and flow in mind that slightly precedes and certainly participates in the selection of language. There's a story, and the writer then finds the words that serve as beats and notes to capture the invisible music. And like all music, that soundless thrum, now represented in language (less obviously, but not so differently than the image is represented), conveys deep emotion. It's possible to evoke emotion from many different aspects of a piece of writing, but I find that my own personal tastes, so far as writers of prose, leans heavily toward writers I think of as musical.

That "underlying rhythmic coherence" is often present in your work. In "We Didn't," for instance, the rhythm of the narrator's language immediately draws the reader into the story.

It's difficult for me to bring a story to its conclusion unless I feel that I've found not just its rhythm but also its sound. It's a feeling akin to understanding a character in order to be able to inhabit that character either on the page or on stage. Sound is, for me, a key to the "character" of the story. Of course, that is an obvious element of writing in the first-person voice. But it's true for me in the third person, as well. Rhythm is one of the primary components of what goes into making up that sound. Gardner has another great line in which he talks of description as a writer's connection to his unconscious. The same could be said about sound.

An interest in music can't hurt. Is it essential? Probably not. I know numerous writers who are comfortable reading the most cutting-edge post-modern experimental literature and, yet, whose musical tastes don't extend beyond golden oldies or rock's central lament of American teenage angst: I WANNA BE A BIG STAR. I don't think it's possible to specifically demonstrate the notion of using music as a literary model, although there have been instances when I've tried to capture the ecstatic riffing of, say, an Eddie Palmieri song or the way *The Rite of Spring* begins to chug in order to build its tension. That's all subjective, though. Does a reader ever hear such things in the work?

But in discussing the connection between poetry and prose rhythm, one is on solid ground. I read at least as much poetry as I do fiction; I record notes that I later use for both fiction and poetry in verse.

The language and movement of your prose poems is often similar to your short stories, particularly the shorter pieces that sometimes seem

like poems in *The Coast of Chicago*. When you write, how important is it to know where you are going or, for that matter, what form the material will take?

Sometimes I think I know where a piece is going; sometimes, rather often, I don't. Even when I do think that I know, a chance digression, a juxtaposition or, say, a flat ending can alter the course. A response to a perceived problem or the failure of the piece to live up to its conception can result in its salvation in some unexpected way. Several of my stories, such as "We Didn't" and "Pet Milk," were, in early drafts, poems I was unable to resolve until I allowed them greater narrative latitude, which in turn led to populating them with characters. They became stories with poems encoded in their DNA. Because such reconceptions and accidents have happened so often, I'm now more comfortable treading water between modes and forms, allowing a piece time to exist as a UWO—Unidentified Written Object—accumulating and shedding skins until some design is discernable and it identifies itself as fiction, poetry, nonfiction, or some hybrid.

In your story "Paper Lantern," you create a seamless transition of thought for the narrator, who views an event that causes him to drift from the present into a memory. How do you weave the two settings—memory and present situation that calls forth that memory—while composing a story?

The time machine at the start of "Paper Lantern" and the heightened emotion of the story once it enters extended flashback are, of course, comments on one another and also one and the same.

Writing is the most abstract of the arts. I envy music, painting, and dance their physicality, their sensuality. A legitimate challenge for a writer is to swim upstream against abstraction and try to make writing as sensual as the other arts in which the sensual is taken for granted. The Italian poet Montale is one of my primary examples of such a writer. Of course, as Beckett does, one can go in the opposite direction. But the abstract nature of writing also makes it a medium with tremendous agility. On the turn of a phrase, of a single word, a piece of writing can travel between emotion and thought or between past, present, and future. Because of this great power, narration (which is by nature about a time line) and especially fiction, with its magical relationship with a reader (as opposed to other narrative arts, such as film or theater), is the perfect vehicle for time travel. To my mind, no other art is better suited to emulate memory. Flashback is a primary tool in fiction. Flashback is wholly natural to fiction, whereas in other narrative arts, such as film, it's gimmicky. Directors and playwrights who've managed to use it, such as Miller in *Death of a Salesman* and Fellini, have broadened the reach of their respective arts. Their explorations of the subjective nature of time through flashback devices not natural to their genres, which are located in the present and in real time, is a measure of their genius. In fiction, even the most pedestrian yeomanlike writers have access to movement back and forth in time. Flashback is a tool that can be used for a variety of effects, including introducing exposition. But it is also the tool by which a storyteller conveys the power of memory, and memory is a selective, compressive power—a state of being other than what might be called ordinary reality.

How do you know when a poem or story is finished?

This is a good question, one I've heard asked several times before—most recently just this last summer after a reading that Marvin Bell and I did together in Prague. The where and when it was asked has stayed in my mind because I was unable to answer the question then and don't think I can answer it now. The question itself is simple, direct, and goes directly to the heart of the process of creation. That's a place of considerable mystery and complexity. The question might be answered intellectually, say, in terms of completing a design. But for me, finally, the reason that one piece stays in a drawer waiting for further gestation, while another gets sent out into the world is essentially gut level. I think there's some instinctive calculation involved akin to the calculations predators do to arrive at a decision as to whether the energy expenditure it takes to run down prey will ultimately be worth the nourishment the prey affords.

A legitimate challenge for a writer is to swim upstream against abstraction and try to make writing as sensual as the other arts in which the sensual is taken for granted.

You are legendary for holding on to your work for long periods and editing incessantly before having it published. What do you tell beginning writers about editing?

Something that's obvious, I suppose, but that took years for me to see, is how little schooling in craft most beginning writers have had. There's enormous emphasis on reading, and I applaud it. Writers certainly need to be avid readers. One of many reasons writers read is to instruct themselves in the craft. But most classes that young would-be writers have taken are literature interpretation classes. Seldom, if ever, is craft mentioned in literature interpretation or survey courses. I think most literature teachers take craft for granted, if they consider it at all, and they're far more comfortable discussing philosophical ideas, analyzing psychology, or detailing various political agendas than they are in talking about how a particular piece of writing was fashioned.

Take dialogue, for example. Most writers know how to punctuate dialogue; few have ever been asked to practice it or consider its myriad uses, yet it's as important a tool as any a writer has.

Take point of view. Most people can identify point of view in a story, but again, few have really considered the various ways point of view can be manipulated. They've come from classes in which they've read and debated gender wars and multicultural issues—all enormously important—but no one has ever asked them to notice how a writer uses transition, even though it might be argued that the art of writing the short story is the art of making transitions.

Stuart Dybek on the Editorial Process

Do you have someone read your work in progress?

When I was a student at the Iowa Writers' Workshop, I shared an office with Tracy Kidder [*The Soul of a New Machine*]. We began reading and critiquing one another's work way back then, and we have continued to do so over the years since. Occasionally, I'll send work—especially poems—that I find myself laboring over to other friends, as well, but that's more the exception than the rule. I did a lot more of such reciprocal critiquing when I was younger, especially before I began publishing steadily. It was important to development, and I always urge young writers to strike up such relationships.

How do you deal with editorial suggestions you don't agree with?

My basic mind-set so far as editorial suggestions go is gratitude that a keen literate pro has taken the time to offer an opinion that might help improve the work. And on the whole, that has been my experience—that is, on numerous occasions editors have prompted changes for the good. I consider that positive mind-set to be a healthy attribute for a writer.

Gratitude is, of course, not to be confused with relinquishing control over one's work. On a few occasions I have encountered editing that crossed over into being invasive and wrong-headed. Sometimes while the suggestion might be wrong-headed, what's behind it can be useful. For instance, an editor might mess up sentence rhythm in trying to get more clarity. So it's up to the writer to heighten clarity but also to preserve the prose rhythms. Usually, in instances where there is disagreement, if a writer digs in, even a pushy editor will back off once satisfied that the writer has genuinely considered the suggested change.

So I emphasize craft not, I hope, in some workmanlike way, because I don't believe that about craft. I believe craft is the way the writer makes magic, the gifts through which the writer transcends his or her limitations and participates in a power borrowed or stolen from the gods. Craft, like ancient gifts the gods gave mortals, gives you a power over language that isn't wholly your own.

I think craft can be taught as a series of "movements," the way dance or the martial arts are taught. One learns, for instance, the certain feel and sound of opening a story, how to locate and explore a resonant image, how to sense out a title, the change of gears that often signals closure, and hundreds of other like moves, and, as in dance or karate, these moves become instinctive, available for lightning-quick reactions and recombinations.

Models are, of course, important and obviously are found through reading—reading carnivorously, as writers do,—but the practice of these techniques and the discussion of their uses is what the art of writing is about. I'd like to think that's my emphasis when I teach.

What is essential for new writers to learn about the craft of writing?

That there's magic in craft. Craft makes us better than we are, smarter, wiser, sharpens observation into vision, quickens reflexes, allowing an intellectual activity to be more blessedly instinctive. The practice of the craft of any art is so allied with not simply the expression of imagination but the very *experience* of imagination as to become indistinguishable from imagination.

Craft, like ancient gifts the gods gave mortals, gives you a power over language that isn't wholly your own.

Craft is important to you as a writer and as a reader. What else do you expect from a short story?

I hope for a short story to surprise me into a more intense vision of life. But then that's as much a response to what I expect from art in general. But why be so reductive? Poe demanded an effect from a story. Stories can console, enlighten, seduce, mystify, broaden one's sympathies, enlarge one's experience. I don't insist that a story deeply move me; there are, after all, other kinds of more intellectual pleasures, especially in a medium like language. But by temperament, I do favor stories that communicate strong emotion and strong imagination. And in this age in which agendas and attitude take the place of individual thought, imagination and strong emotion are, unfortunately, not especially typical of either literature or some of the other arts, such as painting.

What are your thoughts on the state of the American short story?

Predictions of the demise of the short story have almost come to seem like a feature of the genre itself. It's a genre I love. Some of my favorite works of literature, some of my favorite books in world literature, are story collections or novels in stories—James Joyce's *Dubliners;* Isaac Babel's *Red Cavalry* and *Odessa Stories;* Sherwood Anderson's *Winesburg, Ohio;* Franz Kafka's stories; Jorge Luis Borges's; Ernest Hemingway's; Eudora Welty's. . . .

I love the intimacy of the short story, the intense chamber music quality.

It's always so difficult to assess the work being done in your own time. The present is contentious and messy, as it should be. It hasn't been winnowed as yet. I'm not going to try to start winnowing here in terms of individual writers. It's almost a reflexive statement, though no less true for that, that one looks for original voices. That quality, almost by definition, is always in short supply. I will venture to say that, in my opinion, if there is a single significant problem for the American story to solve, it is the problem of privilege. Writers who I generally admire address privilege in some way, whether it be thematic or through tone or choice of subject; something about their perspective, on some level, no matter how subtle, recognizes that privilege in America needs to be acknowledged, if not directly confronted.

invitation to the story

RICHARD FORD

Richard Ford, the first novelist to receive the PEN/Faulkner Award and the Pulitzer Prize for the same novel (*Independence Day*), has become a spokesman for the American short story in recent years. Aside from his own fiction, Ford has edited numerous anthologies, including *The Granta Book of the American Short Story, The Granta Book of the American Long Story, The Best American Short Stories, The Essential Tales of Chekhov,* and two volumes of Eudora Welty's work for The Library of America.

Born February 16, 1944, in Jackson, Mississippi, Ford became a favorite among the American school of dirty realism with the publication of his first story collection, *Rock Springs*. In his second collection, *Women With Men*, Ford changed the tone of his short fiction and wrote three long stories focusing on relationships between the sexes.

In *The Sportswriter*, published as a paperback original in 1986, and its sequel, *Independence Day*, Ford demonstrates his range as a novelist by exploring the life of one character, Frank Bascombe. Ford's other novels range from a Faulkneresque portrait of Mississippi in *A Piece of My Heart* to a hard-edged story of drug deals and a Mexican prison break in *The Ultimate Good Luck. Wildlife* is a gentler story of a young boy faced with his mother's adultery set against the backdrop of forest fires in Montana.

Aside from teaching occasionally, Ford's sole profession has been writing. After a brief period as a law student, he received his M.F.A. from the University of California at Irvine.

He has received fellowships from the Guggenheim Foundation and the National Endowment for the Arts. He taught creative writing and literature at Williams College, the University of Michigan, Princeton University, and Northwestern University. He maintains several residences, including a home in New Orleans with his wife, Kristina.

Books by Richard Ford

A Piece of My Heart (novel), Harper & Row, 1976
The Ultimate Good Luck (novel), Houghton Mifflin, 1981
The Sportswriter (novel), Vintage Books, 1986
Rock Springs (stories), Atlantic Monthly Press, 1987
Wildlife (novel), Atlantic Monthly Press, 1990
Independence Day (novel), Knopf, 1995
Women With Men (stories), Knopf, 1997
A Multitude of Sins (stories), Knopf, 2002

It's been more than twenty years since the publication of your first novel, *A Piece of My Heart*. How do you look back on your body of published work, particularly the early novels?

I don't think about it unless somebody comes along and makes me think about it. I'm not a person who looks back at something and revises my opinion of it, particularly work I can no longer affect, change, or improve. It goes without saying that if I were to set out to write a book called *A Piece of My Heart* today, I would probably do it differently. But that's not what's going to happen. There's a wonderful story by Borges called "Pierre Menard, Author of the *Quixote*." In that book, a man named

Pierre Menard decides he is going to write a book. The book he wants to write is *Don Quixote.* He hopes to write, without access to the other book, exactly *Don Quixote.* That, in a way, is Borges saying something about the nature of how we look at time, how we look at the past and past events, how we would like to change them or repeat them. But we can't; that's an absurdity. I'm happy about all my books. The thought that somebody might read *A Piece of My Heart* or make a movie out of *The Ultimate Good Luck* thrills me. I'd be neurotic if I constantly picked away at those earlier accomplishments. I'm not neurotic.

Two of these accomplishments, *The Sportswriter* and its sequel, *Independence Day*, differ both in sentence structure and in tone. Was the change in Frank Bascombe's life something you wanted to establish through this?

I wanted, without knowing how it would eventuate, to have *Independence Day* record change in Frank. I didn't know what the change would be because there ain't no Frank. I make Frank. Frank existed in one book; then when I started to write *Independence Day*, he didn't yet exist in that book. I knew a good working conceit for a sequel would be for the book to record a change in Frank's persona. But I didn't know how it would work. The opening sentences in *Independence Day* are as they were when I first wrote them. Virtually unchanged. That was the mood, tone, sentence weight, and syncopation that were first available to me in *that* book. I thought when I was writing it that it was the same prose as *The Sportswriter.* It was only after I put the two books up side to side, late in the process of writing *Independence Day*, that I realized the sentences are much shorter, less complex, generally more succinct in *The Sportswriter.*

Did you reread *The Sportswriter* before you started work on *Independence Day*?

I deliberately did not. Eventually, I had to skim through it to try to be sure the street names were the same. A couple of times, I had to be sure

I hadn't simply repeated myself with a certain image. It's a complex and involved clerical process to write long novels. When a book is related to another, that just exaggerates the clerical morass.

Is there a third Bascombe novel planned?

I was thinking of having Frank be a Negro. I was thinking of having him become a woman. That's just a way of saying, "Yes, I have." I have to imagine a third book that is so distinct from the other two it's almost not qualified as a sequel. So I'm in the process of accumulating the information about that. I've been doing it for a year, and I'll go on doing it for a couple of years while I do other things. I think probably in a couple of years I'll sit down and see if anything makes sense. As it was, there was an impulse in me when *Independence Day* was published to think, "Well, I've written two. Maybe I could write three." But at that point all I could figure out was what I could write next—what happens the next day after *Independence Day* was over. And to me that's not what a sequel really is. I need the intervention of time to cut me off from any of those stylistic conceits or sentence structures so that I can hatch something new, if indeed I can hatch anything at all. I know a lot of things already about how I would like to write that third book: where I would like it to take place, where I would like it to be set. I don't have yet, and I'm kind of sensitive to this, that big conceit that I had in *Independence Day.* But that's okay. I hope to find it.

You wrote "The Womanizer" during a plane trip from Paris to the United States, and *Independence Day* took four years to complete. How different were these experiences?

When I was on that plane coming back from Paris, I was writing, I guess I'd say, feverishly. I had all this stuff bubbling out of my head, and that doesn't happen to me much because I have the instincts of a novelist. Even when I'm writing short stories, I pace myself so as to always be fresh and not run myself into the ground. With a novel, I don't want to work myself silly because I'll get frustrated and write beyond my capacities to be good, and the next day I'll have to throw stuff away. I am measured in how I work. I go at the thing, and then I stop. I do this all during the day, all during the week, all during the year. So it was different writing that story on the plane. I sat down on the plane and realized there were some things I had to write down. I started writing, then the plane left, and I was still writing. When I got back, the story wasn't precisely finished, but it was drafted out. It was unusual.

How did you make the transition from novel to stories?

There isn't really anything difficult about that. You just stop doing one thing and start doing another. First you wash the dishes, and then you dry them. One minute you do this kind of work, and another minute you do that kind of work. It may seem to be a feat, but it isn't. When I was tired or wanted to stop writing *The Sportswriter*, I would write a story.

One of the things my mother taught me was to try to make everything seem as normal as you can. Don't let the world dictate to you that there is something more difficult than your experience tells you it is. I don't want many things, so it should be possible, given the modest number of things I want, to do them. In a way, writing may create magic in the heart, but it is not performed magically. I wouldn't be able to do it if that were the case.

What kind of relationship do you have with your characters?

Master to slave. Sometimes I hear them at night singing over in their cabins. And sometimes, I'll wake up at night and write down what I hear. Other than that, they don't have an existence that I don't confer on them. I'm kidding, of course. But they don't talk to me. They don't tell me what to do. I make them do whatever I want them to. I'm basically practical, cut-and-dry about characters. They're made of language. They're not people, and I can change them as such. I can change the color of their eyes, their genders, their races. They are totally subservient to me. Which isn't to say that I always plot out their every action. I act on a whim at times, and they have to exist upon that whim. I'm disdainful of these aesthetes who talk about, "My characters wouldn't do that," or, "I just start writing it and then my characters write the book." Horseshit, is what I say. It's a ruse to get out of taking responsibility for your mistakes. Authorship means I authorize everything.

Writing may create magic in the heart, but it is not performed magically. I wouldn't be able to do it if that were the case.

Is this also true of your settings, which are often the starting points of your stories and novels? You've said you aren't necessarily concerned with getting the setting "right." For instance, if you're writing about Mississippi, it doesn't have to look like Mississippi looks.

It can't because Mississippi only looks one way. It looks the way you see it when you get there and get out of your car and walk off into the cotton field and look out at the levee. I can try, through the agency of language, to provoke you into that mental picture, but right away, you understand that language never gets anything that accurately—nothing that's physically provable. Anyway, language is more interesting to me in its poetic and noncognitive qualities than is the mental picture I might betray. So I'm willing to alter the mental picture on behalf of certain pleasures of language. In any case, landscape in my stories is always just background to what the characters do. Plus, even if you could be "accurate," different readers would always envision it differently.

You seem to have a strong interest in language and the weight of words within a sentence. Where did your interest in language originate?

I don't know. From reading Faulkner. Maybe from getting immersed in those long, sometimes endless sentences, and sometimes losing my antecedent, losing my pronoun reference, and sometimes losing all sense of where the sentence is going and still liking it. Maybe from being dyslexic and having to pour over sentences so gravely that I became more attached to the physical qualities of the words than to their referents. From being a slow reader and always weighing the word as I read it just as I do now when I write it.

I grew up in Mississippi, and for reasons I can't begin to tell you, I grew up making word jokes and puns—and Eudora Welty was the same way. We weren't particularly educated, but we were inventive with words. I've always assumed we grew up with a strong sense of irony and absurdity in Jackson because of the basic absurdity of racism: words meaning different things from what they seemed, and so on.

I'm basically practical, cut-and-dry about characters. They're made of language. They're not people, and I can change them as such. I can change the color of their eyes, their genders, their races. They are totally subservient to me.

Did reading Faulkner at a young age and noting his attention to language allow you to see the possibilities of writing fiction?

I can't very well say no, because you read his sentences and you see what they do, how lush and profuse they are. I never really wanted to do that, although I think for a while I was kind of immured in it because I wanted to write about the South, and that came with it. But I don't think Faulkner was particularly stylistically influential in terms of the types of sentences I wrote or the ones I write now. I recognized when I read Faulkner that he was one kind of writer and that he was probably not the kind of writer I was ever going to be if I was moved at times to imitate him. There were other writers who were influential to me on the level of the sentence. Ford Madox Ford was a very affective writer for me. Pinter, Borges, and other writers, too. My view of what sentences are is a licentious view. Sentences are not conceptual formulations the writer sets out to fulfill. They are spontaneous, invented things you have to restrain somewhat to make sense.

You restrain your narration, but what type of process do you go through to create dialogue?

That's a thing I do first by ear. I try to hear the sentence. I write a sentence I like tonally that has the right number of beats in it, that sounds right, and then I see if it is interesting. If it isn't, I start rearranging it. I end up changing its tonal qualities to adapt to what sense it makes or promises to make, and then I develop a new tonal structure for it, a new structure of sounds and relationships, and then sometimes the sense changes. That's one way invention occurs. It's much like rhyming poems or poems in metric patterns. The poet starts trying to figure out how he can accommodate sense with the poem's sound structure, and then the poem develops. You start out with a set of understandings you don't finish with, and that's good; you've learned something.

Much of your work is in the first person. Do you feel more comfortable writing from that point of view?

No, that's just the way a lot of the stories turned out. I did notice something, and I can't account for it right now, but in stories like "Empire," "Occidentals," and "The Womanizer" (all stories written in the third person), I have a much harder time finding redemptive language for events and characters. Those stories all turn out to be—and I don't know if it's just coincidental—harsher stories. The moral quotient to those stories tends to be of a more negative kind. They tend to be stories that indict their characters more than the first-person stories. Why? I don't know. But I'd like it not to be so.

Do you think you have more flexibility, then, with a first-person narrator?

I don't feel, when I'm writing a story in the first person, any different from how I feel when I write a story in the third-person view. There are no tactile distinctions about those two methods for me. You can almost, in a falsely spatial way, say that from a third person you're above the earth a little more, whereas with the first person you are close and personally involved with the characters. Maybe the first person enjoins the reader and the writer to be more sympathetic to the character. Maybe to be godlike is naturally harsher.

***The Ultimate Good Luck* was originally written in the first person, then you changed it to a third-person narrative.**

I didn't like it in the first person because it was too short. There wasn't much of a book there. I showed it to my friend, writer Geoffrey Wolff, and I said, "I wrote this book to the end as I understood it to be, but it's just one hundred fifty pages long. That just isn't enough. It doesn't feel like enough of a book." He read it and said, "Well, you're right. It's not a story, and it's not a novel." He said, "You may have to try it in the third person." I thought that was an interesting idea, and when I started doing it, there was the book waiting to be imagined but in another intellectual mode. I was teaching at Princeton then. I was young and ignorant and didn't know how to do it. I certainly had no idea how hard it would be or how much a different narrative mode using the same focus character would change or cause me to reimagine a story. That was a learning process. It made me realize I had to be more scrupulous when I start a book so that I can try to anticipate mistakes.

Several of the stories in *Rock Springs* are set up as stories within stories. The narrator addresses the reader, announcing the story. Many of the stories also end in hope. Are these elements you wanted to carry throughout the collection?

You're talking about the deliberate invocation of storyness and the deliberate attempt to find something affirming about the story. Both things are deliberate on my part. I want a reader at the beginning of a story to understand that he or she is reading a story. I'm trying to make a clear, almost contractual arrangement with the reader of the story, which says, "Okay, now quit thinking about this and that. Here's a story. It's made up. It's a contrivance made of words. It's not your life. It's something else. It's special. I made it as well as I can. Enter into it. Take pleasure." I think that submission and entry are pleasurable for a reader, or they can be.

The other is another matter. That's something I kind of stumbled on. The first two books I'd written had a rather dark view of the world. My friend Walter Clemens, who's dead now—he was the wonderful book critic for *Newsweek* magazine—told me once that he thought I had somehow short-circuited my sense of humor by writing *The Ultimate Good Luck*, and he wished I hadn't done that. In the process of musing about Walter's remark, I began to realize that in those two books, what I had been looking for and what I would probably always be looking for was drama of some kind of high order. And I had begun, out of youthful ignorance and ardor, to associate darkness—emotional, spiritual, moral darkness—with high drama. It's not unheard of. But I realized I could no longer sustain identifying darkness with drama. I just sort of ground to a halt. I needed, and this was at my wife Kristina's suggestion, to write something that was optimistic or that concerned redemption of a secular kind. And that, with a couple of notable exceptions, has remained my purpose. When you get to the next to last movement of the story and you have one more movement you know you are going to write, you have the option of making that last movement anything you want it to be. My impulse is always to say, "Sometimes I'm defeated. How can I contrive this ending to be the proper ending and to give the reader something affirming?" It's just an instinct. I am, basically, an optimist. I think every writer has got to be an optimist. It's in the character of literature.

Throughout your career, you've edited anthologies, including *The*

Richard Ford on the Short Story Market

How optimistic do you feel about the market for short stories?

That's always been difficult. Eudora Welty, all through the late 1930s and 1940s, didn't want to write any novels. She preferred stories. We've sold a lot of copies of my collection *Women With Men.* It went into the third printing after only three weeks. I think books of stories, probably not commensurate with the number of books of stories that are being published, do okay. If the publishing industry wasn't doing fairly well with collections of stories, they wouldn't be publishing them.

As a writer, you can't worry much about things like that. You can't fight battles for which you have no armor. You're not, as a writer, in the publishing business. As long as publishers are publishing short stories, then you should be writing them. If they finally hang the shingle on the door and say, "Sorry, no more short stories," then maybe you should no longer write them.

***Granta Book of the American Long Story, The Essential Tales of Chekhov*, and two volumes of Eudora Welty's fiction. Why have you focused so much energy on other writers' works?**

Well, for my colleagues, really, and for readers. And also to keep myself reading. If you write all the time and your life is taken up with trying to find something interesting to write and letting yourself be talked into doing this or that, most of your energy is spent writing. I don't feel I read enough. I take these projects on so I can read something I haven't read before. The Chekhov project is a case in point because I was reading many of those stories for the first time. I was interested in the *Granta* project of long stories because I wanted to read those stories again. They were stories I wanted to champion. The case of Eudora Welty's work was a matter of doing something I felt compelled to do because of the excellence of her work and because this was such a good opportunity to have it all consolidated into one place. Ultimately, though, these projects are for others but also for me, too. I do get paid for it, but not much.

You grew up across the street from a house in Jackson, Mississippi, that Eudora Welty once lived in. How do you look back on this coincidence?

My family came to North Congress Street a good while after she had gone. When I was growing up at that place, 736 North Congress Street, I never knew Eudora Welty had lived in the house across the street. It was only in the 1980s that I found out from somebody, maybe her, that she had lived there. She always liked to say, "We were neighbors." And I'm happy to think so, too. It is a sweet coincidence.

You and she became close friends, and with Michael Kreyling, you edited two volumes of her work for The Library of America. How did she feel about your involvement?

She was glad for mostly personal reasons. I was sort of the neighborhood boy, and so I think she felt that I would do as good a job as I could, and indeed, I didn't have to do much. People who were involved in that project did much more than I did, however: Michael Kreyling, who was my co-editor, and Noel Polk, a Eudora Welty scholar at the University of Southern Mississippi who did important reconciliations of Ms. Welty's manuscripts. My job, I sometimes think, was largely ceremonial, but I am happy to be associated with the project because, for us Mississippians, her work embodies something indestructible and incontestably good. I cared for Eudora. I was her literary adviser and her neighbor.

The subject of luck runs throughout your work. Have you developed any theories on luck?

I've always been struck by how things happen in your life in unplanned

Richard Ford on Keeping a Community of Writers

You have written about your friendship with writer Raymond Carver. What does a literary friendship involve?

A literary friendship is one like any other friendship: It offers the faith that someone will act on your behalf, if by acting on your behalf one doesn't have to betray oneself. For writers, I think, specifically, an ongoing interest in the work one does is essential, a willingness (and this is hard) to not always give the most favorable answers to questions when the truth is asked for. A willingness to be amiably candid, if value is put on that.

The two of you became friends when you were just beginning your writing career. How did your career progress from then?

Before any really serious good luck came my way—and good luck is always just temporary, I think—I spent years writing and experiencing the normal vicissitudes of a writer's life in America, which is to say working a long time and not having many readers, having publishers drop you, having your books not picked up for paperback, normal things. I didn't think any of it was exceptional and still don't. When days finally came that I had a bigger readership and things seemed to work out for me better for a while, my habits as a writer, my expectations for what my work would enjoy and what pleasures I took from being a writer, were already well established. It would have been hard to shake me off the ground I thought I was standing on. Even if the ground grew in elevation, I have always had the certainty that it will redescend.

What is the importance of keeping your colleagues in mind this way, of being a part of a community of writers?

It's very important in a way I would probably not be able to specify. Some of its particulars are—and I'm fierce about things like this—that we writers not run each other down in print. I know that because I did it once, and I didn't think I was right. It's important that we try to be as much as we can be forces for good in the lives of our colleagues. I was at an American Booksellers Association convention one day, standing in line waiting to get a hot dog. Tim O'Brien [*The Things They Carried*] grabbed me and said, "God, I haven't seen you in a long time. How are you?" That was important to me. He and I started off together as young writers. I hadn't seen him in years, but there was that sense, and we both felt this without having to say it, that we've been through this together. It's probably a small thing—like Shriners meeting other Shriners. But I liked it. I know we both have the same kinds of aspirations, which is to make a contribution to the world in some way using our best selves. I don't always like my colleagues personally, but I regard them highly as people who are writers. I write them fan letters, and they do the same for me.

ways: Your father dies on a Sunday afternoon; your dog gets run over by a car; you have a child, and the child suddenly dies. Everything you've done in your life has been designed to prevent these things, at least if not from happening, from happening in a way that totally surprises and defeats you. And yet they do. So much of the world is driven by that randomness, which I sometimes call luck. I've always preferred the old adage turned on its ear: Design is the residue of luck. I think everything, basically, is subject to unexpected intervention and that our character as human beings, if we can be said to have character, has a lot to do with how well we accommodate, how well we try to invent a vocabulary and a moral scheme that allows us to take responsibility for our actions in a universe that is much affected by randomness. That's how we stay cogent to ourselves.

Of course, some things aren't random at all. Some things we or others predictably cause, and we must own up to them.

Luck also seems to reverberate in your life: the chance upbringing near Eudora Welty and being invited to a writers conference and meeting Raymond Carver when you were both beginning. How do you look back on these encounters?

In the aggregate, that is how everything happens. There are courses that cause people to collide. I used to have a friend who wasn't a very good friend. When I would publish something or when someone would write something complimentary in the press about me, he would, in a suspicious way, say, "How do you think that happened?" or "Do you know someone there?" He was always slightly impugning any good luck I had. And I always think of it as being just good luck.

The truth is that those kinds of collisions take place one way or another. Sometimes it is just the quality of one's work that wins out, and sometimes you're in the right place at the right time. Sometimes it's a mistake. But I've never had the feeling that in the literary world the fix was in. It isn't profitable enough to want to fix. Consequently, it's just nicely timeless and free. I do still believe that all good writing will eventually find a readership. I mean, so much *bad* writing does. Why shouldn't the good enjoy its small victories?

You've said your writing schedule becomes more intense the deeper you're involved in a project. How do you find your rhythm?

There really isn't much of a rhythm. You quit one day and start the next and try to catch the way things sounded the day before. There may be something of a rhythm when you work at something many days in a row. I can detect it when I break it. If I write six or eight days steady and the work is going in a fairly harmonious way, if something comes along that causes me to take three days off, then I'm aware that something has been interrupted. So if it's a rhythm, then okay. In an odd way, I don't really like to work that much. But I have found over the years that in the context of my life, it satisfies me to work. It's a little bit like eating spinach. You are not supposed to like spinach when you're a kid, but people make you eat it. After a while, you begin to like the taste.

You've said your choice to become a writer was an arbitrary one, made when your mother asked you what you wanted to do. Is that really how it started?

Yes, but I must've been thinking about it. There's such a long time between now and 1968 when that conversation happened. At the beginning, when you say you would like to be a writer, you don't really know what you are saying. You're saying a sentence that seems plausible that nobody can refute and that doesn't cause anybody embarrassment. You set about doing it. After many years, it begins to have the appearance of genuine purpose. But at the moment of embarkation, I didn't know what I was saying. I could have easily said I wanted to be a chimney sweep. I guess if I'd said that, I'd have probably gone on to do it.

Were you writing before that decision?

I had been in law school until three days before. I had been at Washington University, and Stanley Elkin was the adviser to the literary magazine then. I remember hauling out one of the stories I had written as an undergraduate and dressing it up, smoothing it out, getting it proofread, and taking it over to that magazine. Of course, it got rejected. But there must have been something percolating in me in 1966 and 1967 that made writing stories attractive. What was left after law school were those words about me becoming a writer, totally ridiculous words, baffling to my mother. She didn't say no to the idea, but she just looked at me with a sort of wan despair.

You've said if it weren't for her, you wouldn't be a writer.

True, but if it weren't for my wife, I wouldn't be a writer, either. If it weren't for a lot of other people, I wouldn't be a writer. My mother, at least I can say, never discouraged me from being a writer. She never thought it was a terrible idea, though I don't think she understood it very well. She told me when I was young, and later when she was dying, "You must make yourself happy. Go toward those things that make you happy. Stay away from those things that make you unhappy." Now, I don't believe that just deciding to be a writer will make you immediately happy. But some inner peace may be conferred upon you by trying to do something you consider inherently good. My mother was instrumental in that way. All through the years between 1968 and 1981, when she died, I was trying to write books, and she was respectful of that. It's important that your parents not impede you, that they not castigate you or reproach you for doing something they didn't do or something they may not understand. She was always firm in her conviction that if this is what you want to do, then do it.

I do still believe that all good writing will eventually find a readership. I mean, so much *bad* writing does. Why shouldn't the good enjoy its small victories?

It seems that, for a writer, work and life can be more connected than other professions. How has this affected your relationship with your wife and friends?

I guess, at an early stage in life, it felt a little queer to always be home, but then I got over that. Sometimes, when I was an unknown writer who was staying at home writing books and there wasn't any product and no evidence that I was actually doing anything, people would laugh about it—being a househusband and not doing anything. That ended, though. I don't think it's had a big effect on my relationship with other people at all. When I started to publish books, the naysayers slipped to the back row. As far as my relationship with Kristina is concerned, we started out in life this way.

The year we were married, 1968, was the year I started trying to write stories. So we never had a life that didn't involve me staying at home writing stories or that didn't involve her getting in a car and going to work, which she did and does to this very minute. She was certainly never reluctant to have me at home. We are pretty conventional people in most ways. We have a house with pictures on the wall; we have dogs running around. I have a motorcycle and a car. But at the same time, we are not much inhibited by convention. We don't let it tell us what's right and wrong. This is the way we've always set out to live. It didn't seem to me to be radically divergent from what other people did. It was never an issue.

Some critics have branded you a "male writer." Although many of your male characters are decent people or people who are trying to be decent, the women are often the stronger characters.

People who brand me a "male writer" haven't read my stories. I like to hunt, and I like to fish. I used to box. I've got a pretty wife. Even if the fiction doesn't bear that out, I still get typecast as a certain kind of guy. I rather hate to think, though, that I've been writing books all these years, working this hard, for only half the population. I would never do that. If I believed I was doing it, I would quit. I would say, "No more of that." Women and men are so much alike as human beings, and they need to be addressed in ways that cause them, by the agencies of that address, to seek out the places they are alike rather than just hide behind the gender distinctions.

How do you and your wife respond to comments like that against you and your writing?

I've been surprised by how long it's held on. When you first make your entrance in the world as a writer, there isn't much for the press to hang on you. So they hang whatever they can hang on you, often something superficial or invented. Maybe living in the West as I have or being a Southerner as I am or being the kind of guy I seem to be, that made sense at one moment. But for it to persist so long is silly. I think what Kristina felt when she first saw it was, "Well, you are kind of a male guy. You are not ashamed about being a man, and you do have certain tastes that are traditionally male pleasures." I get mad in a sort of flash way when I see somebody dismiss me for being something I'm not. You really have to start worrying when they get it too right, when somebody's got you all figured out. But other than that, please spell my name right.

What do you think is the role of writers in American society?

In America, writers are totally marginal and not taken too seriously, which may be freeing. Here we have become a country of professionals, and writers are not professionals. We are amateurs. We don't have any rules for governing our daily lives or for our quasi-, would-be vocational lives. We are inventing new things all the time and working within and outside established modes. We don't fit in, but we're not left out completely, either. A writer is a person who looks at the world from across a frontier, writer V.S. Pritchett said. That's kind of the way it is in America. Our role as writers is to try to write about the most important things we know and hope that other people will agree about their importance. I don't, however, think the concerns of novels finally formulate the public consciousness much. In fact, we're always tugging at the coattails of American culture. We're followers, not leaders. We're always writing about things that have already occurred. In that aspect of the arts, we are always slightly retrospective. There's almost no way in which narrative art can be avant-garde. It's always reacting to something in the culture.

Our role as writers is to try to write about the most important things we know and hope that other people will agree about their importance.

voices in mind

ERNEST J. GAINES

Ernest J. Gaines was born on January 15, 1933, and raised on a plantation near False River, in central Louisiana, the area that serves as the setting for much of his fiction. Though he left the plantation to join the army and to later study in California, the stories that he heard and observed on the plantation form the foundation of his work. In his fiction, he views struggles of love, race, and family beneath the microcosm of the plantation.

Gaines attended graduate school at Stanford University, where he was a Wallace Stegner fellow and, later, writer in residence. He received the 1993 National Book Critics Circle Award for his most recent novel, *A Lesson Before Dying*, which became a *New York Times* best-seller six years later when it was chosen for the Oprah Book Club. *A Lesson Before Dying, The Autobiography of Miss Jane Pittman,* and *A Gathering of Old Men* were all made into feature films.

Gaines has received an American Academy of Arts and Letters Award in Literature, a Guggenheim Fellowship, and a MacArthur Foundation Fellowship. In 2000, Gaines received the National Humanities Medal. "A

Long Day in November," from *Bloodline*, was selected by Richard Ford for *The Granta Book of the American Long Story*.

Gaines and his wife divide their time between San Francisco and Lafayette, Louisiana, where he is writer in residence at the University of Louisiana at Lafayette (formerly the University of Southwestern Louisiana).

Books by Ernest J. Gaines

Catherine Carmier (novel), Atheneum, 1964
Of Love and Dust (novel), The Dial Press, 1967
Bloodline (stories), The Dial Press, 1968
The Autobiography of Miss Jane Pittman (novel), The Dial Press, 1971
In My Father's House (novel), Knopf, 1978
A Gathering of Old Men (novel), Knopf, 1983
A Lesson Before Dying (novel), Knopf, 1993

You've said you write your stories to be read aloud. Do you think there's an advantage to oral storytelling?

When people hear stories, they identify more closely with the characters. When I read aloud, people always come up to me and say, "I understand it much better now that I've heard you read it. I can hear the characters' voices much clearer." Quite often, writers use dialects or words and phrases we are not familiar with, but once we hear it, we tend to understand it.

Dialogue is something you said you're proud of in your work. Does this go back to the sounds of words?

In dialogue, I'm dealing with the sounds I've heard. One of the reasons I suppose I often write from first person or multiple points of view is because I want to hear the voices of different characters. Omniscient narration becomes a problem because, for me, the omniscient is my own voice narrating the story and then bringing in characters for dialogue.

I think my ear is pretty good. As a small child, I listened to radio a lot. During that time—this was back in the late 1940s—there were always great dramas on radio. I liked listening to them because I had to follow the story through dialogue. I like reading plays, and I like listening to the ways people speak. Sometimes I have to rewrite and rewrite to get the exact phrases I want. I stick with south Louisiana and not places with accents I don't know anything about.

Does this oral approach help when you are editing your work?

I usually record my work. If it sounds good, then it is. I never read my work to anyone else and say, "Okay, what do you think?" Editors recommend certain things, but usually, at this point in the game, I can stick to my guns and say, "This is how it's written, and this is how it sounds." I know about this stuff because I write about south Louisiana, and I feel my ear is pretty good for the dialects of south Louisiana, at least better than the people in New York who have never been here.

You also have a great talent for character development. How did you find Miss Jane Pittman's voice?

I did a lot of research to get the historical facts right, and I read quite a few slave narratives to see how they expressed themselves. I grew up on a plantation on False River, and I was around older people—my aunt who raised me and the older people who visited her because she was crippled and couldn't walk. I had those voices in mind when I created Miss Jane Pittman. She was not based on any one person or any two people, but on the kind of experience I felt someone who lived during that time might have gone through. I had read enough, and I could recall the sounds and the dialects and the limited vocabulary of the older people on the plantation to create an authentic voice for Miss Jane. The first draft was told from multiple points of view with people talking about her after she had died. I did that for more than a year, and then I realized it was not exactly right. I needed to get her to tell the story, so I concentrated on one voice rather than several voices.

Some people believe *The Autobiography of Miss Jane Pittman* is an autobiography with an introduction by Ernest J. Gaines.

Several people reviewed it as an autobiography, and many bookstores keep it on the autobiography shelf. There was a famous magazine in New York that called me for a picture of Miss Jane because they were reviewing the book. I said, "You know, that is a fictitious character." They said, "Oh, my God!" They had already written the review, and they wanted a picture to go with it. My agent had tried to sell it to a couple of women's magazines, but they turned it down when they realized a man had written it. As long as a woman would have written it, it would have been great. I was in Orlando, Florida, talking to some people, and one guy said, "Mr. Gaines, may I ask you a question? How long did you have to interview that old lady before you had enough material to write the book?"

Have there been some characters' voices that were easier to find than others?

I feel I got inside Jim in *Of Love and Dust* easily because I was thirty-three years old when I started writing that book, and I created him to be the same age. He uses the same language I grew up around living in Louisiana. Also, it wasn't too difficult to find Jefferson's voice that's seen in his diary in *A Lesson Before Dying* because I wrote the diary after I had been writing the novel for five years, so I felt I knew his character.

Are there particular works of literature or films, such as *Rashomon*, that helped shape the way you deal with various points of view in one story?

I saw *Rashomon* many years ago, and I suppose that has had some effect on me, as well as Faulkner, Joyce, and whoever else's work I've read. They say if you steal from one person, you are a plagiarizer; if you steal from a hundred people, you are a genius. You don't pick entirely from Faulkner, entirely from *Rashomon*, or entirely from Hemingway. You learn from all of them, just as all writers have done. You learn from people you read.

Ernest J. Gaines on Point of View

Is point of view one of the first decisions you make when you begin a story or novel?

I change point of view when one doesn't work for me. *A Gathering of Old Men* was originally told from one point of view, that of the newspaperman, Lou Dimes. Then I realized he could not tell the story. He could not see Snookum running and striking his butt the way you would if you were trying to make a horse run faster. He could not see Janie going to that house and so many other small things that could make the story better. He would have never known the thoughts of these people. So much of the story is internal. There is little action. You don't see Beau being shot. What you see is Beau lying there and all these other people talking and thinking. I knew I had to write it from multiple points of view.

I recommend taking the easiest route in writing, not to make things harder than they really are. If you can tell a story better from the omniscient point of view, then tell it that way. If you can tell it better from first person, tell it that way. I never say, "Well, I'm going to tell some first-person stories and some omniscient ones." I think, "How can I tell my story? What's the easiest way to tell it without cheating?"

Who and what else have you been influenced by?

I've been influenced by the great French filmmakers of the 1950s—Truffaut, for example, particularly *The 400 Blows* and *Shoot the Piano Player.* When I was writing *A Lesson Before Dying,* I saw a film on television with Danny Glover, and it had tremendous effect on me. Danny Glover plays a social worker who visits prisons. There's one prisoner who will do anything to annoy him. I realized that this is what happens when you keep going back to a prison to visit one guy. He will always do something to irritate you. That's how I decided to have Jefferson not speak, or say something to aggravate Grant.

What I'm saying is that you learn from all these things. You learn from music, from watching great athletes at work—how disciplined they are, how they move. You learn these things by watching a shortstop at work, how he concentrates on one thing at a time. You learn from classical music, from the blues and jazz, from bluegrass. From all this, you learn how to sustain a great line without bringing in unnecessary words. I advise beginning writers to keep their antennae out so they can pick things up from all these sources, not only books, but everything life has to offer, but books especially, which are the main tools they have to work with. They should not close their ears or eyes to anything that surrounds them.

There was a famous magazine in New York that called me for a picture of Miss Jane because they were reviewing the book. I said, "You know, that is a fictitious character."

You've recommended the book *Max Perkins: Editor of Genius* by A. Scott Berg. How do you think about that style of hands-on editing exemplified by Perkins?

I like Maxwell Perkins because of all the great writers who were around him. A. Scott Berg did a wonderful job with that book. He did a lot of research and brought out the different characters of F. Scott Fitzgerald, Ernest Hemingway, and Thomas Wolfe.

I knew some good critics and editors. Malcolm Cowley, who had the sense to rediscover Faulkner, was a teacher of mine at Stanford. Wallace Stegner was my mentor at Stanford. He was the person who brought me there. Ed [E.L.] Doctorow, who later became famous as a writer himself, was my editor at Dial Press. I have a good editor at Knopf now, Ash

Green. These people are wonderful editors. They are not as famous as Max Perkins, and not all writers are fortunate enough to get great editors, but I've been lucky. You need a good editor because every writer thinks he can write a *War and Peace*, but by the time he gets it on paper, it's not *War and Peace* anymore; it's comic book stuff. If you have an honest editor who knows what literature and writing are about, he can give you good advice. You don't have to necessarily follow it all. It's good to get the material away from you after you've finished something, to send it out and let another person comment on it.

I had a wonderful agent, Dorothea Oppenheimer, and she saw everything of mine for thirty-one years. Whenever I wrote something, I sent it to her. We had our fights. When she would criticize me, I would say, "Well, you don't know what you're talking about. I'm the writer." But I would apologize later. I think those editors and agents are necessary.

You began work on what became your first novel, *Catherine Carmier*, when you were sixteen years old. It went through many rewrites and titles. What did you learn through this?

I tried to write a novel that later became *Catherine Carmier*. Of course, I sent it to New York to a publisher, and they sent it back. We had an incinerator in the backyard, and I burned it. I was falling back in my class work, so I started concentrating on school. When I was twenty, I went into the army. I wrote a little bit. When I was twenty-two, I went to San Francisco State University to study literature and theater writing. Then I went to Stanford and was writing short stories during that time. Someone gave a lecture, and he told us that young writers would have a hard time publishing a collection of stories. So that day, I put the stories aside and said, "I've got to write something I can publish." That was in January of 1959.

I didn't have anything else for a novel but that one story I tried to write fifteen years earlier. I started rewriting it, and I wrote about fifty pages and won the Joseph Henry Jackson Award, which was an award given to California residents. That helped me get through 1959. I got jobs at the post office, a print shop, a bank. I would write in the morning and get these little part-time jobs in the afternoon. From 1959 to 1964, I wrote that novel over and over. I must have written it more than ten times. Each time I rewrote it, I came up with a different title. I was always changing things: Somebody would die in one draft, and another person would die in the next. Malcolm Cowley saw it, and several other editors saw it, but no one was ready to publish it. I worked on it for about five years, but it is still a simple story about a guy coming back to the old place and visiting the old people, and he has changed so much that he doesn't fit in anymore.

When I was writing that book, I used Turgenev's *Fathers and Sons* as a model. I read something from it every day. It's about a young doctor who has just finished university and comes back to the old place and falls in love with a beautiful woman. He loses her and dies. My character does the same thing, but he doesn't die. He has to go away again.

In that novel, you explore a situation—a young man who leaves Louisiana to receive an education, then returns—that you examine in your most recent novel, *A Lesson Before Dying*.

My characters can't get away. Miss Jane tries to walk to Ohio, but, of course, she never gets out of Louisiana. Charlie in *A Gathering of Old Men* tries to run away, but he has to come back. I guess all my characters are like that; they go far, and then they return. They must face up to their responsibilities.

Your characters seem to know that they must accept responsibility and go on because it's the graceful thing to do.

They have to make the effort to go on, and sometimes it brings death. But they must make that effort before the moment of death. In *A Lesson Before Dying*, Jefferson must stand before he will be executed. Marcus in *Of Love and Dust* can't escape, but he rises before he dies and becomes a better human being. There are certain lines they have to cross to prove their humanity. I could not write about or focus my attention on a character who did not have these characteristics—a person who struggles and falls but gets up, who will go to a certain point even though he knows he might get killed. That's a common theme in all my work: those who cannot escape by running away, and those who go to a certain point even if it means death. For example, in *A Lesson Before Dying*, Grant will not try to run away anymore. I think Vivian is going to keep him in Louisiana.

There's a great sense of optimism in your work. Even though Jefferson cannot escape execution in *A Lesson Before Dying*, he can find peace. Because of this, you turn a potentially devastating book into something redemptive.

I made both Jefferson and Grant tragic figures because I wanted this to be a story about more than just a young black man sitting on death row. I needed someone to go to the prison and teach Jefferson, but also someone who would learn while teaching. Grant is also in a type of prison because he is unable to live the way he would like to live. I had to discover how he could break out of that. Jefferson, of course, finds release in death, and Grant must take on the responsibility of becoming a better person, a better teacher.

Was writing always something you thought you would do?

I did not know I wanted to be a writer when I was a child in Louisiana. It wasn't until I went to California and ended up in the library and began reading a lot that I knew it. I began to read many great novels and stories, and I did not see myself or my people in any of them. It was then that I tried to write.

There were few people on the plantation who had any education at all, especially the old people my aunt's age and my grandmother's age. They had never gone to school, and they didn't have any books. I used to write letters for them. I had to listen carefully to what they had to say and how they said it, the words they tried to use. I put their stories down on paper, and they would give me teacakes. If I wanted to play ball or shoot marbles, I had to finish writing fast. It was then that I began to create. I would write about their gardens, the weather, cooking, preserving. I would talk about anything. I've been asked many times when I started writing. I used to say I started writing in the small Andrew Carnegie Library in Vallejo, California, but I realize now that I started writing on the plantation.

It sounds like it took leaving the plantation to understand that those stories should be told.

Oh, yes. I realized that later. At that time, I was just trying to write those letters as fast as I could. Later, when I tried to write, especially when I went to Stanford, I was encouraged to write about my past. But I had already tried that with the novel I began when I was sixteen years old.

What kind of impact have your many years of teaching had on your writing?

My students keep me aware of things around me, but I don't know that my "style," and I hate using words like that, has changed in any way or if my views on life have changed. Most of my students are middle-class, white females. I learn about their ways of thinking and describing things, their backgrounds and social lives. So when I come to write something of my own, I can use this if necessary. For example, when I was writing *A Gathering of Old Men,* I had someone in mind just like Candy. In fact, she's still on that plantation, and she knows I was writing about her in some ways. I've learned a lot about writing about white females by being aware of my students. I am always picking up things, and sometimes I don't know I am doing it. I am always getting information from the things and people around me, the sounds, the sights, the weather.

Were there goals you set at the beginning of your career?

Well, I thought I would win the Nobel Prize. I thought I would make a lot of money and be able to send it back to my aunt who raised me, but she died many years before any of my work had been published. I told myself I would write for five, six hours every day and try to have enough money to support myself to write. I wanted to have enough money to write as much as I wanted to write, but I never set any goals to be rich or travel the world.

Did you set out to write books with such varying time frames? *The Autobiography of Miss Jane Pittman* stretches more than one hundred years, and *A Gathering of Old Men* follows characters through a single day.

I am proud to have accomplished this, to concentrate on one day with flashbacks, and then to also write something as broad as *The Autobiography of Miss Jane Pittman.* The novels are all about the same number of pages, and the time span in most of them is the same. In *A Lesson Before Dying,* I had to stretch the time to what would be equivalent to the semester of school blacks were getting in the rural South, and, at that time, we were getting less than six months. I knew exactly the kind of time I had to put into that novel as far as story line, when it would begin and when it would end. I never decided beforehand how long a book would be. It just so happens I learned more from Turgenev than I thought I did in the beginning. His novels were short compared to Dostoyevsky's or Tolstoy's. I feel after I've written so many pages, maybe at most four hundred pages, there is nothing else to say, so it is time to close it down. I knew *The Autobiography of Miss Jane Pittman* would be a hundred years and that it would be a longer novel than my earlier ones.

I have been influenced by so many different forms of writing. I studied Greek tragedy when I was at San Francisco State, and I've always thought the idea of having things in a single setting and limited to twenty-four hours was the ideal way of telling stories. For example, "A Long Day in November" takes place within less than twenty-four hours, as do "Bloodline" and "The Sky Is Gray." "Just Like a Tree" takes place in three hours.

In an interview, Walker Percy said the most he could hope to do as a writer was to point out certain truths. What do you feel is your responsibility as a novelist?

I think in writing you try to not answer things, but to perk the interest or the intellect of the reader and let him ask questions. Once the reader begins to ask these questions, he will get some answers that will lead him to other things so he can discuss it with other people. I don't know how to give answers. I try to create characters who develop through the course of the novel, characters who learn and grow before they die and from whom the reader can learn and grow.

I receive many letters from people all over the country and different parts of the world, and most of them come from white males. I think they're middle-aged. Bill Gates said *A Lesson Before Dying* was one of his favorite books, along with *The Catcher in the Rye*, so that's good to hear, but he never sent me any computer stuff. I've always received many letters from students, but *A Lesson Before Dying* seems to have touched a lot of people.

I am always picking up things, and sometimes I don't know I am doing it. I am always getting information from the things and people around me, the sounds, the sights, the weather.

You came into a lot of publicity when Oprah Winfrey chose *A Lesson Before Dying* for her book club. How did you feel when you learned this?

Oprah called me personally, and I didn't believe it was her. She said, "This is Oprah Winfrey. I'd like to speak to Ernest Gaines." I said, "Speaking. Oprah Winfrey? Of the television show?" She said, "We've chosen *A Lesson Before Dying* for the Oprah Book Club. This is all hush-hush until I announce it on my show." I said, "It's okay with me, just as long as I can tell my wife." Oprah came to Louisiana, to the plantation at False River. We spent two days together.

***A Lesson Before Dying* had won the National Book Critics Circle Award in 1993, but did you feel a rush of new readership because of Oprah's influence?**

Oh, yes. Before, the book was selling well, but it was selling to high schools and libraries. With Oprah, it sold to the general public. There were between eight hundred thousand and a million copies printed as soon as she announced it. Everybody knew *The Autobiography of Miss Jane Pittman*, but they never knew who wrote it. Now, they know Ernest Gaines wrote *A Lesson Before Dying* because they saw me on the show.

How do you feel about all the attention?

It doesn't really affect me. I'm happy people are reading the book, but other than that, I just do the same thing. I teach. My wife and I still go to the same restaurants. We still visit our friends, things like that.

from experience to innocence

WILLIAM H. GASS

William H. Gass has earned prestige in each field he has pursued. As a novelist, essayist, philosopher, and translator, he has been placed in the forefront of American letters.

The composition of Gass's first novel, *Omensetter's Luck*, engaged him for fifteen years. *The Tunnel*, which consumed more than thirty years of Gass's life, became legendary in the literary world. More than three hundred pages of excerpts from the novel appeared in numerous publications, including *Conjunctions*, *Esquire*, *The Paris Review*, and *TriQuarterly*, years before the novel was published.

Born July 30, 1924, in Fargo, North Dakota, Gass has written two collections of fiction, *In the Heart of the Heart of the Country and Other Stories* and *Cartesian Sonata and Other Novellas*. His novella *Willie Masters' Lonesome Wife* is a classic text of metafiction that combines photography, graphic art, essay, and fiction. As a postmodern writer, his work has been compared to that of Thomas Pynchon, William Gaddis, and John Barth. In his introduction to Gaddis's *The Recognitions*, Gass comically relates the theory that the entire output of these four writers is the work of a single person.

He has twice received the National Book Critics Circle Award for criticism. He has won four Pushcart Prizes and has received grants from the Rockefeller, Lannan, and Guggenheim Foundations. He was honored with the PEN/Nabokov Award for Career Achievement and was elected to the American Academy of Arts and Letters in 1983.

Gass lives with his wife in St. Louis, Missouri.

Books by William H. Gass

Omensetter's Luck (novel), New American Library, 1966
In the Heart of the Heart of the Country and Other Stories (stories), Harper & Row, 1968
Fiction and the Figures of Life (nonfiction), Knopf, 1970
Willie Masters' Lonesome Wife (novella), Knopf, 1971
On Being Blue (nonfiction), David R. Godine, 1975
The World Within the Word (nonfiction), Knopf, 1978
Habitations of the Word (nonfiction), Simon & Schuster, 1984
The Tunnel (novel), Knopf, 1995
Finding a Form (nonfiction), Knopf, 1996
Cartesian Sonata and Other Novellas (stories), Knopf, 1998
Reading Rilke (nonfiction), Knopf, 1999
Tests of Time (essays), Knopf, 2002

In your fiction, you remind the reader of his role and of your responsibility as the writer. How does this consciousness play into your writing?

For me, the exchange is between the page and myself. It is certainly true that if you are writing essays or writing reviews, while you are not thinking about a specific reader, you are, of course, addressing a reader, telling him something. In that process, you have to remember that you have responsibilities because you are reporting on something that, in a certain sense, is a kind of news. As far as the essay as it becomes an expression of what I'm trying to think about, I don't have readers in mind at all. Walter Benjamin said things of this nature aren't written for readers. Gertrude Stein used to say that she wrote for herself and strangers, but she eliminated the strangers after a while, and then she eliminated herself, which I think is the right thing to do as a writer. You are trying to make this fiction or essay, and if you aim it at anybody, something undesirable happens. What you are writing has its own demands that you try to satisfy. For me, that is a good thing because I don't have much of an audience anyway.

You've talked about a house as a metaphor for a book, where the writer guides readers through rooms.

Yes, but the reader has more freedom than that. As a writer, you are making a verbal space. The reader can leave the tour and go anywhere he wants. Of course, the writer creates the guided tour, but the reader proceeds at his own pace and is quite free to do whatever he wants. He can read the last page first. He doesn't have to pay attention at all.

Do you read a certain way when you are reading as a writer?

I do read in different ways. When I'm teaching, for instance, I try to read as a writer. Many students don't like this because it isn't the way they read. It isn't even the way you ought to read. This type of reading is dedicated to figuring out how a thing is put together. If I am going to start thinking about how this chair is put together, that is quite different from just sitting in it.

Reading is quite different when you are reading in order to talk or write about a text. That is one of the great losses of this profession, either as a critic or a writer. You don't have that innocence or openness that says, "Let me read and have a good time," that you might have had when you started out. Instead, you think, "What am I going to say about this?" or "What is the story telling me about how I am to write?" That isn't a good way for reading, as such. It's rare now that I get to read without any plan or aim.

But if you read a work to discover how it was built, don't you learn more about the text and about writing, even though you may strip the experience of a certain enjoyment?

Yes, you do. And after that, you never go back and just read it. It's like analysis and synthesis. You have the analysis part, and if you can get it back in order and just read it, you should. That is best, of course. Too many times, all I remember about the things I like most, that I've been teaching for years, is that I've been teaching them for years.

Have you come across writers who still make you feel innocent as a reader?

Actually, yes. There are certain writers who are hard to analyze. They are almost seamless, and they have a certain ease that lets you slide through the text without saying, "What the hell is happening here?" These are writers who restore that very quality of innocence. I think Colette is perhaps one of the best examples. She is delicious. As you are reading, you pretty soon say, "Oh, well, let me just have another bite."

What are some of the discoveries you are making as a writer today?

I'm working on a book now that's been in the works for some time. It is all about the sentence, really. I've talked about that subject in a number of seminars. The first time I taught a seminar on the sentence, everybody thought, "How in the hell are we going to spend a whole semester on the sentence?" We didn't get anywhere near the end of our subject. Now, I'm working on the architecture of the sentence, the actual construction. So you get into linguistics and then go in thousands of different directions, just on that subject, which seems to be narrow, but there is always more to learn. The hardest question is not what a sentence is, but what a good one is.

You've been critical of writers who you think write only for the page. What, in your view, should writers aim for in writing a sentence?

William H. Gass on the Importance of Observation

For those who want to write, do you think it's beneficial to learn about other subjects?

I think so. People are different, of course. All people are different in their emotion, psychology, and character, so what works for one person may not work for the next. A writer has to know something, not just how to write. Certainly for me, that is vital. And just as there are certain kinds of readers, as a writer, you have to become a certain kind of observer and examiner of the world. Various writers do that differently. That is, they see and hear things differently than you and I. That is part of their background, and it is what they need to write. Certain writers have a magical ear, and some writers don't have that at all. I'm teaching Katherine Anne Porter right now, and she had the most magnificent eye. She really saw things. There, the eye is education, and it certainly falls outside the academic curriculum.

It's extremely important—especially for prose writers because they are not expected to do it as much—to create a work with a significant body as well as a conceptual structure. Language is basically constructual. The sounds and shapes of words are arbitrary, and you don't want them to seem arbitrary, so you try to bring those sounds and shapes into as close a connection with the sentence's structure and meaning as possible. Traditionally, there are a lot of reasons for this. Most of the structural forms that dominate poetry are mnemonic devices, but it is much more difficult for writers in our position to work with the visual side, and so it gets neglected, at least in the West.

In the East, this isn't so. In calligraphy, the actual writing of the poem is as much a part of what the poet is doing as is the language of the poem. We have a tradition of concrete, or visual, poetry. With it, the placement of words on a page has a notational significance that the reader is supposed to pick up. Stéphane Mallarmé does this all the time. He creates a visual field by putting words in certain places. And then, of course, the sounds of words must be managed as well—something we are more used to. Finally, there is a connection between the sights of words.

Traditionally, prose has just been divided by the page as the page happens to appear. A poet would never allow a stanza to be interrupted in the middle by the turning of a page or having two letters dangling at the end of a line, but that happens to prose writers all the time. My interest is in where the words are put and what visual effect they produce. That tells the reader something about what is going on in the book, as well. These preoccupations remain on the edge of things, but more and more, I think it is being explored and becoming important.

By using a fictional language and, as in *Willie Masters' Lonesome Wife* and *The Tunnel*, other graphic elements within the text, what do you hope to achieve?

It depends again on what you are up to. *Willie Masters' Lonesome Wife* was a kind of odd manifesto; it was part essay, part fiction, and part this and that. Some of the text spoke of difference: "Look, this is what images do, and this is what language does. Look at how they don't do the same thing." But because the images are being used in a painterly way, their use resembles that of linguistic placement. Marianne Moore, for example, always made each of her poems a different shape. That shape is not a painterly shape. It is a notation about the way you are supposed to read the poem. Space is given a function, like a comma, that helps order the meaning of the line or poem. Moore counts the syllables, and then she arranges all the other stanzas to form the shape of the poem. But the questions are, "Why? What does this arrangement do? How do I understand it?" There are so many possibilities. It isn't the same kind of manipulation a painter would aim for. There is constant tension as well as harmony and cooperation in this.

What have you noticed about the reactions to *Willie Masters' Lonesome Wife* since it was published in *TriQuarterly* in 1968?

These reactions change over time. Most of the negative reaction to that piece occurred before it was published. That was true of my early work. It took years to get my work published, and it was hard to even get it published at all. Then, once it was published, to my astonishment, the critics were quite benevolent. But that was early on. After you have a career and people identify a certain position with your work, things change. The early critics of *Willie Masters' Lonesome Wife* were quite kind. They tended simply to enjoy it. Now, people are still reading it, and they are attacking it. By now, the reading of my work, just as it is for so many people, is ideological. When I have a new book come out, it is almost entirely viewed as an ideological thing: "This guy is doing these things because he believes this or that about writing." That is certainly not what I want.

If the book is praised, people say it is because that critic is in my intellectual camp, and if it is condemned, it is because the critic isn't in my camp. That happens retrospectively for books I wrote years ago. Old books become fresh enemies. It's surprised me, the way that works. When I had so much trouble getting anything published, I thought the critics were going to be adamant, but my troubles were with editors. Then, the critics were kind, but after *The Tunnel*, they were not so happy, and they are still not at this point. When you have a track record and a position, you are part of the intellectual war that goes on regardless of whether you like it.

That goes along the same lines as being grouped with certain writers of fiction, as well.

That's right. There is a group of writers I'm associated with in critics' minds, people I actually know and like quite well—no one knows Pynchon, of course—but we don't write alike at all. Paul Valéry said something good about this when he was discussing why he was called a symbolist. He said, "It's because we are all against the same things." I think that is correct. We have an antagonism for certain traditional methods, and when we start going off on our own about that, it becomes a very different story.

You've been noted as saying, "Fiction just is. It isn't supposed to do or cause anything." But you spent thirty years of your life writing *The Tunnel*. What type of relationship did you develop with that book?

The Tunnel was extended, exacerbated. It takes a long time to write a novel, even if it's a bad one. You have to be the same writer through the whole book, and yet you don't want to be the same person for that amount of time. So you have to construct a project that is strong enough to determine the writer of the project. In *The Tunnel*, I had a narrator, William Kohler, who was the whole damn book and whose nature was strong enough that I could reenter it. After a while, it got to be disagreeable to enter Kohler because he is such a disagreeable character. That's one of the reasons it took so long, I think. I didn't enjoy going back and becoming that character.

A lyric poem can be composed in a relatively short period of time, and you can be the same poet and have the same voice. A short story is a little harder, but it's still not as difficult as a novel. During long projects, books become geologically layered. As a writer, you have to hide those layers and make it seem as though the entire text emerged at once.

It takes a long time to write a novel, even if it's a bad one. You have to be the same writer through the whole book, and yet you don't want to be the same person for that amount of time.

How much do you know about a work when you begin to write it?

Very little. I get an idea, and sometimes I even collect a little data, but I'm not a researcher. The data sits and stews for a long time before I start to work. I'm always surprised by my discoveries, and I never outline

William H. Gass on Getting Published

How did you get your first publishing break?

There are two sorts of "publishing breaks." The first is when something of yours is accepted by a magazine or journal; the second is a book publication.

After eight frustrating years, in which I could not get even a letter to the editor published, a distinguished little magazine, *Accent*, not only accepted a story of mine, they decided to devote an entire issue to my work. It was a long famine followed by a brief feast.

My first novel, *Omensetter's Luck*, was rejected by over a dozen publishers before David Segal, a young editor who wanted the book, got a position that gave him the authority to choose one book on his own. Its publication took a devoted agent and editor who would not abandon the manuscript.

How did you find your agent?

My agent, Lynn Nesbit, young and aspiring, searched the literary magazines for talent. She had an eye for it and was smart enough to trust her judgment. So she read me, and wrote me, and found a desperate client. I was not alone. She collected others equally obscure.

Do you have anyone read your work before you send it to your agent?

Now I am copyedited only and have an editor, Victoria Wilson, I esteem. It is good luck. My response to editing of any kind is visceral, irrational, essential. Editing I don't like I ignore or refuse, no matter what. No one reads my work before I send it off, and it goes to my editor and agent simultaneously.

anything. That is another reason it takes me so long. I'm always discovering what I'm trying to do, which is sort of fun, but also exacerbating.

In your collection *Finding a Form*, you note the importance of literature. In "A Fiesta for the Form," you quote Carlos Fuentes's *Terra Nostra*: " . . . nothing truly exists if it not be consigned to paper." What can we hope to gain through reading and writing literature?

Very little. Literature and the humanities in general don't save people. We like to think they do, but they don't. That's one reason, as in *The Tunnel*, I am interested in the Nazi period, where many highly educated and sophisticated people behaved abominably. One could be a great composer or have a mind like Heidegger and also be a fascist. You can't predict that a work of literature will go out and do anything—and how awful it might be if it did, in a certain sense. The futility of teaching is one reason I like doing it. Suppose the students actually believe what you said? That would shut you up in a hurry—for fear you would be misleading everybody.

On the other hand, when I consider the best things that have happened to me in my lifetime, I have to consider various works of art. They become companions for life, in a way. Obviously, they have an effect, but it isn't easily measurable. It isn't necessarily that it makes you a better person in any ethical or moral sense, but it is certainly a part of the enrichment of consciousness. And so these people who were sophisticated may produce finer works, finer performances. It obviously doesn't turn people into acceptable husbands and wives or make them honest, but it presents life as a continual environment of the best things that people have done.

That itself is enough for me, I think—the exhilaration of fine texts or great music. I think you approach it wrongly if you say, "What's in it for me?" People don't go on the grand tour, though they used to, to improve the mind. Today, we don't say, "This cathedral has improved my mind." Yet, art makes life worth living. It leads to a kind of love, the best sort, too, because you don't damage the object of your love, whereas in ordinary life, you are likely to.

mining literary heritage

TIM GAUTREAUX

Tim Gautreaux was born in Morgan City, Louisiana, and was raised in an ethnic and culturally diverse community, where daily habits revolved around Catholic Church activities, cooking, and storytelling. In his fiction, Gautreaux incorporates the region's culture and the lifestyle of its people while he explores moral issues.

He began his writing career as a poet, receiving a Ph.D. in English from the University of South Carolina under the direction of writers George Garrett and James Dickey. He later enrolled in a fiction workshop with Walker Percy at Loyola University New Orleans and honed his craft.

Since the publication of his first story collection, *Same Place, Same Things*, Gautreaux has become one of America's most widely praised short story writers. In *The Next Step in the Dance*, his first novel, young south Louisianians realize the importance of family traditions after they encounter lifestyles in a different culture. *Welding With Children*, his second story collection, followed. Gautreaux's ear for dialogue powers his character-centered fiction, which includes priests, drunks, train conductors, unemployed workers, and card-playing grandmothers with sharp-tongued wit.

Gautreaux has served as the University of Mississippi's Southern Writer in Residence, a program established by John and Renée Grisham. He teaches at Southeastern Louisiana University in Hammond, where he lives with his wife, Winborne.

Books by Tim Gautreaux

Same Place, Same Things (stories), St. Martin's Press, 1996
The Next Step in the Dance (novel), Picador, 1998
Welding With Children (stories), Picador, 1999
The Clearing (novel), Knopf, 2003

You've said that you think every writer is limited to his place of origin. Do you see this as a hindrance?

People own the territory that they are born into. That's the richest ore writers can mine. That sounds like a theory, and like anything anybody comes up with in way of a theory, there are exceptions to it. But that's what I teach. Get in touch with where you're from. No matter where you're from, even if it's a subdivision in Kenner, Louisiana, that is your literary heritage. If you look at it closely enough, you'll see that it is as exotic and unique as some Central or South American culture in the mountains.

I can't understand these people who say that anybody can write about anything and any time if they do enough research because they cut themselves off from the speech of those they grew up with.

Do you see yourself departing from a Southern setting and researching another region and setting a story somewhere else?

The projects I have planned now are all Louisiana projects. I think a writer forms most of his opinions and absorbs most of his nuances in the first fifteen years of his life. Somebody with creative sensibility is born with a lot of antennae. A schoolteacher can tell you that children are much more receptive up to seventh grade than they are after. Information is just pouring into them because they are wide open to all sorts of things. That's why I think that when they grow up to be writers, their youth is what they mine.

The dialect in your fiction is genuine, but you don't speak that way. Does this precision come with observation?

Growing up in Louisiana (where pretty much everybody around me was poor), I was exposed to many different levels of language. Next door to me when I was growing up was a Cuban family. On the other side were black children whom I played with. Living behind me were some hillbillies. Across the street were old Creole ladies who talked with a black French accent. My father worked for a tugboat company in Texas and picked up a Texas accent.

As a result, when I was a kid, I was good at mimicking people, changing my voice to various types of accents. I spoke that way until I became educated, around the age of seventeen. Uneducated people have a much richer language than educated people, and it is because they are forced to improvise. After you go through college, you have acquired standard, formal English that you're supposed to speak. People who are raised with parents and in a neighborhood where everyone speaks standard, formal English don't understand the richness of nonstandard speech.

The idea of the "frontier" is based on old tales and humor. Could you talk about this tradition and why you feel your writing is more closely related to it than to the notion of "Southern" writing?

I don't think of myself as a Southern writer. I'm just a writer who lives in the South. When I was a kid, one of my favorite books was B.A. Botkin's *A Treasury of Mississippi River Folklore*, and that book had a lot of Mike Fink yarns in it. Mike Fink was a keel boatman on the Mississippi River before the days of machinery. He was a raftsman. I also read the old Davy Crockett yarns. What those had in common was a kind of energetic hyperbole characteristic of much of America's early campfire storytelling tradition. Mike Fink used to say he was so fearsome that he could grin the bark off a tree at twenty paces. That type of hyperbole is wonderful, but it's hard to do. In my story "Died and Gone to Vegas," it's that exaggerated, spontaneous narration of story that imitates the campfire tradition of two hundred years ago.

Somebody with creative sensibility is born with a lot of antennae.

That story has been referred to as a Cajun *Canterbury Tales*.

It is, and it emerged mostly subconsciously after I finished the first draft. I said, you know, these people all want to go on some kind of a pilgrimage. It's not Canterbury; it is the secular shrine of Las Vegas. And, of course, that comes from this culture because every old lady in Louisiana wants to go to Las Vegas. If they had a vote on whether they should go to Las Vegas or Rome, even if they are Catholic, they'd say, "Well, there are no slot machines in Rome."

How far back in your memory does storytelling go in your family?

Before television and air-conditioning and before people were mobile, family members would gather more often. Families were closer in the old days because once a family would generate in a community, it tended to stay in that community. We're talking about the 1940s and 1950s. People would sit on the front porch until 4:30 or 5:00 in the afternoon because the house was too hot to stay inside.

My uncle had a large camp south of New Orleans in Hopedale, and the family would go down there about every weekend. The men would drink beer, and the women would gossip. There was always dancing because there was a jukebox, and the kids would just do whatever kids did—buy firecrackers and mooch money for the slot machines or to buy Cokes. When the kids ran out of things to do, they went over to sit with the adults. The big people were always telling stories. The men would almost always tell the stories, although the women would sometimes tell them too, but they preferred telling elaborate stories about their medical operations.

The men would tell stories about work. To me, they were ancient, but they were in their sixties and seventies. They were retired riverboat men, tugboat pilots, or railroad men. My father was a tugboat captain. Their tales had a certain structure and were spontaneous; one man would begin, "Yeah, one time I jumped off the back fantail of the *Johnny Brown* when she got her hawser wrapped around a propeller, and I had to chop it out with a hatchet under water." The other old guy would say, "Well, that ain't nothing. I was on the Third District Ferry the time the *Sipsey* came between the hulls and cut the pilot house in half with a smokestack." Another one would say, "Wait a minute. That tugboat wasn't named *Sipsey*."

There would be this fantastic interweaving of stories because one man would make up facts, and the others would catch him, and their "facts" would throw the story off on a tangent. These sessions taught me about the spontaneity, the organic structure, and the emotion that is involved in storytelling. Today, I see the short story not primarily as an intellectual endeavor but as a cultural artifact tightly bound with a necessary narrative structure.

Were you drawn to storytelling from an early age?

Somebody bought me a portable typewriter for Christmas, and in the mid-1950s I got a pen pal from Canada. One of my childhood pastimes was typing two- and three-page letters to this guy in Canada every other day. He would tell me about what things were like in Canada, and I would tell him about things here. After a while, I ran out of things to talk about, so I started making up stuff.

Was that your first experience in fiction writing?

Probably so. Lying to pen pals.

Tim Gautreaux on the Novel Versus the Short Story

What form do you think you're better suited for, the novel or the short story?

They are totally different animals, and you've got to realize that from the first sentence. An inexperienced writer doesn't know the difference, and that is what gets him in trouble. When I'm writing a short story, I realize that every word in it has to be relevant to the thing. You cannot waste the reader's time for one millisecond in a short story, just as you can't in telling a joke. A short story is like an automobile engine—every part is functional and has a purpose.

That's what Walker Percy taught me. Now, the novel I see as a big, elaborate short story, in that you still can't waste the reader's time. You're going to decrease your tale's effect by boring the hell out of the reader with an essay on a character's motivations when you can let him know what a character's motivations are with one turn of the head.

The novel, as far as line-by-line technique is concerned, has a lot in common with the short story, but I think I know the difference between a short story concept and a novel concept. When I got the idea to write the story "Waiting for the Evening News," about a man who wrecks a train and runs away, I saw that the tale was driven more by event than character, which is a tip-off that it was a short story topic, not a novel.

A novel I wrote that was never published, *Black Bayou*, concerns a family that discovers a toxic waste dump on their property. The old man who owns the property relies on his son, who is a lawn mower salesman in west Louisiana, to come back and help him with his dilemma because he's too sick and old to deal with it. Generally, event drives a story, and character drives a novel.

Your editing technique consists of several methods, doesn't it?

When I started teaching technical writing, I became more sensitive to little mistakes in short stories. Let's say there are fifty things wrong with the first draft of a story. I can approach the second draft by attempting to go after all fifty things, or I can focus on one thing, such as sentence structure.

So I make a pass going only after sentence structure. I decide which compound sentences should be made into complex sentences, where to bust long sentences into smaller ones. Then I arrive at a level of coherence, flow, and readability. Then on a second pass I look for stuff to cut. Generally there's a lot. Then on a third pass, I look at dialogue.

Then I've got it fairly clean, but I check for underdeveloped sections and a wrong ending. For that, I've got to show it to somebody else. I show it to my wife or my agent. Every writer has a blind spot, and he's going to overlook certain obvious things. Endings are the hardest things. That's where experience in poetry writing comes in handy, because good endings are often the result of a careful manipulation of the connotative values of images. Sometimes you've got to end with a picture that tells the story.

When I get it back from my readers I go through it again and fix things they've noticed, and it still might not be right. The agent might send it around, and I'll get it back with a note from an editor saying it's too long or there is some other problem with it. Then I have to take it apart and do it over.

What is the most difficult part of the editing process for you?

Generally, every sentence I write is two words away from being good. For me, the hard thing is to study each sentence when I'm revising and make it as good as I can by cutting, adding, or changing at least a couple of words. Ultimately, each word in a story is the result of decision. And the wrong word in a sentence is like chocolate syrup in soup.

How do you respond to editorial comments you don't agree with?

I generally trust an editor and go with whatever he or she suggests. If

I don't understand why an editor wants something changed, I'll ask for the reasoning behind the change. Sometimes the editor just needs an explanation of a detail or idiom that he or she doesn't understand. But unless the recommended change is a big mistake, I just follow directions. Most editors have a vision, or at least a notion of what's good for their readers, and I trust that. And it's really foolish to alienate an editor over a trifling edit.

In 1977, you took a writing seminar under Walker Percy at Loyola University New Orleans. Did Percy play a role in opening the field of fiction to you?

When you work under the aura of a great writer, it is always influential. You actually see somebody who is productive and successful and is doing something good as a writer.

Just being around him was helpful. Percy would focus on basic things about novel structure: You've got to get the thing off the ground; you can't go on tangents when you write. When you teach creative writing, you say basically the same things over and over. The things I say to my beginners who have never written a word of fiction are the same things I would say to God if He asked me how to write a short story. It's all pretty basic. And that's what Percy said.

What advice do you give beginning writers?

Believe everything your teacher tells you, even if you think he's wrong. Understand that if you're writing fiction it will probably take twenty years before you begin to know what you're doing, so develop the habit of patience. If you want to write well, you've got to read well.

You've said that when you started writing, you wrote many failed novels and "crippled" short stories. Have you revised these?

I go back and fix busted stories; it's a hobby of mine. Writing is rewriting. The only reason I would leave an older piece alone is if it would take too much time. I might be able to write a completely new manuscript in the time it would take to fix a messed-up old one. The new one will be better, and the old one will always be patched. After you weld something that's broken, you can always see the seam.

How daunting is it to finish a novel and realize it doesn't work?

You can't let that bother you. Rewrite it or pitch it. I think what hampers a lot of writers is an inability to deal with their own bad writing. A lot of us write things that we don't want to cut because we feel doing so is like sawing off a little finger. But if a patch of writing is overdone or irrelevant, it needs to come off—like an eleventh finger.

How attached do you remain to your work after it has been published, especially after you read reviews of your work?

I've been lucky. So far I haven't had a really bad review. I'm sure that if somebody really puts a pasting on something I've written it won't be fun to read, but I'll try to learn from those things. Generally, negative comments don't come out of thin air. They are based on something. One reviewer of *Same Place, Same Things* said there was a kind of sameness to the structure of the stories. That sent up a red flag with me. I went back and I checked the stories to see if there was some validity to what he said. Naturally, there are similarities in the stories as far as setting is concerned and social level of the characters, but I didn't agree with his comment. Nevertheless, I do take reviews seriously.

You mentioned earlier that you learned about storytelling by listening to your father and his friends. What role did your mother play in this development?

A very rich one. The women tended to sit around and gossip and play cards. They were colorful in the way they expressed themselves, in their attitudes, particularly the older women. A lot of these women had husbands who either worked at nautical trades or in the oil fields, and they

Tim Gautreaux on the Necessity of Conflict

Your stories often take the reader through an event that changes a character's life, usually within the first paragraph.

The purpose of telling a story is to get people involved. Why would you not want to get a reader's attention? If you start to tell a joke, would you start with five sentences of explanation? No. You begin by saying, "A Jew and an Arab got onto a streetcar." There's an immediate conflict there. A joke is the archetype of all human entertainment. Like the joke, the basic story structure is composed of initiation of conflict and then the development of that, called rising action, which leads to either a climax or an epiphany, and last there is a falling action. That structure is not just peculiar to the short story. It is a natural organic thing that the human mind craves.

The people who experiment with the short story often turn out things that are hard to read, and it's because they experiment with the wrong thing. They could experiment with point of view, with the time period, setting. But instead they choose to fool with the one thing that will trip them up and ruin the story, and that is basic narrative structure. They will do something like Washington Irving does in "Rip Van Winkle"—start out with 850 words of description of the Hudson River Valley. I've had to beat students with a stick to read "Rip Van Winkle." They say it's boring, and they are absolutely right. That story is put together like a Yugo.

weren't around for fifteen days of the month. So most of the women were pretty self-sufficient, and you see this in my characters, particularly the older women. They are fantastic cooks, and they use cooking as power.

What role does your wife play in your work, aside from reading drafts? How has your profession affected your relationship?

I've taken writing very slowly. Ambition, though, has not been my long suit. I've also understood that the important goal was not to write and be published, but to write well. I've considered myself more of a teacher than a writer all these years, and a husband and a father. I've put twelve million hours in honey-do projects into this marriage. That has always been first.

People would ask ten or fifteen years ago how I would find the time to do any writing with two young kids and a marriage and a mortgage. I told them, I do what I can. I've been lucky to have some writing success. But you know where that writing success springs from, don't you? It's from building a life with a woman for twenty-six years and raising kids. How could I write the scenes in "The Courtship of Merlin LeBlanc" unless I had kids? How can I write about the relationship between Colette and Paul in *The Next Step in the Dance* without living through normal conflicts that are part of a marriage?

Does it come down to writing what you would like to read?

Who knows where my stories come from? It's amazing what appears on the word processor screen. I've read that a woman is born with all of the eggs she is ever going to produce. I think a story writer is sort of like that. Sometimes, when a story is successful and complete, I feel like I've given birth to something.

Do you feel a responsibility to show readers something that verifies a truth they know but have not realized they know?

Writing provides a certain amount of self-discovery. Much that a writer expresses comes from his subconscious, that realm of the nearly known. He might not ever talk about, for example, the erosion of the institution of marriage, but he might embody the concern in a story or novel.

Flannery O'Connor said that when she was writing "Good Country People," she didn't know what was going to happen in the story. She was surprising herself, and she knew it was a good story because if she was surprised, certainly the reader was going to be surprised. What she means by being surprised is that the story blossoms and the blossoming is connected to the previous events of the story. She didn't know that Manley Pointer was going to open a Bible and there was going to be whiskey inside the hollowed-out text. When she wrote it, she probably said, "Yes, this is where this story has been going from the first sentence."

Do you write in a similar fashion as O'Connor did, or do you outline before you begin to write?

I wrote a two-page, double-spaced outline for *The Next Step in the Dance,* which I revised as I wrote. The first draft was out of control because I wrote it in little snippets of spare time. I have to have a big block of time to work on a 120,000-word manuscript. When a semester would start and I would drop it for a month, I would forget what I was writing about. I'd come back to the manuscript and think: Who are these people? Why was I so interested in them?

Barry Hannah [*Airships*] called me and asked if I'd like to be writer in residence for one semester at Ole Miss. I went up there, and I was separated from the ringing phone and the grading for about five months. I jumped on that novel and the characters never got out of my head. I rewrote it, cut it, rearranged it, added to it. I sent it off to New York and shortly after received a contract offer.

How long did you work on *The Next Step in the Dance*?

Maybe eight years of diddling around with it and not knowing where it was going, then finally having that block of time. I was writing two novels at the same time, and it took a long time to come up with the first draft of *The Next Step in the Dance,* and a tremendous amount of time to come up with the first revision. Then I sent off an early version of it to New York.

With a novel, you get the manuscript together and you send it off, and if you don't have an agent, that baby's gone for five or six months. Then all you get back is a one-paragraph rejection letter with some comment like, "Well, this is wonderful and richly detailed, and so on," but the letter's got "It's broken and we don't want it," written all over it. You send it off again, and it's gone for another half year.

At some point in your life, you had to make the decision that you wanted to be a writer. How did that decision come about?

It's not like deciding to become a CPA. For me, at least, writing is just something I do, the way other people swim or play canasta. I never took it seriously. I wrote because I enjoyed it. I'd always written, all the way back to when I had a pen pal when I was eleven years old.

There was one big moment of departure, and it happened when I sent a story to *The Southern Review* in 1989. They sent me a letter containing compliments that said they didn't have room to publish it. I got a little miffed, because I thought this story was appropriate for *The Southern Review*, and I had faith in it. But that is pure, foolish vanity.

At any rate, I stuck that story in an envelope the day I got it back from *The Southern Review*, and I sent it to C. Michael Curtis at *The Atlantic Monthly*. He said it was okay until the ending, where it turns talky and peters out, and that if I ever tinkered with the ending they would look at it again. I took that story and rewrote the ending. It was about a one-thousand-word rewrite, finished within six hours of the mail carrier coming. I put it back in the mail, and Curtis bought it. I couldn't believe it when I got the acceptance letter. That is when I began to get some confidence that I could do better, serious work and have a broad audience.

inhabiting the other

SIRI HUSTVEDT

Obsession, secrecy, and voyeurism pervade the fiction of Siri Hustvedt. In *The Blindfold*, Iris Vegan enters an affair with her professor and slips into sexual ambiguity as she identifies with the male character in the novella that she and the professor translate. In *The Enchantment of Lily Dahl*, a waitress in a small town participates in local theater as a stranger moves into town and captures her attention. Juxtaposed with the production of *A Midsummer Night's Dream*, her life spins out of control as her suspicions build.

Born February 19, 1955, in Northfield, Minnesota, Hustvedt attended St. Olaf College and later moved to New York. She received a Ph.D. in nineteenth-century British literature from Columbia University and has taught at Queens College.

Her writing career began with a collection of poems, *Reading to You*, some of which were originally published by *The Paris Review*. She has also translated works from Norwegian, including, with David McDuff, *Fyodor Dostoyevsky: A Writer's Life*. *Yonder* collects essays ranging from an exploration of Charles Dickens's *Our Mutual Friend* to personal reflections of the home.

Hustvedt lives in Brooklyn, New York, with her husband, the novelist Paul Auster (*The New York Trilogy*), and their daughter, Sophie.

Books by Siri Hustvedt

Reading to You (poems), Open Book Publications, 1983
The Blindfold (novel), Poseidon Press, 1992
The Enchantment of Lily Dahl (novel), Henry Holt, 1996
Yonder (essays), Henry Holt, 1998
What I Loved (novel), Henry Holt, 2003

Your first published book, *Reading to You*, contains several prose poems. What are the differences for you between writing prose and verse poetry?

When I was in graduate school at Columbia, I wrote only poems. Then I got stuck, and I didn't like what I was doing anymore. I had a teacher at Columbia who is also a poet, David Shapiro. I told him I had run into a wall, and he said, "When that happens to me, I do automatic writing like the surrealists." The first draft of the prose poem "Squares" in *Reading to You* was written in a single night. I wrote thirty pages and then spent about two and a half months editing those thirty pages down to ten. I never wrote another verse poem after that.

That poem contains a scene similar to one in your second novel, *The Enchantment of Lily Dahl*.

Writers have obsessions that never get away from them, even if they write different books. "Weather Markings" includes a suicide: A boy hangs himself in the barn. When I was a child in Minnesota, that suicide took place just up the road from my house, and the story *marked* me. "Weather Markings" comes out of the Midwest, out of Minnesota, and *The Enchantment of Lily Dahl* is set there, too.

Your poems contain several identifiable elements from your life. You

use your sister's name, and Minnesota often serves as the setting. Do you find it easier to write poetry from experience?

I've always liked the distinction M.M. Bakhtin makes in *The Dialogic Imagination* between the single voice in a lyric poem and the many voices in a novel, between a univocal tone and a polyphonic one. There are poems that destroy the single voice by borrowing from many sources. For me, however, the argument, dialogue, harangue, and noise of lots of voices are part of the excitement of writing novels.

It's intriguing that you mention Bakhtin. He wrote extensively about Dostoyevsky, and you are cotranslator of the biography *Fyodor Dostoyevsky: A Writer's Life*. When did your interest in Dostoyevsky begin?

I read *Crime and Punishment* when I was a teenager, and it was a cataclysmic book for me. I reread Dostoyevsky in college because I was studying Russian intellectual history, and ideas are central to his novels. I began reading *Crime and Punishment* for the third time the day I arrived in New York, which was in September of 1978. I didn't know a soul in the city. I sat in my tiny room on Riverside Drive and devoured the story of Raskolnikov. I finished the book in two days. That obsessive reading was probably an emotional response to my entrance into the urban world.

But Dostoyevsky was also an epileptic, and I feel close to lives influenced by neurological events. Since I was twenty, I have suffered from severe migraines. Once, I had a migraine that began as a seizure, and I was actually thrown against a wall. I have had auras, hallucinations, and euphoria before attacks, all of which were, of course, far less dramatic than Dostoyevsky's *grand mal* seizures. Nevertheless, I am convinced that these altered states have a strong influence on personality. Neurologists have associated epilepsy with religiosity (St. Theresa of Avila was probably an epileptic) and, interestingly, also with the urge to write.

Your interest in translation appears in your creative work. In *The Blindfold*, the narrator translates a fictitious German novella, *The Brutal Boy*, with her professor.

I think of *The Brutal Boy*, or *Der Brutale Junge*, in *The Blindfold* as a vehicle for a larger act of translation in the narrative: Iris translates herself into the novella's protagonist, Klaus. Like a translation, she is not identical to the original but a version of it. She wanders around New York, telling people her name is Klaus, and through this character, she permits herself small acts of subversion. She cuts her hair, wears a man's suit, and writes graffiti on a city wall. The strange thing is I have always felt that she becomes him to save herself, but more than that, I don't know. It's mysterious to me.

You seem to have a strong interest in the physical act of creating written language. Your poem "Squares" begins, "He was making a paragraph on a yellow page."

I think it's because I find written language strange. It is odd that we can look down at those little signs and understand them. Reading and writing are peculiar activities, and yet when I write, there is an odd confluence of the physical and mental. I often need the physical act of typing to bring something out. It is not enough to just think. The words seem to come through my fingers. I prefer typing to writing by hand because I need the distance of print.

My husband, Paul Auster, likes the words to leak out of his body mediated by only a pen. He needs to write by hand first. It seems to me that my handwriting obfuscates the text. These are differences of work and style, but I think they are deep and related to style itself. You discover over time what you can do. Not everything is a matter of choice. As a young person, it became clear to me that no matter how much I admired Wallace Stevens or Henry James, I could never write like them.

Do you share your work in progress with anyone?

My husband edits my work and I edit his. We make suggestions, point out weak passages to each other, and so on. His comments are invaluable to me. If an editor suggests changes that I don't want, I don't make them.

How do your books begin? With an image, an idea, a character?

Every book is different. Its beginnings are generally vague and unconscious. *The Blindfold* began with an experience that triggered an uncanny feeling in me. I didn't want to re-create the experience but rather the feeling—that discomfort that I remembered. *The Enchantment of Lily Dahl* started with a story I had heard in my hometown about a young man, a twin, who had gone into a diner, ordered breakfast, eaten it, and then blown his brains out in public. The story grew from there—the theater in the book, the doublings, and the suicide were all generated from that small true story. *What I Loved*, my newest novel, began with a picture in my mind of a very fat woman lying dead on a bed in a room. I have no idea where it came from, but it insisted itself on my imagination, and the novel grew from there. It does deal with problems of hunger, illness, painting, and art, as well as losing people one loves.

In one of the biographical notes, you mention you were going to write five Iris stories—stories about the character who came to be the narrator of *The Blindfold*, which is a novel in four parts.

Five is a nicer number than four. There is a true middle that way. I started writing a fifth part of *The Blindfold*, which was about Iris's childhood. It came out of unhappy experiences with peers in my childhood. I worked on it for three months, and every day was a miserable experience. I remember riding the subway during that time and feeling that I had cut open my heart. It was something deep and painful, but it was not art. I gave what I had to Paul. He read it and said, "Just forget this." I threw it away and was immensely relieved. I realized that the book was done because I was sick of Iris. If you're sick of a character, you can't go on. So that novel ended up with four parts, not five, which is less elegant, but a quartet has something going for it, too.

Did they start as separate stories?

The first one was just a story. After I finished my dissertation at Columbia, I had the urge to write a story that came out of an uncanny experience I had had as a student when I met someone through an ad on a bulletin board. The true story and the fictional story are different, but they share what I felt: uneasy and disturbed. I wanted to turn that feeling into a story. After I had written it, I knew I wasn't finished with Iris.

Both of your novels begin with characters watching someone.

I didn't notice the similarity until later. The voyeurism in *The Enchantment of Lily Dahl* is fully carried out in a way that it is not in *The Blindfold.* Lily watching Ed at the beginning of the book leads to an intricate network of people looking at and spying on each other and then interpreting what they have seen, often wrongly. The two men Iris sees across the airshaft from her apartment never become part of the book's plot. Their presence is atmospheric and erotic, part of Iris's loneliness and longing. Art itself is a form of voyeurism, of course. You have to stand back in order to see. I'm not plagued by voyeuristic fantasies, and yet it keeps coming up in my work—watching, looking, fascination.

Lily and Iris both look out, but they also go through introspection in the novels.

Introspection is not separate from the drama of looking. I believe human beings are formed by and through others. If you lock a child in a closet early in his life, he will never be normal or have a normal relation to language. We find ourselves in the eyes of another person. There is no self-consciousness without the other. You are yourself, but you are always also the other looking at yourself. In an important way, we are always doubled.

***The Blindfold* was written in first person and *The Enchantment of Lily Dahl* in third. Did the novels begin with these points of view?**

I wanted to write a third-person narrative after I finished *The Blindfold.* It was hard for me. The tone wasn't easy to get, and I struggled with it for a long time. It's a narration that's close to Lily, but the story is not told in her voice. In early drafts, I toyed with entering the points of view of different characters but dropped the idea. For Lily, a nineteen-year-old girl, I needed the freedom of the third person because the narrative voice required a greater flexibility and range of language than Lily has access to.

The use of autobiographical material, as you've mentioned, can be seen in both novels.

I suppose the use of autobiography is both conscious and unconscious. It's like an itch I can't get rid of. Whatever it is, it's inevitably something I don't understand, something ambiguous and often frightening. In *The Blindfold*, I kept moving closer to my fears. *The Enchantment of Lily Dahl* began with the true story of a suicide in a restaurant. I was not a witness. I heard about it, and I knew the brother of the person who killed himself. It is a strange thing to commit suicide in front of an audience, and after I finished writing the book, I understood that the whole novel was born of that death performed for others. The play inside the book, Martin's bizarre theories about language and the world, the obsessive questioning about what's real and what's performance, what's art and not art—all of it came out of that single explosion.

In the first section of *The Blindfold*, Iris says, "Just for the moment, I decided to pretend that the thing really can be captured by the word."

Language is arbitrary. Because I'm always writing, I often feel a vast distance between a word and what it refers to. At the same time, language produces the real to a large extent. The relation between language and this room, for example, is pretty slippery. Without language, this room would look entirely different. Words cut one thing from another and make us see each thing as a distinct identity.

Language and culture can't be separated, and this interests me. Language is a social contract, an agreement about what things mean. I suppose that the more abstract language becomes, the harder it is to grasp and find agreement. When I read novels, I see people, places, rooms in my mind. I make up a whole world. I wrote about these mental images in my essay "Yonder." But when I read philosophy, I don't see pictures. I don't really see the text on the page, either. I feel the motion of the sentences, the necessity of the logic, which are too abstract to be made into images.

Art itself is a form of voyeurism. You have to stand back in order to see.

This attention to language is obvious in your collection of essays, *Yonder*. In the title essay, you talk about going to Norway and dreaming in Norwegian with English subtitles.

That was one of my great dreams—a concise formulization of the bilingual experience. I hadn't lived in Norway long; I was only a couple of months into my year there. The double-ness of living in two languages was perfectly expressed through the subtitles. It was like watching myself on the big screen.

When I was living in Iris's (and my) apartment near Columbia on 109th Street, I had another remarkable dream. All the poverty material in *The Blindfold* comes directly from my own experience. Those were the years of Reagan, of right-wing thinking, of calling ketchup a vegetable. Anyway, I dreamed that Ronald Reagan and his wife, Nancy, sponsored a competition called "Poverty's Best Dancer." I entered the contest and tap-danced my heart out in front of the president and his wife. I won. Again, that dream was an amazingly succinct expression of my life at the time in relation to the wider political climate. Writers can learn a lot from the efficiency of dreams.

Art runs throughout your novels and several of your essays. When did your interest in art begin?

I drew constantly as a child. When I was a little girl and people asked me what I was going to be, I would say an artist, a painter. So I think I'm satisfying the urge to make paintings by writing about them in a book. I've always been interested in pictures and paintings, and I have a better memory for images than I do for texts. I'm always misquoting Paul and misquoting myself. I don't remember the exact words, but pictures I remember, not always perfectly, but pretty closely. I'm sure that is just physiological.

When Iris in *The Blindfold* describes the painting *The Tempest* by Giorgion, she forgets about the man in the painting because she has become that man and is looking from his perspective.

I took that experience from my own life. I saw that painting in college as a slide in an art history class, and it made a huge impression on me. Four years later, when I was twenty-three, I was in Venice and I went to see the real painting. I remembered everything about the painting, except the man in the foreground. The role of the man in the painting is as a voyeur. He seems separate from the nursing woman as he stands there looking at her. I had entered his place in the painting and blotted him out. For Iris, the loss of the man has even greater resonance because she actually takes on a male persona in the story.

This brings up the role of the reader in art, filtering what has been written and making it his own.

I think every reader writes the book. That's why there are so many different views of a single work. When a book is published, I'm always amazed at the radically different responses it produces. Of course, there is a hierarchy. Some readings are a lot better than others. When I was teaching at Queens College, students would sometimes write papers about a book or a story in which they made grievous errors. When I confronted them, they would sometimes say, "But that's my opinion!" And I would say, "But you can't tell me that the hunger artist runs away when he doesn't. There is a text. There are words." At the same time, I think there

Siri Hustvedt on the Editing Process

How do you edit your work?

I do endless rewriting. Paul says, "Siri, you don't revise; you rewrite," which I think is true. If there is something I don't like, I throw it out and then remake it. It's as if I need a certain speed to redo the whole thing. I also edit sentences carefully, but that's later. When I'm making drafts, I produce hundreds of pages of work.

How do you edit a sentence?

I remember Paul and I had a conversation about vowel sounds in sentences. Sometimes repetitions are nice, and sometimes they're ugly. That's where you find yourself at the end of the day. How do I avoid repeating that vowel sound or that ugly unintentional rhyme? There are too many *t*s in this sentence. I have to change it. There are some truisms in prose, however. Strong verbs are nice. Use necessary adjectives but not hysterically. Of course, that's a matter of style, too. Rococo prose is beyond my sphere. It grates against the Midwestern, Protestant personality. Sometimes I admire it, but I can't do it. It's too decorative. I tend to banish words, to throw out sentences I've made if they're elegant just to be elegant. Showing off is to no purpose.

Is it difficult to cut something you realize is overwritten?

It's not hard because I do become an engine for the work. I'm happy to be corrected by myself or by a reader like Paul. There comes a time when I'm so close to a book, I can't see it anymore. Then I have to put it aside and get Paul to read it. That usually comes only after years of work, however.

Even when you're not writing, is your current project always with you?

You are always writing a book, even when you're not at your desk. I write at night in my head, which is pleasant. I begin to compose the next paragraph before I fall asleep, or I hear the characters having conversations with each other. Sleep is good for books. Movement is also good. Sometimes when I'm stuck, I go to the bathroom, and the act of getting up and walking loosens the thought, and the words come to me when I'm away from the computer.

should be enough room in a book for people to invent it. If you give too much information, you can push the reader away.

You mentioned your interest in art when you were young. Were you also writing at that time?

I was proud of terrible poems I wrote in the third grade, verses in which I rhymed "true" and "blue." In the fifth grade, I wrote a novel, which shouldn't impress you too much. It was forty-two pages of huge handwriting. My parents saved it. The story was straight out of English novels for girls and was called *Carrie at Baxter Manor.* Its middle chapter had the exciting title: "Danger." Martin in *The Enchantment of Lily Dahl* has a book called *Baxtor Manor* among the volumes that clutter his apartment—a private joke for me alone. By the time I was fourteen, I was loudly declaring to everybody that I was going to become an "author." I was a pretentious little idiot, but I think pretension is necessary for all writers. You have to get over it later, but it's good to live out various personas. That's what writing novels is—enacting other people.

How did the ideas for your novels begin?

Ideas usually begin as a single image, feeling, or a real event. As I said,

Siri Hustvedt on Her Early Influences

What writers did you read growing up?

When I came of age as a reader—after children's books and fairy tales—I found myself enthralled first with two poets, Blake and Dickinson, and then with nineteenth-century novels. *David Copperfield* was a gigantic book for me, as was *Jane Eyre.* Jane's story is maybe the greatest ever written for pubescent girls. I read it to my daughter when she was ten. She loved it. Then she insisted on hearing *Wuthering Heights,* and I hesitated. It's a darker book, beyond good and evil, but she loved it, too. I remember I paused during the reading and said to Sophie, "They're not so nice, Catherine and Heathcliff, are they?" And she said, "No, they're not, Mom, but they love each other so much!"

The Enchantment of Lily Dahl began with a real suicide. There is a café in Northfield, Minnesota, where I grew up called The Ideal Café. The real suicide did not take place there, but I used it in the novel to bring together the book's characters. That novel is written almost as a stage piece. It unfolds visually, a fact that reverberates with *A Midsummer Night's Dream,* the play inside the book.

The café was a convenient place for characters to enter and exit. The real Ideal Café was like that. People dropped in and out, even when they weren't eating. Two of my sisters, Liv and Astrid, and my best friend, Heather Clark, worked there, and I heard lots of stories. There were stories I thought I had invented, which turned out to have their origins in real life. For example, Boomer Wee, a minor character, is an Elvis fanatic. After Heather read the book, she pointed out to me that the café's owner had a bust of Elvis in the restaurant. Obviously, I knew it but couldn't remember it.

How did you get your first publication?

In 1981, I sent a poem to *The Paris Review.* I had never offered a poem to any magazine before, with the exception of my college literary magazine that refused everything I sent. *The Paris Review* took the poem called "Weather Markings," sent me a ninety-dollar check, and published it in the fall issue of 1981. There was something magical about the first experience. It was followed by rejections elsewhere, but the extreme gratification it brought has never quite worn off.

You mentioned your husband, Paul Auster. How does it work that you share a profession?

When we met, Paul was not a famous writer. He had published poems with small presses, had translated a lot of poetry and prose from the French, and had written a number of essays, some of which were printed in *The New York Review of Books.* He had finished the first part of *The Invention of Solitude* and was working on the second part, "The Book of Memory." He was a poor, struggling writer, and so was I—even though he had a lot more to show for himself.

Books were certainly part of our attraction to each other. I remember an ecstatic moment early in our love affair. Paul had his arms around me. He looked at me and said suddenly, "Whom do you prefer—Burroughs or Beckett?" I said, "Beckett," and he said, "So do I." That sealed it.

The truth is, however, that Beckett is more important to Paul than to me. Beckett was the great literary presence Paul had to overcome in order to be himself. I never had a writer-father, maybe because I'm a woman. I think most male writers have to struggle with what critic Harold Bloom called "the anxiety of influence," and it may be that, like it or not, men find themselves at the center of the culture in a way women don't. We're on the side. This doesn't mean that women don't have to fight influences, but rather that we are less likely to situate ourselves in some great tradition. For example, I love George Eliot, but I never had to get over her.

Many people assume that writers who live together must be locked in a competitive battle. But, honestly, if you love someone well and are loved in return, that nonsense doesn't come up. I lived through Paul's struggles and disappointments. *City of Glass* was rejected by seventeen New York publishers, but their stupidity did not slow him down. Now that novel is translated into twenty-seven languages, and people read it all over the world. It keeps selling. I loved his work right from the start. When I read *The Invention of Solitude* before it was published, I thought the man was a genius. The fact that he has become an internationally celebrated writer has always seemed to me a confirmation of my good literary opinion.

Do you work together?

He reads his work to me more frequently than I read to him. I've been working on a novel for two and a half years now, and Paul hasn't seen it yet. But he will see it, and what he says will be important. Paul's sentences are finished much earlier than mine are. He constructs a book paragraph by paragraph. I write and rewrite whole books over and over. We are honest with each other and brutal if need be. When you know the person is on your side, criticism is good. Usually when Paul tells me something isn't working, he confirms a doubt I've already had.

What kind of stretch was it to write the essays in *Yonder* after having written two novels?

I sat down at my desk, and the essays just ran out of me. I felt free. These are not academic pieces but real essays—from *essayer*—to try. They are attempts at thinking on the page. One thing leads to another. The great master of this associative form was, of course, Montaigne.

I like to look at a painting for a long time and then try to say something about it. That is what I did with Vermeer's painting *Woman With a Pearl Necklace.* Essays are wanderings from here to there, a theme that comes up in the title essay, "Yonder." That piece was commissioned for a book of essays by women about the idea of home. I felt uncomfortable appearing in a book with women only, but I accepted, expanded the essay into a meditation on place, and wrote it. It was too long for them and so it was rejected, which was just as well. I'm grateful to that editor, however, because the commission sparked "Yonder," and I'm glad I wrote it.

In that essay, you describe reading as a "yonder place, neither here nor there."

If the definition of yonder is between here and there, then reading fits. The reader situates himself somewhere between the immediate here of the world in which he reads and the there of the book. He enters a state that is between himself and the voice of the book. Reading is also entering a dialogue of sorts because a book is nothing until it lives inside the reader, who makes the book come to life.

And that "between" is a strong theme in your novels, the question of identity.

People are made through other people in time. The self is a narrative, not a fixed entity. There are countless cultural fictions that lie about the self. "Just be yourself," is one of them. For writers, there's "Find your own voice." Existing in time means that we have a flesh-and-blood body that moves through space and time, and it changes. The continuity of that self lives only in memory. What I believe is anti-Cartesian, and it flies in the face of the current vogue-ish thinking that proposes that genetics is everything. It's the new Darwinism. Some people are more stable than others, and some are more fragmented. Coherent or incoherent personalities are obviously made from both genetic factors and from a person's life story, but to what extent and exactly how remains mysterious.

In "Yonder," you focus on basic, universal questions.

I think it's important to ask the first question if you can find it, the blooper question children always ask. Too many essays begin at the seventeenth question. Everything really interesting, it seems to me, comes before that. You might sound really stupid, but it's always more interesting and you are more likely to get closer to the truth than if you are muddled by all the received knowledge of the culture. I think, particularly now, people are getting deadened by it.

What role does reading play in your writing?

When I am writing a novel, it is hard to read other novels, especially good ones. I remember reading J.M. Coetzee's *Life and Times of Michael K* and thinking, "Why am I not doing this myself? This is so good." I had to put it away.

Between novels, I can read fiction with a lot of pleasure, but mostly while I'm working I read nonfiction. I like to read books for laypeople about the brain and memory. I like to read history and biographies. I read a lot of psychoanalytic case studies. I've done a lot of reading about personality disorders from all points of view.

My newest book is narrated in first person by a sixty-eight-year-old man who was born in Berlin. I read about the Jewish community in Berlin in the 1920s and 1930s. Most of this doesn't appear in the novel. It's just background for the story to take place in New York many years later. But I wanted to know; I wanted to have it right even if it's never mentioned. I think sometimes hiding behind the curtains of a book is that knowledge. I knew I wasn't going to get it wrong.

This sounds like a different direction for you.

I am always eager to write a completely different book from the one I wrote before. I knew that it was time to write as a man. Both of the other books were from a female perspective. For this particular book, I wanted a voice from the center. It had to be a male voice. Nevertheless, he's a Jew and an intellectual, which puts him outside the heart of the culture. He is me, too. He was just waiting to come out, I suppose. That's one of the mysteries of making art—all the people we carry around inside us.

pleasing the masters

HA JIN

Ha Jin began writing in English fifteen years ago with no expectation of success. He was born on February 21, 1956, in mainland China and served in China's People's Army. When he moved to the United States in 1985, he left his wife and young son behind, planning to return to China after completing his Ph.D. at Brandeis University. His wife managed to join him in 1987. After the massacre in Tiananmen Square, their son reunited with them. Jin became a U.S. citizen in 1997. His simple but elegant novel *Waiting* won two of America's most prestigious literary prizes, the 1999 National Book Award, and the 2000 PEN/Faulkner Award.

Jin is the author of three collections of poetry, *Between Silences*, *Facing Shadows*, and *Wreckage*. His first short story collection, *Ocean of Words*, won the PEN/Hemingway Award. The stories in this collection concern Chinese soldiers on the Russian front during the Cultural Revolution and offer comparisons in theme and structure to the stories of Chekhov and Babel. It was followed by another collection, the Flannery O'Connor Award-winning *Under the Red Flag*, and *In the Pond*, a novel. Jin teaches at Boston University.

Books by Ha Jin

Between Silences (poems), University of Chicago Press, 1990
Facing Shadows (poems), Hanging Loose Press, 1996
Ocean of Words (stories), Zoland Books, 1996
Under the Red Flag (stories), University of Georgia Press, 1997
In the Pond (novel), Zoland Books, 1998
Waiting (novel), Pantheon Books, 1999
The Bridegroom (stories), Pantheon Books, 2000
Wreckage (poems), Hanging Loose Press, 2001
The Crazed (novel), Pantheon Books, 2002

You served in China's People's Army for five and a half years. You hadn't had much formal education, nor had you been widely exposed to literature. Is it true that when you were on the front you found a Chinese translation of *War and Peace*?

Someone made that up. I was a regular soldier on the front, where it was very difficult to get any books. They just weren't available. Later, when I transferred inland to headquarters one hundred miles from the front, I began to have access to literary books, but nothing like *War and Peace. Don Quixote* was passed on to me, but I had it for only one day. I couldn't read all of it before I had to pass it on to someone else.

Since Mao had closed the schools in China at the start of the Cultural Revolution, was that your first experience with literature?

I don't know if it was a genuine experience because I didn't have time to read it carefully. My first real experience was with two textbooks my parents sent to me that contained ancient Chinese poems. I read many of those poems and memorized some of them.

When did you decide that you wanted to study literature?

In the early days, when my parents sent those textbooks, I was interested in good poems and literary works. This didn't mean that I wanted to study literature. When I decided I wanted to go to college, I planned to study science. I wanted to be an engineer. We were living in peace, and I realized that I needed some kind of education. When I took the exams, I couldn't compete with the science majors because I didn't go to middle school or high school. You can't teach yourself chemistry; you need a lab. So I was a rather weak applicant. Then, I became more interested in the humanities, but not in writing. Philosophy was my first choice, then classics, then library science or history. English was my last choice.

What perspective has living in America and writing about China given you?

The distance is important because it has given me a detachment and a deeper understanding of the Chinese situation and experience. The fact that I'm writing in English has also given me a new perspective. If I wrote the stories in Chinese, they would be different. I don't mean that they would be inferior, but they would be different kinds of stories.

What kind of writer would you be if you wrote in Chinese?

Perhaps I would write mainly poetry. For Chinese writers at this moment, poetry is more promising. It can do more for the language. In the beginning, writing in English gave me much uncertainty and risk. Writing prose is less risky in English than writing verse. It somehow made me feel more like a writer. But I continue to write both.

You became a U.S. citizen in 1997. What prompted that decision?

It was almost a natural part of the immigration process. For many years, I didn't have a passport. I couldn't travel, but I was writing in English and living in this country. America is a great place. Why not live here? Citizenship is not that important for a writer. Craft is what is most important. But I'm grateful for being accepted as a citizen. It gives me a place to stay.

Ha Jin on Writing in a Non-Native Language

How did you decide to write in English?

The decision was hard. It was largely a practical one. When my son came out of China after the massacre in Tiananmen Square, I looked for academic positions and jobs related to Chinese—as a translator or a teacher of Chinese—but I couldn't find any work because there were other applicants with degrees from colleges in the States. Since I didn't have any degrees in Chinese, English was the only way.

It took me one year to decide to write in English. I didn't know, and I still don't know, how far I can go with the language. It was, especially in the first two years, physically painful. I had fevers. I always say it's like changing your body, in a way. I made a conscious effort to undergo the transition and to think in English and try to immerse myself in the language. Gradually, I got used to it. This doesn't mean that the uncertainty is no longer there. It's always there. But I can take it as part of the process.

Do you remember when you began to think in English?

Even before writing in English, I was thinking in the language. Once I started writing in English, this became more frequent. When I wake up, I think in English, but when I dream, it's always half in Chinese and half in English.

Your wife and son arrived in America years after you had moved to study at Brandeis. What was your wife's reaction to your decision to write in English?

When she came, she couldn't read a word of English and couldn't speak it at all. Now she reads and speaks it well. She was stubborn about my writing. She said, "You're a born writer." She believed in me more than I believed in myself. She's the one who said that I wouldn't have any chance writing in Chinese, that I had to write in English. She was clear about this from the beginning. When I finish a piece, she reads it. This doesn't mean that I always follow her advice. But I do listen to her suggestions and revise. I like her basic, simple responses as a human being, as a regular reader.

There's a strong tradition of writers living outside their culture and writing in another language about their homeland. Do you see yourself in that tradition?

I think a writer can write only about what is close to his heart. For many years, China has been the subject I am obsessed with. I didn't know anything about any other place when I moved here and began writing. China had to be the subject. But gradually, I think my subject matter will be different. I haven't returned to China in fifteen years. It has become unfamiliar, remote. In other words, American life is now closer to me. I think in a few years I will be more comfortable writing about the American experience. But it takes time. I have to do it step by step, and I won't rush.

When you were a student at Brandeis, you gave a poem, "The Dead Soldier's Talk," to your professor, who then called his friend, a poetry editor at *The Paris Review*, and the editor accepted it on the spot.

That's a true story. Frank Bidart was teaching a poetry workshop at Brandeis. I was a graduate student at that time, so I wasn't allowed to take the class for credit, but I sat in and observed. I was taking another course that was in conflict with this workshop, so I couldn't always attend, but I sat in every other week. I wrote that poem, then showed it to him. He was excited about it, and called his friend Jonathan Galassi, who was an editor at *The Paris Review* at the time. The poem was accepted over the phone.

That says a lot about the clarity and precision of your writing.

As a writer, I try to be lucid and transparent. V.S. Naipaul [*A House for Mr. Biswas*] is this type of writer. He aims for clarity in his prose. Writing this way is a conscious effort on my part. I think lucidity is a virtue. It doesn't mean you can't be subtle. Chinese people would say that my writing is too plain, that it's not literary enough. But this is the way I work. It doesn't mean that over time I won't develop. For me, the style of those early stories was right.

Since you've written about experiences and events set in China but your books aren't available there, do you feel cut off from your native readership?

It's none of my business. Once a book is written, it assumes its own life. I can't do much about a book after its publication. I have to let go and concentrate on new work. If the book is strong, it may penetrate some barriers. It is beyond my reach, and it's impossible to interfere with it after it's published.

Do you think American readers need to have an idea of the last thirty years of Chinese history to fully understand your work?

I don't think so. I try to reduce the historical element of my work. I focus on human psychology and human experience. I use history only as context. On the other hand, I have to make the experiences of my characters as concrete and as historical as possible. Only through history can history be conquered. We cannot do anything in a vacuum.

Critics have commented on the violent acts in your work. How do you keep these acts from reading as vulgarity on the page?

It depends on what the story means. I wrote only two scenes related to rape, but many critics continue to mention those scenes. I feel they are both essential to the story. In my prose, I can't resort to vulgarity at all. The purpose of writing is to write against vulgarity. As writers, we can't make violence for the sake of sensationalism. I have to bring out the human qualities of my characters in the story. There were other moments of violence, not just rape, that were normal in China at the time I was living there. I think poetry comes from being able to find humanity in brutal scenes.

> I think a writer can write only about what is close to his heart. For many years, China has been the subject I am obsessed with.

You've said a person must accept failure and adopt a sense of hopelessness before he can become a writer. What do you mean by this?

When I started, I was absolutely uncertain how far I could go, whether a book or even a story could ever be published. People said I was crazy. Friends became estranged because they thought I was a hopeless case. I had to accept this as part of the psychology of being a writer. I didn't expect to reach any success. I just wanted to make writing something I could do and enjoy doing. That's why I think it's important to accept failure. It's always a possibility in the craft of writing. There are many great books in the world. If we put our work in the context of the great books before us, then we can't think of success. In another sense, as writers, we can't talk about success at all. There is only humility.

Was it essential for you to work on shorter forms before attempting a novel?

Writing stories taught me a lot. Through that process, I became more skilled and in control of many aspects of fiction writing. It's good to start with short pieces. It doesn't have to be a short story but just a short piece.

This way you gradually build yourself up and train yourself to become a more capable writer. That doesn't mean I will now only write novels and forget other forms. For me, short fiction and poetry are essential and important. I think one of the most ambitious achievements a writer can aim for is to write one great story. For instance, Shirley Jackson's work basically rests on the achievement of a single story ["The Lottery"]. One story is sometimes enough.

What affect have your prose and verse had on each other?

Writing poetry can teach you to be more careful with words, their nuances and sounds, and the rhythms of language. But poetry and prose are different. Poetry depends on your ability to condense. Anything that is not essential must be let go. In prose, you try to bring out the abundance of the experience and make it as rich as possible. These forms work on different principles. The way they affect each other isn't always positive. For instance, if you write a lot of fiction, you may tend to be dramatic with your poetry. Sometimes poetry doesn't need much drama. It needs lyrical intensity. If you become a good lyric poet, your prose language often becomes purple. That's not good for prose because it needs harshness and concrete tangibility.

Do you feel more comfortable in one form?

I'm more comfortable as a short story writer. Short fiction is close to poetry in terms of impulse. I can stretch a story into a novella, then a novel, but I feel more at home in the form of short fiction. Other forms—the novel and poetry—are more challenging because I'm not as capable in them. I always want to do something I can't do. As long as I have good ideas—as long as I'm bothered by something—I can figure out a pattern of experience and make a story. Of course, this takes time and a lot of energy.

When I teach, short stories are something that I can pick up, work on, then put down. I can't do that with a novel. I have to be in the novel a long time and think about it—sometimes I have to live in it—and that involves too much time while I'm teaching. I need a lot of leisure for it, and I don't have that often. With a short story, that's possible. In the case of poetry, it depends on luck. When I finish one poem, I don't know whether I will write another one. It's absolutely uncertain. With short fiction, I can will a story into existence.

You've said that you write slowly and go through many drafts, but since 1996, you've had six books published. Had you been working on these books for many years?

The material had accumulated over the years. I couldn't get my first few books published. That's one of the reasons for the buildup of manuscripts. Some of them sat around for a long time. *Waiting* stayed on my shelf for nine months before I sent it to a publisher. I didn't know where to submit it. I knew that Zoland Books, my former publisher, couldn't do much marketing for the book. I think that was good for me, especially as a beginner, because it taught me patience. Every time a manuscript was returned to me, I would work on it and see that there were possibilities for improvement. I think that's part of the process that helps a writer to develop his ability.

How do you create a story? Does it begin with an image, a voice? Your character Kang from "Love in the Air," in *Ocean of Words*, is a telegraph operator. One night at work, he hears the voice of a female operator from another city and imagines a life for her.

It depends. Sometimes a story can be purely willed into existence. For instance, in my story "The Bridegroom," I researched and read about the subject, and then I wrote a story based on that research. It is best when I am bothered by something and have to write about it in order to calm myself. But that is not common. Often, when I start to write a collection, the first few stories are made from something I have had on my mind for a long time. Then I have to research and gather material for the rest of the book.

What is your editing process?

It's crazy and endless. Usually, I write longhand and then rewrite it when I'm putting it on the computer. I like the state of the screen because the text is fluid, and it gives me the feeling that nothing is fixed, that I can do anything. But I have to keep a record; otherwise, I may lose some good passages. It takes a long time for me to make the text relatively fixed on the screen, and then I print it and work on hard copy, using different pencils over many drafts. I don't know how many drafts I go through in hard copy. I take it to the point where I don't think I can do anything about it. But nowadays, I have deadlines to meet. This is not good because the work is not fixed and finished yet. A manuscript somehow has its own demand of time and of how much energy it needs put into it. I try to always give myself enough time to edit so I can meet its demands.

How do you know when you've finished a book?

No matter how I try, I cannot improve anything in it.

What do you do when an editor makes suggestions that you don't agree with?

Most of the time my editor doesn't suggest big changes. If I don't agree, I keep or put in what I think is right, because the author will face the criticism eventually.

Who are some writers you find instructive or who offer good examples in terms of craft for beginning writers?

I often use Shirley Jackson's "The Lottery," Faulkner's "A Rose for Emily," and Hemingway's stories in the classroom. That doesn't mean I learn directly from them, though sometimes this is the case. I like to read

Louise Gluck, Frank Bidart, Alice Munro, Tracy Kidder. There are a lot of writers, even bad writers, who are useful.

There are different kinds of readings. Sometimes I read for nourishment, and this is when I read the best literary works. Sometimes I read to get information and to learn about a subject. I read the National Book Award nominees for 1999 to see what these writers are doing. I follow writers who are writing about immigrant experience, for instance, Chang-rae Lee [*A Gesture Life*], Jhumpa Lahiri [*Interpreter of Maladies*], Gish Jen [*Who's Irish?*]. Besides those, I read great writers like Saul Bellow, Flannery O'Connor, and Grace Paley. Especially Bellow. His sentences are wonderful, as are Cheever's.

Waiting **stayed on my shelf for nine months before I sent it to a publisher. I didn't know where to submit it.**

Your sentences are sounded out and constructed in a style similar to Cheever's.

Cheever is a superb stylist and an example of the highest achievement in short fiction. It's different, though, because Cheever uses American idiom. Because my subjects are different, I cannot use true American idiom. Sometimes I can't refrain from using it, but, in the process of revision, I take it out. I have to make the writing suitable to the subject. Gradually, I think this won't be a problem because I'll be writing about American life, and American idiom will be a natural part of this.

Did you run into problems with the language when you began writing in English?

I never asked anyone how the language works, how words are used, what the proper idiom consists of. I teach writing, so I should at least have that little pride of learning the language by myself. I checked dictionaries and read books to find the right usage. I labored a lot, especially in the first few years. Sometimes a phrase would take a few days to fix. But gradually, I accumulated inertia. I don't mean to say that things have gotten easier, but they are less frustrating than before.

What are some discoveries you made as an evolving writer?

I think that if I really understand my material and speak from within the story, often the story will have its own demand for style. I think that's clear. For instance, look at *In the Pond* and *Waiting*. If you take out one sentence from each novel, they sound different. *In the Pond* is a comedy, and *Waiting* is a tragedy. The subject matter, the story itself, determines the style. Style is supposed to serve the story, not vice-versa. Sometimes as writers, we make mistakes and try to devise a style and make it fit the story.

What is your favorite part of the writing process?

The final editing, after which you know you are finally done with it.

Some writers say that there is one moment in which they realize they are writers. Was there a moment like this for you?

It was a process. Before I started teaching at Emory, I had published a book of poems, but I was halfhearted about writing. I didn't know what I was going to do. But I was working step by step. Once I was hired by Emory to teach poetry, I became serious because it became my profession, and my livelihood became dependent on it. I don't mean to say that it was a purely practical decision made in order to earn the bread. There was more to it than that. I wanted to observe the masters, the writers I care for and love. I write with the hope that if one of the masters were alive and read one of my stories, he would be pleased. On the other hand, there was a pure, practical reason that I decided to become a serious writer, and that is the instinct for survival. That's the biggest reason for me.

Ha Jin on Point of View

Many stories in *Ocean of Words* are in first person. *In the Pond* and *Waiting* are both third-person narratives. How do you decide on point of view?

This is important. Isaac Bashevis Singer [*Gimpel the Fool and Other Stories*] once said in an interview that a writer should depend on the third-person narrative. He has a good point because the third person is where you can bring out all you have as a writer. When I finished the stories in *Ocean of Words*, I put them together and realized that many of the stories were written in the first person. Some of the voices were similar, although they belonged to different narrators. I had to dismantle some of the stories in order to keep the book vocally diverse.

Gradually, I've come to realize that the third person is vital. That doesn't mean I won't write in the first person. I sometimes have to. But it's limited compared to the third person. Omniscience gives you different views of the same thing, as if the novel is a house and you can enter different rooms and see various views. If you write in first person, you have to let the reader know how the narrator has gained access to the information. The narrator has to be a witness to the experience. That limits you in many ways, including language, because the language has to fit the personality of the narrator. There are other kinds of limitations, as well. The first-person voice, really, cannot be as rich as the third person. But there are different kinds of first-person voices. For instance, it can be a communal voice, like the one in Faulkner's "A Rose for Emily." Third person may be the most important tool a writer has. To speak as yourself, sentence by sentence, and not in the voice of a character, is interesting. That is one way to show your strength as a writer.

That seems like a great challenge, that something you write should please the masters of the craft.

I think that when you constantly read a lot of good literature, you become close to writers, even if they are dead. It's important to read the classics and to have some books that you carry close to your heart. I want these books to be my companions when I work.

This doesn't mean that if you learn from the masters that you can write like them. That's impossible. You always have to be yourself. You always have to write something different. Originality doesn't necessarily mean that the work is good. Novelty and originality are sometimes not distinguishable. But I don't mean you shouldn't be original. Mastery and personal development don't contradict one another. The first step is mastery; then you can think about how to make something new.

You were a juror for the Neustadt International Prize for Literature. In the past thirty years, twenty Nobel Prize winners were previous nominees, winners, or jurors of the prize. What would be the ultimate achievement for you as a writer?

How can I say that? Really, I have to look at it book by book, story by story, and poem by poem. Writing is not something you can draw a map for. It's like building a house without a plan. You can only build the work piece by piece. Luck also plays a big role in this process. I can't think about what type of writer I will become, but I know where I was born. I am from mainland China. I grew up in another language, in another culture. In the English language, there has been a wonderful tradition of prose writers. I think I am close to the tradition of writers like Conrad and Nabokov, who wrote in English though it wasn't their first language. I continue to follow their way rather than to be involved in a cause or a new wave. I want to write literature.

vision of an artist

CHARLES JOHNSON

Though perhaps best known as the National Book Award-winning author of the novel *Middle Passage*, Charles Johnson prefers to think of himself as an artist. "I sometimes see myself mentioned as 'the novelist Charles Johnson,' but I don't think of myself in that way," he says. "I don't call myself a writer; I call myself an artist. I create things. Today it might be a cartoon. Next week I might write an introduction to a book. Then it might be a short story."

Born in Evanston, Illinois, on April 23, 1948, Johnson's first artistic inclinations were as a cartoonist, but his pursuits have always been wide-ranging. In keeping with his earliest aspirations, he has published two cartoon collections, *Black Humor* and *Half-Past Nation Time*. Other early interests, including martial arts and Eastern religion and philosophy, continue to enter his writing. Johnson has also worked as a journalist and contributes regularly to various magazines. In 1970, he forged what would become a longtime relationship with PBS when he became the host of *Charlie's Pad*, a series on cartooning. He went on to write many scripts for the station, including *Booker*, which won a Writers Guild Award. He recently contributed original short stories to the PBS companion book *Africans in America.* Johnson is currently studying Sanskrit.

As a student, Johnson wrote six of what he now calls "apprentice" novels over a two-year period before meeting novelist and teacher John Gardner at Southern Illinois University. Gardner served as Johnson's mentor and helped him through his first published novel, *Faith and the Good Thing,* which explores black folklore, humor, and magic. A story collection, *The Sorcerer's Apprentice,* and three novels followed. *Oxherding Tale,* which he calls "a metaphysical slave narrative," tells a humorous and philosophically charged story of a mulatto slave. With *Middle Passage,* the story of Rutherford Calhoun's attempt to flee debt and marriage by stowing away on a slave transport, Johnson became the first black male novelist since Ralph Ellison to win the National Book Award. His most recent novel, *Dreamer,* explores the life of Martin Luther King Jr.

Charles Johnson lives with his wife in Seattle, where he is the Pollock Professor of English at the University of Washington.

Books by Charles Johnson

Black Humor (cartoons), Johnson Publishing, 1970
Half-Past Nation Time (cartoons), Aware Press, 1972
Faith and the Good Thing (novel), Viking Press, 1974
Oxherding Tale (novel), Indiana University Press, 1982
The Sorcerer's Apprentice (stories), Atheneum, 1986
Being and Race: Black Writing Since 1970 (nonfiction), Indiana University Press, 1988
Middle Passage (novel), Atheneum, 1990
Dreamer (novel), Scribner, 1998
Soulcatcher and Other Stories (stories), Harvest Books, 2001
Turning the Wheel: Essays on Literature and Buddhism, Scribner, 2003

When you were twelve years old, your mother gave you a journal and told you to write. Did she have any idea what she started?

She started lots of things, most of which didn't succeed: clarinet lessons, piano lessons, dancing lessons. None of that stuck with me because I wanted to be a cartoonist. My mother had many artistic interests, and she shared those with me. I found the journal attractive because it gave me a place to write my thoughts. You're absolutely free, in a journal, to say whatever you want.

And that's why she gave it to me; she wanted to read it. But I couldn't get away from it after I began. It evolved into a kind of writer's journal, which I continue to use. I put them aside once I'm done. By then, it has served its purpose of helping me clarify some of my thoughts. I think a journal is an extraordinarily good tool for beginning writers because it helps them get accustomed to thinking about experience in language.

I tell my students that it's difficult to write sometimes, just to get to the writing, to sit down and finish a story. But if you write each day, even just a paragraph in your journal, you're never outside the creative process. When I write fiction, I hardly touch my journal. I sometimes spend five or six years on a book, so there might be a big gap between journals, but that wasn't true in the beginning because I was writing a book every ten weeks.

If you write each day, even just a paragraph in your journal, you're never outside the creative process.

You knew your mother read your journal. In a sense, she was your first reader. Did that help you realize there could be an audience?

After I realized she read it, I hid my journal. I would never think of sharing that with anybody, though I think my wife took a peek when we were first married. The intention when you write for others is entirely different from when you keep a journal. Sometimes when I go back and look at my journals, I see whole essays I've written. With a little editing, they could be excerpted and published. But most of the time, I'm trying, basically, to take my own temperature.

When I first started teaching at the University of Washington, I had my students turn in a writer's notebook twice in a ten-week period. I told them, "I don't care what you use it for, but let me recommend that you write character sketches. Maybe you'll see an image when looking out the window that strikes you. Write that down. Clip a newspaper article. Just show me that you're observing the world." Some of the students got so hooked that they didn't want to leave their journals with me over the weekend because they needed them.

Every writer needs something like that. I clip articles all the time, things I think I can use later. They can be about anything: woolly mammoths, statistics about social life in America. When I revise my work, I set six to eight hours aside to go through all of my journals and clippings, just to see if there's one thought I might have had twenty years ago that's useful, and often there is. More than anything, it's a memory aid. The heart of writing is rewriting, revision. So the writer's notebook is critical; it helps me recall what I thought and felt about certain things.

A first draft of a novel or story should be written with the intention of seeing if you have something worth pursuing. You begin to clean up in the second draft. You take out what doesn't fit, and you fill the holes of the first draft. It's not until the third draft that you can settle down and begin to revise. After that, you might go through twelve or twenty drafts to improve and refine. To me, that is not a lot to ask. Nothing is perfect. I'm not going to say certain things don't approach perfection, but the goal is to have something that is as consistent, coherent, and complete as you can make it in that moment. If you revise thoroughly, that moment might be a long moment. It might endure for decades as a work. Writing well is the same thing as thinking well.

Can you remember any stories that came from searching through your journals?

I'm on the Washington Commission for the Humanities, and a few years ago we held an event called "Bedtime Stories." I asked writers to write bedtime stories. I had to write a story, too. But I didn't have an idea for one until four days before the event. The only thing that bugged me at that time was taxes. I racked my brain. I went through my notebooks and found one line: "What if the government decided to tax people's dreams?" In one night, I wrote a story called "Sweet Dreams," which is about a man who goes to have his dreams audited at the Department of Dream Revenue. I had fun with that story, and the audience went nuts—they just rolled. In that desperate situation, I went back to my notes and found a germ that could grow.

You mentioned your six "apprentice novels." Did you think of them in those terms when you wrote them?

Every time you do something, you try to do your best. I wrote those books over a rather quick time—two years. I never intended to become a writer. All of my orientation from childhood to college was as a cartoonist. But then, one idea for a novel occurred to me, and I had to write it because it wouldn't leave me alone.

Setting out to write a novel was something I was familiar with because I had friends who were writers. One very good friend, Charles A. Gilpin, to whom I dedicated *Faith and the Good Thing*, wrote six books by the age of twenty-six, then died of a rare form of cancer. I wrote my first novel, and it was rough. I needed to know more. I started another one immediately to see if I could improve things like character and plot description. Then I wrote a third novel to see if I could improve structure. By the time I got to the seventh, I had read every writing handbook I could find. I understood a lot, but there were certain things I still didn't know.

By good fortune, I happened to be at Southern Illinois University, where John Gardner [*Grendel*] taught English. According to editors who had looked at my work, I needed to learn two things: voice and rhythm. Those were two things that John was quite good at. He was a narrative ventriloquist. John paid an extraordinary amount of attention to rhythm, meter, and cadence. And he was also familiar with philosophical fiction, which was what I focused on for those six books that I couldn't nail.

From the beginning you've been motivated to write philosophical fiction?

I asked myself, what can American philosophical fiction achieve? My background is in philosophy, and in that first book I tried to achieve the American philosophical novel, of which we don't have many examples. At that time there were about five or six people who worked in that vein, including John Gardner, William H. Gass, Walker Percy [*The Moviegoer*], and Saul Bellow [*Humboldt's Gift*]. This was a natural way for me to develop because as a graduate student in philosophy I read philosophers who wrote fiction—Camus, Sartre, Santayana.

That's my little corner of the literary world. I've done other things because they interest me, but that's home base. Gardner represented what I've come to refer to as, stealing a phrase from Northrop Frye, "the educated imagination." The imagination is one thing, and that's fine, but if it isn't tempered with a base in the theory and practice of literature, then it's a wild imagination. That's not the kind of literature I'm most attracted to. I want literature to be intellectually vigorous. I want it to fit within the history, at least of the Western world, of the evolution of our literature. Why write? There's got to be a reason. Sartre writes about this in *What Is Literature?* It contains wonderful chapters: "What Is Writing?" "For Whom Does One Write?" "Why Write?" He says a writer writes because he has something to say that has not been said. That's why I write, and that's the kind of writing that I want to read.

There are objective problems in science that are handed down over generations, mistakes that were made, questions that were not resolved. It is the same with literature. There are books that need to be written, stories that need to be explored. There are subjects that never get treated. There may have been a book that treated a subject a hundred years ago, but botched it, making that book obsolete. If this is the case, we need to revisit that subject again.

It's all about the evolution and the efflorescence of meaning and the exploration of possibilities. Most of our writers have not done that. This is an enormously complex world. They're eating cloned beef in Japan. We have technology that didn't exist twenty years ago. Some people compare the Internet to the Gutenberg Press. We are entering a period that will be as radically different as 1899 was to the 1920s, when we had a new science, a new poetry, a new evolving fiction and all the trappings of our world today did not exist. I suspect that the next ten to fifteen years will be just like that. It's a remarkable time to be alive. Some people say that everything has been written. Not so. We have entirely new situations. These stories are dying to see print.

Has this always been a concern for you? Several of your novels deal with subjects that have received little or no attention in fiction.

Nobody had ever written a novel about Martin Luther King Jr. This shocks me. There are libraries of nonfiction, and I looked at as much of that as I could. I spent two years reading and looking at documentaries and speeches before I wrote a word because I didn't know who King was. It astounded me that a figure of King's magnitude had not been in our imaginative literature. Now I understand why this was probably so. King is hard to write about.

And by the same token, there was no novel about the slave trade until *Middle Passage.* There was nothing that put people on the boat and took the reader through the daily routine of what happened on the ship with specificity and detail. *Middle Passage* was actually the second of the six books I wrote in two years. I wasn't ready to handle it properly, and I told it from the wrong viewpoint. But I had begun the research, and I kept it up. I continued to learn about the Middle Passage. When I returned to the book in 1983, I didn't need to do any more research on the slave trade. What I didn't know was the sea. So I spent six years looking at all of Melville and Conrad. I looked at nautical dictionaries and films relating to the sea. I took copious notes about what was on board. As they say in theater, how do you dress the set of a slave ship? What are the props? Everything has to be as exact as you can possibly make it. These are stories that need to be written. Fiction writers need a little time to catch up on these matters. And they will.

I want the next thing I write to be that kind of book. My questions right now are: What is civilization? Where are we? What does it mean to be American these days? Do we have shared values, or are we all coming from different Balkanized places? Are there many Americas? And what does that bode for the future? These are pressing questions.

How does writing historical fiction differ from writing about history? How are they related?

To write a novel, you have to know the history, and then you have to make up a story. I truly admire what historians do because fiction writers base what they do largely on that. But as a novelist, you have to know everything. When I tackled a figure as eminent as Martin Luther King, I had to learn many things about him. I didn't know, for instance, what his favorite sermon was, and it was important for me to learn that.

I didn't know that he smoked.

Many people never knew that because he never let the camera take a picture of him while he smoked, except once or twice. There's one picture of him where he's leaning forward at a bus station, talking to Andrew Young, and there's a cigarette in his hand. When he died, there was a cigarette in his hand and somebody took it out. He had gone out on the balcony to smoke, and that's when he got shot.

As a writer, I need to know these things. One thing I couldn't discover was the brand of cigarettes he smoked. I needed to know the ordinary, everyday things. How did he shave? All of these things characterize an individual. Writers need to know all those details about a fictional character. For historical characters, it's great because the historians have already done all the work for you. But what you have to have is a story. History is made of stories. History and fiction are means of interpretation based upon narrative—beginning, middle, and end—which, of course, is an artificial structure. You choose a piece of time that you want to work with. In that respect, the historians and the novelists are like brothers and sisters in their efforts.

Do you think fiction writers are able to enter history in a way that historians cannot?

One thing I like about *Africans in America*—which is the product of a ten-year project of historians working under the direction of Orlando Bagwell—is that it is the first history book I've ever seen that has short stories in it. It would be great to see more historical books like this because fiction writers can get into the moment and sink the reader into it in a way that historians can't.

I've talked to the historian Stephen Oates about this. I truly admire his *Let the Trumpet Sound*, which was one of my touchstone books for *Dreamer*. He said that he always wanted to go further with his book on King, but he felt that as a historian, one hand was tied behind his back. He had restraints that I didn't have. I could be speculative. I could connect things. One of the things I was delighted with about *Dreamer* was that I figured out what paper King was writing for a college course when he met Coretta. I could have her ask him what he's doing, what he's working on, and he could say, "Well, I'm working on this paper about. . . . " There are a couple of episodes in *Dreamer* like this.

King didn't have a religious conversion as a child. It was in Montgomery during a night when he couldn't sleep and was wondering if he should bail out of the movement when he heard God talking to him. King gives this event only three or four sentences in his writings, but I wanted to spend some time with it. There are possibilities grounded in the historical record, but a historian might not reference these events and put them in

Charles Johnson on Editing and Publishing

What are some things you learned the hard way about writing and publishing?

What I learned of greatest importance after I published my first novel, *Faith and the Good Thing*, in 1974 is that when I send off a novel manuscript it needs to be as perfect as I can make it.

How did you find your agent?

I was introduced in 1973 to the Georges Borchardt Agency by my friend and teacher John Gardner, who was brought into the agency by, I believe, Stanley Elkin.

What is the most difficult part of the editing process for you?

First drafts are always hardest because I have to despoil all the possibilities inherent in a story idea. After that, revision and rewriting—which is 90 percent of writing—is the real joy.

How do you deal with editorial suggestions you don't agree with?

If I believe the editor has identified a real problem but has given me a solution that is inappropriate for my own aesthetic vision, I simply come up with a solution I like better. If the editor has erred in seeing a problem where there is none, then I ignore the suggestion entirely, especially if I've intentionally done something that is risky and fresh and I've thought about it a hundred times before submitting the manuscript.

Do you have anyone read or comment on your work before you send it to your agent?

I have scores of friends all over the world whom I share prepublication drafts of my work with—my wife and children, literary critics who have published (or are at work on) studies of my fiction, friends who are poets, playwrights (like August Wilson), novelists, essayists, filmmakers, screenwriters, and teachers of philosophy and literature at many colleges and universities. Quite often they give me helpful comments.

How do you know when a story or novel is finished?

I know a story is finished when I have revised it so thoroughly that a single sentence cannot be removed without disrupting the music and meaning of the sentences before and after it. In other words, when everything in the story is so complete, consistent, and coherent that every dimension of the story feels organic and interconnected, like parts of a living body from which nothing can be torn without disturbing the whole.

larger contexts. One of the things I want to do as a novelist is look at all the pieces, come to some decision, and connect things. It's all there if you want to do the work.

Each of the stories in *Africans in America* has a different tone and structure. Did you set out to accomplish this variety?

I worked on *Dreamer* right up until the time that the stories were due. I wrote all twelve of the stories in *Africans in America* in one month, January 1998. It came down to about three stories a week. I quit living my life and wrote the stories because I had no choice: The deadline had arrived. I discovered that I could make it engaging for myself if I wrote each story in a different form. I use first person, second person, third person. There is an all-dialogue story, a story written in the form of a newspaper article. It was fun because I was able to shift forms aesthetically.

Almost every one of John Gardner's exercises from *The Art of Fiction* shows up in those stories. There's one I had given my students for twenty years that I had never tried—a third-person monologue. I used that exercise in "Confession."

You wrote those first six apprentice novels over a two-year period. And then you met John Gardner. How did he help change the way you wrote?

When I first started writing, I loved the work of Richard Wright, John A. Williams, and James Baldwin. They had distinctive visions. I hadn't gotten to my own vision yet, though I was trying to get there with a philosophical novel. One of the things that can seduce a young writer, unfortunately, is the publishing industry, which likes writers to turn over products quickly. So a lot of writers produce rapidly, one book a year. One of the things I realized is how to deepen a work rather than just get it done.

It wasn't so much what John said. I'll talk about it this way: Gardner's idea was that you shouldn't go on with the next sentence until the last one is correct. You should not write below the best line you've ever written. He was a perfectionist in that way. He could sit and write for seventy-two-hour stretches. I've never seen anybody work that way. He was totally devoted to the craft of fiction. It was a religion for John. If you want to understand the craft, you must give total commitment. John would read my work and give me some comments, and I would say, "I'll go back and do that, but let me get to the end of the book first." He'd say, "You can't do that. You've got to get this part right now."

I realized that I could get deeper into something with each draft, that revising is like filling a cup. Basically, what happens is that you fill the cup and it spills over. You add more layers, and things pop up in the fifteenth draft that you had never dreamed of when you first began. These things lead you forward, and the book grows out of its own potential rather than following an outline regardless of the other possibilities. This process also results in having to throw lots of pages away.

For *Oxherding Tale*, I threw away 2,400 pages to get 250. It was 3,000 for *Middle Passage* and easily 3,000 for *Dreamer*. There are issues I pursued that were fascinating, but they didn't belong in the book. If I hadn't pursued those issues, I would not have gotten to other things that did belong in the book. I keep all those drafts. There might be a paragraph or a line that might be useful in something else. There is a section in *Dreamer* where Chaym Smith shoots heroin. I wrote that scene in another novel back in the early 1970s. When I was writing that scene for Chaym, I went back and found the passage so I wouldn't have to do the research again.

Sometimes there are nuggets of good writing that have to be cut when they don't fit, but some of it is publishable. There's a book called *Literary Outtakes* that includes poetry and passages from stories and novels that didn't make it into the final products. They are great, but they just didn't fit. The book contains a passage of *Oxherding Tale* in it.

If you want a really good example of what I'm talking about, look at *Juneteenth*, Ralph Ellison's second novel, which was edited by John Callahan. He edited the 2,000 pages of that novel down to 350 pages of a story, more or less, so we could have something after Ellison's death. In the edited version, we read that the main character receives a letter from a woman. Well, Ellison actually wrote the letter, and it takes up a whole chapter—and is probably magnificent in itself—but Callahan decided it didn't fit. Ellison probably would have decided the same thing. But you have to be open to every possibility.

How much does *Dreamer* differ from your original idea for the novel?

I worked on *Dreamer* for six years. The King stuff was easy. That was based on historical research. The hard part was writing about King's double. That was my original idea for the novel: Suppose King had a double. I tried it as a short story in the 1980s, and it didn't work. The double was tough. I tried him as an uneducated man who several of King's supporters had to bring up to speed, and that didn't work. Finally, through a series of coincidences, I discovered who this guy was, who he had to be. I went to a black writers conference in California. As I was leaving, the man who brought us there for the conference, Ricardo Quinones, gave me a copy of his critical book *The Changes of Cain.* Quinones's book contains two thousand years of the Cain figure, from Genesis through Byron, where he is a reprehensible, devil figure, to his birth as the new antihero.

When did you decide to use the Cain figure as the double in *Dreamer*?

I didn't connect the dots until my agent called me after she saw the program. She said, "What about Cain as the double?" As soon as she said that, I found the structure I had searched for, the scaffolding that I had tried to discover for six years. I rewrote the book in about six months from that angle. The material became new to me; it was energized in a completely different way. Things take time to grow and become richer. Sometimes, it's just luck. When I work on a novel for five or six years, my senses are open; I look for anything that relates to the book.

When I was writing *Dreamer,* I asked myself, "How would Martin Luther King do this? What would he think about that?" That kind of dialogue was in my head all the time. It is an exhausting process, but I think it is the only way to create a truly rich work. Perhaps I picked that up from Gardner. I am sure I got that sense of devotion to the work as a gift from him. There's something else I got from him that relates to this. He talked about moral fiction a lot. People sometimes misunderstood that. People often thought he meant moralistic fiction, and that's the opposite of what he wanted.

What did he mean by "moral fiction"?

John saw fiction, novels, in particular, as being a process. A scientist goes into the lab with a hypothesis. He says, "What will be the result if we do this?" At the end of the experiment, the original hypothesis may be confirmed or denied, or a whole new question may appear. According to John, it's the same with fiction. He liked to use Dostoyevsky as an example. Dostoyevsky thought, "What if God does not exist? What would that allow us to do? Does it allow us to commit murder?" Dostoyevsky couldn't go out on the street and commit murder, but in fiction we have mimesis. He could create Raskolnikov and explore these questions without going through the actions himself.

My question in *Dreamer* was "What if King had a double?" I didn't want to close off any possibilities. And by the end of the book, my idea about King and the Civil Rights movement was completely different than when I began the process. I now have new perceptions. In *Dreamer*, as it turns out, Chaym never gets to be King's double. The long speech King gives in the church in Evanston, Illinois, was originally written for the double. Then I realized that he would not be able to do that. This is about Cain and Abel. This is about inequality on some basic level. So Chaym doesn't get a chance to be, in the full sense, a stand-in.

As a writer, you may have a modification of your original idea, or the whole idea may go in a different direction. That is what Gardner meant by moral fiction. It's why you don't close off any ideas, and it's why you don't preach. Fiction is about discovery. It is trial and error, as in a scientific experiment. When you complete a project, you should be transformed.

Gardner said that when somebody writes a book and puts everything into it, including that person's best jokes and images, he isn't ready to write another book for about two years. He needs to step back, live life, absorb the world. When I write a book, I write it as though it might be the last thing I ever do. I convince myself that this is it—my last will and testament in language. Gardner was big on the idea of emotional honesty. You need to go to those places that are emotionally difficult to visit, things that you don't want to confront, precisely because you don't want to confront them.

Did John Gardner offer you any advice as your work began to be published?

He said the real danger for a well-known writer is that you don't get edited; nobody touches your stuff. He said that when you submit your manuscript, it has to be perfect. You can't expect an editor to work through every line. You have to do it all yourself before you send it in. But you still need a good copyeditor and a good editor to ask questions like, "Don't we need a scene for that? Isn't this an idea you want to reinforce later in the book?" You need another eye, but you don't always get it. John taught me that I had to do much of that work myself.

In what other ways did he instruct you in your writing?

I was working on my seventh book when I met John. He was never my teacher in a classroom setting. I met with him in his office. He would give me suggestions about how to fix problems. I would usually go back and change the scene in a way that we hadn't talked about because I needed John, as an editor and friend, to identify the problem. That's the issue—the problem. I would find the solution. The solution has to come out of the writer's own sense of how this world works. John often told a story about a woman who approached him after a reading. She said, "I like your fiction, but I don't know if I like you." He said, "That's fine. That's the way it should be because I'm a better person when I write. I'm talking to you right now, and I can't revise what I say. But when I write, I can fix it." He believed he could fix language, even if it took 20 drafts, and make it more accurate so that it would not hurt anyone. And writing may be the only time in your life that you can be "right" because you can revise yourself.

What is your best advice for young writers?

Learn the theory and practice of our finest literary predecessors, in the West and East, white and black, if your goal is to contribute significantly to, as Matthew Arnold put it, "the best that has been known and said in the world."

Which of your books was the most difficult for you to write?

The most difficult was *Oxherding Tale,* which I spent 5 years writing and threw away 2,400 pages on to arrive at the final manuscript of approximately 250. It was the most difficult because, frankly, there was absolutely nothing in American literature like its fusion of the American slave narrative with Eastern philosophy and literary forms (as well as the English picaresque novel), and about 2,000 years worth of Western intellectual history.

Which of your books are you most proud of?

I'm most proud of *Oxherding Tale.* I whimsically call it my Platform Novel, first because it is the foundation for all my books and stories that came after it, and second, I call it that as a playful reference to the Buddhist "Platform Sutra of the Sixth Patriarch."

It seems like *Oxherding Tale* was the book you believed you had to write.

Yes, that's true. *Faith and the Good Thing,* my first novel that was published, was a fun book. I wanted to write a novel with black folklore, humor, and magic. The serious book I had in my soul was *Oxherding Tale.* No one understood what I was doing at the time. Alex Haley's *Roots* was popular then, and that book helped to form the way people thought about black American life and literature. *Oxherding Tale* is a slave narrative, and it's a philosophical novel. It deals with not just Western philosophy but Eastern philosophy as well.

If I hadn't written *Oxherding Tale,* I couldn't have written *Middle Passage.* I had to make a lot of the same decisions in both of those books about how to write in a historical context for a contemporary audience. For instance, the first-person narrator of *Oxherding Tale* is black and educated. I had to ask myself how to create a nineteenth-century black man with these qualities. I worked those issues out in *Oxherding Tale,* and the knowledge was there at my fingertips for *Middle Passage.* If I hadn't written *Oxherding Tale,* I wouldn't have written another novel. I wasn't interested in any other book.

You've put a lot of pressure on yourself to be a spokesman and innovator of black fiction. In the introduction to the Plume edition of *Oxherding Tale*, you wrote that you believed your level of success with the book would have an impact on more than just your writing, that the entire field of black literature could be opened if you achieved success. "Black fiction—as I imagined its intellectual possibilities—hung in the balance," you wrote.

I did. I still do. I think that every black writer in America since the nineteenth century has been expected to write a certain way. Those expectations can smother the possibilities of creative expression. If you are writing only about racial oppression—and only about racial oppression in a particular way that, for example, white readers understand—you're missing something. Sartre said that if you're a black writer in America, you automatically know what your subject is: It has to be oppression. Maybe that was true in the period of segregation. But there was also Jean Toomer, who wrote *Cane* in 1923. He looked at everything, beginning with the nature of the self.

It is not true that if you are a black writer in America that you automatically know what you are going to focus on, but that is a trap black writers can fall into. Why did nobody pay attention to Zora Neale Hurston [*Their Eyes Were Watching God*] until the 1960s and 1970s? I'll tell you why. Richard Wright's *Native Son* and *Black Boy* are works of genius in the naturalistic tradition, and they defined black writing. He is the father of black literature. Hurston did not write about racial oppression. She wrote about relationships and culture. Her work was trapped in the background for a long time because of the conception of what black writing should be.

I knew when I began writing *Oxherding Tale* that this was going to be a danger. Some people couldn't conceive of black philosophical fiction, even though we have Toomer, Wright, and Ellison as examples. I was determined to make the things that interested me the focus of the book. It is a slave narrative. I did not want to deny the history of slavery, but this book is not merely about legal or political slavery. It's about other kinds of bondage:

sexual, emotional, psychological, and metaphysical. The main character, Andrew Hawkins, has to work his way through all these types of bondage, some of which are even more fundamental than chattel slavery. Eastern philosophy was very useful to me in that exploration, as it is in all my books.

Writers, especially black writers, have to fight against limitations. Why shouldn't you be able to write about anything? That kind of freedom is not given to black writers. You have to fight for it. You have to claim it.

In what ways have you claimed your territory?

I'll tell you what I did with my editor when I was writing *Oxherding Tale.* I gave him a ten-page, single-spaced outline. He wrestled with it. Midway though our conversation, I said, "I may not write this book. I think I might write a three-generation black family drama." His eyes lit up, and he said, "Yes. I can sell it to the publisher right now."

I went home and wrote him a letter stating that I never intended to write that book. I wanted to see what he would say. And I knew what he was going to say. He was going to jump on that idea because everyone was excited about *Roots*, but that was not the book I wanted to write. I didn't want to feed an audience something that just reconfirmed its own assumptions and prejudices. There are other things I'm interested in. That is what *Being and Race* is basically about. It is about shaking up those presuppositions, not just through black literature, but through black American life itself. I think Ellison did a marvelous job of this in *Invisible Man.* We are mostly invisible to each other. One of the things that literature ought to be about is liberation of perception and consciousness. Our voices need to be freed so that we don't fall into those traps that diminish or limit other human lives.

I think that every black writer in America since the nineteenth century has been expected to write a certain way. Those expectations can smother the possibilities of creative expression.

You've actively tried to do this with each of your novels. Even when the character is a slave on a plantation, he's not the slave we've read about in other works of literature.

Most people don't know anything about the history of slavery. They know a bit about Frederick Douglass, who was an incredible genius. And there are others like him, but Hollywood and literature give us images like the ones in *Gone with the Wind.* This is what *Africans in America* addresses. It clarifies the history of slavery.

When I was in junior high school, we read no black literature. I remember when my teacher in junior high school talked about slavery. She botched it. Slavery comprised a paragraph in our history book, and she passed right over it. I don't blame my teachers; their educations were flawed. They did not know about Harriet Tubman and Sojourner Truth, so they couldn't deliver it to us. Black studies started around the time that I went to college. The people teaching the courses were black graduate students in history and philosophy. I was pulled in with about twenty others to be discussion group leaders.

I got the idea for *Middle Passage* from one of the graduate students who was involved in the group. He showed us an image of a slave ship with little figures arranged spoon-fashion. That image burned itself in my mind. The next quarter, I wrote my research paper on the slave trade. That was the beginning of *Middle Passage,* maybe about 1970. By 1971, I had written the first draft of the novel.

I don't fault my teachers for not knowing this history, but by now we should know it. I am shocked by how much general American history people don't know. For instance, the automatic stoplight was invented by Garrett Morgan, a black man. The phrase "the real McCoy" refers to a black man, Elijah McCoy, who invented the lubricating device for machinery. All this stuff is invisible, as Ellison would say. And then there are bigger things, as in all the black people who fought in the Revolutionary War for the crown and for the continental army. Most of that history is not known, and that's where we get assumptions, prejudices, and misinformation, which causes a lot of suffering. Literature can address some of that. It is entertainment, but all great literature also enlightens. All entertainment doesn't enlighten; it doesn't have to do that. Great literature does both, and that's difficult.

You've juggled quite a lot—writing novels and short stories, studying and writing about Western and Eastern philosophy, writing for TV and film, cartooning, working as a journalist, learning and practicing martial arts, being a husband and father.

When I was in my twenties, it was all about skill acquisition. I still work in that way. I'm now in my second year of Sanskrit studies, and I love it. We have intensive seminars, two or three days in a row, six hours a day through the American Sanskrit Institute. I have always wanted to read original Buddhist and Hindu texts. I can begin to do that now.

Life is about learning and growing, and if you stop doing that—and I put these words in King's mouth in *Dreamer*—you might as well be dead. You sometimes have to fight to find those spaces that will allow you to grow and develop, but that's what life is about. It's like when a person learns a language. The second new language seems easier than the first. And the third is easier than the second. It's the same way with the arts. Many writers, like Ralph Ellison, begin as musicians, and then they suddenly realize the commonality between music and poetry or music and fiction. The arts become easier as you move from one to the other. If you write fiction, you should be able to write nonfiction. If you write a novel, you should be able to write short stories. These are all part of the same universe, so to speak. It's about crossing boundaries, which isn't that difficult. There are certain things that I will never be able to do because they involve different concepts, like the hard sciences. But on the continent of art, there are similarities in the ways the creative imagination works. Most artists can cross boundaries quite easily.

You started with cartoons and journalism, then you went on to philosophy and fiction. Do you think your experience in these fields aids you as a novelist?

The novel is one thing that I do. The novel can be anything. It allows you to do things the short story cannot allow you to do. The short story is a defined form, beginning with modern stories in the nineteenth century. We see its evolution from Edgar Allan Poe to O. Henry to people who reacted against the rigidity of the story, like Sherwood Anderson and Margaret Atwood. When you write a short story, you have to do a specific thing. There is no waste, and there is always a structure, always a formula. The novel, on the other hand, can go in any direction. It can be a slave narrative, a folktale, anything. There can be unresolved matters. If it's original fiction and not formulaic, there is a world of possibilities to explore, and it can be any length. The novel is flexible, but I don't privilege it as a form.

It bothers me when people put things in categories, boxes. All these boxes are arbitrary. Saying, "You belong in this box, and you belong in that box. And this is a better box than that box," is like segregation, apartheid. It's all creation, and the processes are so similar that it doesn't really matter. Whether it's journalism or a well-done drawing or a philosophical work, it's about clarity of thought and expression. I know when I write a short story that certain things must happen within the narrative. But I never tell myself that I'm writing a short story. When I sat down to write the stories in *Africans in America*, I didn't say, "What's a short story?" I said, "What I have here is Phillis Wheatley, and she's working on a poem early in the morning and her mistress comes in and asks her what she's doing." I try to follow characters through a story. It's like Gardner said, you have to know the form from within. Students get hung up when they ask themselves, "How do I write a short story? How do I write an essay? How do I write a novel?"

Don't worry about it. The engine of fiction is character. Everything comes out of the people. All you have to worry about is knowing who they are. This may involve research. You must know your characters and their situations. If you are faithful to how they would respond to things and you don't treat them as puppets to illustrate your own ideas, then you'll have revelations and you'll have a story or a novel. Readers want to know who these people are. Are these people I'm interested in? Do they relate to me? If they do, I must follow through with this because their stories may have implications for my own life. The hardest thing for writers is to get to the heart of a character, to create a character with more than one dimension, who is not just a prop that walks through the story.

You lived a long time with the idea of Martin Luther King for *Dreamer*. Where will you go from here?

I'm not ready to write another novel that involves heavy research.

Charles Johnson on Ralph Ellison

When you won the National Book Award, you gave tribute to Ralph Ellison. What did you learn from reading his work?

I've read *Invisible Man* many times. I was in my teens the first time, and I didn't get everything. Every time I go back to Ellison, I find something new. It's sufficient to say that the most important thing he ever said, and which is represented in all of his work, is that Americans have to learn over and over that we are individuals and we have the responsibility of individual vision.

The other day, August Wilson asked me, "What do you think makes a great writer?" I said, "A major writer is someone who has a major vision." You usually can't explore that vision fully in one book. It's broad and specific at the same time. A major writer is someone who interprets the world for us, and it usually happens over a lifetime, a body of work, an oeuvre.

Maybe I'll choose something close to home, a topic that I already know something about, and that would take about two years. I'm talking to an editor about writing a book that would be like a *Souls of Black Folk* for the twenty-first century, something that looks at black consciousness in a philosophical way, but for a broad audience. It would cover the post–civil rights period. I've already covered much of that material in some of my books, so I'm not sure that I want to write a race book. I'll spend about two years on the next novel, which is sufficient if a lot of research isn't necessary. This is my year off to think about it and do other things. The Buddhist review *Tricycle* printed an article I wrote on Buddhism in black America. I truly enjoyed writing that piece. I think I've waited my whole life to write that article. When I'm working on a novel, there is not a lot of time for these other things. Everything has to be focused on the book and the subject. But when I'm not writing a novel, I can learn and do other things.

August Wilson recently gave me the three volumes of Borges's works: the collected short fiction, poetry, and nonfiction. A body of work is like a house. In one room, there are novels. In another room, there are short stories. In the next room, screenplays. The next floor contains drawings and comic strips. It's a round, diverse body of work. When an artist creates a body of work like this, it is all about interpreting this world we live in. There is a unity that is brought to that—whatever the subject may be—by the personality and vision of the artist.

in search of a world

VALERIE MARTIN

Valerie Martin was born on March 14, 1948, in Sedalia, Missouri, and was raised in New Orleans, the setting for several of her novels, including *Set in Motion, A Recent Martyr,* and *The Great Divorce.*

In her novel *Mary Reilly,* which was made into a feature film, Martin retells the story of Robert Louis Stevenson's *The Strange Case of Dr. Jekyll and Mr. Hyde* through they eyes of Dr. Jekyll's housemaid, a nameless, minor character in the original book. Told in the guise of Mary's diary, Martin's version of this story includes strenuously researched details of the daily life of a housemaid in nineteenth-century England.

Martin's story collections include *Love* and *The Consolation of Nature.* She is also the author of a biography, *Salvation: Scenes From the Life of St. Francis.* Her work has appeared in *Black Warrior Review, Ploughshares,* and *New Orleans Review.*

She has taught writing and literature at the University of New Orleans, the University of Alabama, Mount Holyoke College, the University of Massachusetts, and Loyola University New Orleans. She lives in New York.

Books by Valerie Martin

Love (stories), Lynx House Press, 1976
Set in Motion (novel), Farrar, Straus, & Giroux, 1978
Alexandra (novel), Farrar, Straus, & Giroux, 1979
A Recent Martyr (novel), Houghton Mifflin, 1987
The Consolation of Nature and Other Stories (stories), Houghton Mifflin, 1988
Mary Reilly (novel), Doubleday, 1990
The Great Divorce (novel), Doubleday, 1994
Italian Fever (novel), Knopf, 1999
Salvation: Scenes From the Life of St. Francis (biography), Knopf, 2001
Property (novel), Nan A. Talese/Doubleday, 2003

Throughout your career, you've experimented with point of view. *A Recent Martyr*, in particular, has drawn attention for its unconventional style. Much of the story takes place in the narrator's mind, and she relates many events that she could not have witnessed. What was your experience in writing from this perspective?

A Recent Martyr has the most unconventional point of view of all my novels. It was partly for that reason that it sat a long time before it was published. After about twenty publishers rejected it, an editor told me he'd take it if I would change the point of view. I didn't want to because it was important that the story took place inside Emma's imagination.

How did you decide on that type of narration?

I had written *Set in Motion* as a straightforward, first-person narrative. I was trying to move toward a third-person narrative, but I wasn't quite ready. I liked the idea of Emma's preoccupation with the two people in her life, Pascal and Claire. In the novel, it is almost as if she is trying to tell their stories, and to do so she has to imagine scenes, which makes her an unconscious narrator of her own life. What we imagine about other people's lives is sometimes more revealing than what we imagine about our own.

In your second novel, *Alexandra*, you use a first-person, male point of view.

Alexandra, for me, was a real lark. It was a sort of mock Gothic, extremely funny. Claude, the narrator, doesn't know what's going on. It's not that he's naive; he just doesn't catch on at all. But the reader does. That's another fun thing to play with, as far as point of view is concerned. Claude was in some ways an experiment ultimately fulfilled later in my character Mary Reilly. The reader knows everything about her. It's like watching a play: A character goes into the room where the audience knows there is a burglar behind the couch, and the character sits on the couch. I was trying to have that sense with the reader of *Mary Reilly* from page one—the sense that she can't know the story she tells, but we, as readers, already know it. *Alexandra* was a preview of that.

Has one form of narration been more difficult for you than others?

I guess *The Great Divorce*, a novel with several points of view, was the most difficult. In some ways, *A Recent Martyr* was difficult, too, because Emma narrates scenes she couldn't know about. I didn't feel as bothered by that as other people seemed to be. I think that people do that all the time; they imagine what happens and flesh it out by telling stories. Emma has to put it together from what others have said to her, from stuff she knows about what people would do. I guess that was the hardest part about writing from an unreliable narrator's point of view, for me. *Mary Reilly* was the easiest. Once I got started, it just took sitting down and writing steadily without scratching out.

Was that a daunting task, to take on a classic work of literature, in this case Robert Louis Stevenson's *Dr. Jekyll and Mr. Hyde*, and write the story from another perspective?

It was, and it wasn't. *Dr. Jekyll and Mr. Hyde* is such a small book that you can actually know it in its entirety. It wasn't like taking on Nabokov, as a young Italian woman (Pia Pera) has recently done. She wrote a novel in the form of Lolita's diary. I was using a book that is in the public domain, so there was no worry about lawsuits. Stevenson was a generous writer. He wrote with other people, his son-in-law, for instance, so I don't think he would have minded.

What we imagine about other people's lives is sometimes more revealing than what we imagine about our own.

Using the character Mary Reilly, Dr. Jekyll's housemaid, as narrator, gave you room to make the story your own since that character isn't even named in Stevenson's novel.

The only real mention of Mary is toward the end of *Dr. Jekyll and Mr. Hyde*, when they go into Jekyll's house because the butler has brought the lawyer over to see what is going on. When they go inside, all the servants are lined up, and they are upset because Jekyll has locked himself in his laboratory. One of the maids starts crying, and the butler tells her to hold her tongue. For me, that is Mary Reilly. That was my starting point. Why would the maid cry because her master has locked himself in his laboratory? And why would the butler snap at her? Everything about her comes from that brief scene. I thought when I started the book that I would write up to that scene where she is weeping, but in my book she isn't there when the lawyer comes in. She is in the laboratory with Jekyll.

Stevenson layers stories within stories in his book, and you do the same in *Mary Reilly*, which is told, for the most part, in the form of Mary's diary.

Stevenson's book is modern in its construction. It's small, but it contains three accounts: one by the lawyer, Jekyll's own statement, and a letter. They're all documents, in a way. The style is inviting; the sparse documents play off each other. My book also has three documents: the opening piece, which is about the diary, Mary's diary, and the editor's afterword. I was trying to echo what Stevenson did.

Aside from being familiar with Stevenson's novel, what other types of research did you conduct while working on *Mary Reilly*?

I chose the Victorian period unconsciously, not realizing how much I knew about it. I've always enjoyed Victorian novels, reading about politics and the whole class structure of England, particularly life in London during that time. I did go to London halfway through the book, mostly to figure out some scenery. I was looking for a house that, in my imagination, would be Jekyll's house. I did find one.

I also found some diaries written by people from that period. One was written by Hannah Culwick, who was a servant of a lawyer and who married her employer. They had a strange and kinky relationship. She always wanted to remain a servant. She was resistant to any notion, including marriage, that implied that she should not be valued for the work she did. She took great pride in the fact that she was strong and could do manual work. I was thinking of that type of character.

I also found a cook who kept wonderful diaries. Having access to their food, she did mean things to the people she worked for. She was different from Hannah. A lot of people at that time were documenting the lives of the working class. I found hundreds of books on the period at Mount Holyoke, where I was teaching at the time. I discovered in one of those books a photograph of an anonymous housemaid who I think of as Mary. I also found a schedule of a maid's duties, hour by hour. It was quite killing, the amount of work she had to do: up at 5 A.M. and a full day until 9 P.M., with every hour accounted for.

At the end of the novel, the editor of Mary's diary talks about straight-

Valerie Martin on the Film Adaptation of Her Novel

What was your reaction when you were approached about *Mary Reilly* being adapted for film?

I was delighted. I think all writers want to have movies based on their novels. I thought it might pay for my daughter's college education, and in fact, it did. I was able to disconnect myself emotionally because I knew about others who had gotten involved in that process. To me, it was strictly that they would take it, do what they wanted, and then give me money.

What do you think of the film?

I like the first part and the look of the film. I had high hopes for a while, but as it was being made, it became clear that it wouldn't meet my expectations. There were lots of troubles with the script and on the set. And then there was a problem between the director and the producer.

Did you read drafts of the screenplay?

I did, and I made suggestions. The screenwriter, Christopher Hampton, made so many changes that I think at one point there were twenty different endings.

Have you found that the film has changed some perceptions of the book?

I think people who read the book before they see the movie will be disappointed. And for the reverse, well, you always expect the book to be different. I don't think the movie caused many people to buy the book, and I don't think many people who had already read the book went to the movie. The two seem curiously unrelated.

ening Mary's punctuation but leaving her speech patterns.

I think if I would write that novel today, I would change a few things, like using "mun" instead of "must." Hannah used "mun" instead of "must," and I saw that usage somewhere else, as well. One thing that makes Mary's voice work is something I've noticed from teaching people who are learning English, and that is that they always have trouble with the verb "to be." Mary does, as well.

Literature is often grouped in two categories: writing, which constitutes writing by men, and women's writing. Why do you think the two categories are spoken of as separate entities?

My dad said to me one time that he thought my books were good for a woman writer. And that was a high compliment.

I don't see much difference between the two. There are some generalities. These days, men seem to be more preoccupied with the kind of word play that women don't often become preoccupied with. I can think of few women who are engaged in the fracturing of language the way some experimental male writers are. But then you have somebody like Raymond Carver. I think he wrote in a style that a lot of women would be perfectly content to express themselves in. There is nothing terrifically male about his writing. It's simple, and it's not sentimental, especially the stuff he wrote after Gordon Lish was his editor. For the most part, everybody is pretty much involved in the same game because there are so many different things you can do with the novel. The novel that questions the structure of society is one I think women tend toward. My daughter is a philosophy student in graduate school. She told me it's common for women who are interested in philosophy to focus on ethics, whereas men are drawn to language analysis. There is a similar dichotomy in the novel—a fascination with what language says about what kind of people we are and the investigation of how we should live.

You've said you can't teach someone to write, but you can show him which books to read. How much can a new writer learn directly from someone else?

How much can be done? Essentially, writing is a gift; some people have it, and some people don't. When I encounter someone who has it, it's really fun. The sad thing is that some people who really want to write just can't. I have some sense that no matter what they do, there is something blocking them from being able to write in a way that satisfies even them, and that is not wonderful to see. But every now and then, you get a student who you think will never write, then he practices, wins prizes, and might become the next Philip Roth.

What is your best advice for writers trying to make it in this competitive marketplace?

My advice would be to ask yourself what the *it* is that you are trying to make. Would you still want to write if your work was never published and you had to spend your whole life working in a shoe store to support your passion for writing?

If your answer to this question is yes, then my next piece of advice is to finish the first book, send it out, and move right on along to the next.

Do you think the quantity of books being published hurts the chances of young writers to stand out?

I don't think it really matters. I think books survive no matter what. It's nice that there are a lot of competent writers. When the real thing comes along, when you see a young writer whom you admire—for instance, Kirsten Bakis's *Lives of the Monster Dogs*—it makes you think, well, this is great. There is a lot of life out there, a lot of energy. Writers need other writers. There is a lot of stuff I read that I don't think is particularly exciting. It gives me that sleepy feeling. But should it not be published? No, I don't think so. What should not be published are celebrity biographies that publishers pay millions of dollars for. But novels—you can't have enough of them.

How many rejections did you receive before publishing your first book or story? Were any especially memorable?

There were, of course, lots of rejections. The most memorable was one, mildly accusatory, that read: "There are more than a billion people in China, and I feel certain that any one of them is more interesting than anyone in this novel."

How do you edit your work?

I try to write every day when I can. I write by hand and use a word processor later. I write from the beginning of a book or story to the end. I don't let myself go ahead. As I work, I start to put it on a word processor, so that as I get to the end of a novel, most of it is ready to print. Then I usually print a draft, work it over, put in changes, and that's it. I wind up having to rewrite my endings because nobody ever likes them. I think *Italian Fever* had six different endings. So that's always a problem, but it's what I've come to expect.

How do you deal with editorial suggestions that you don't agree with?

First I try to ignore the suggestion, then, if the editor is insistent, I try to make some very minimal change, such as changing one sentence in a scene that has been described as problematic. It's surprising how often the response to this is "Now it's perfect."

Other than *Mary Reilly* and *Italian Fever*, your books have been set in the New Orleans area, but you have written most of your books while living in other locations.

I like to write about New Orleans when I'm away from it. I wrote *Set in Motion* and *Alexandra* in New Orleans, though I was gone by the time I wrote *A Recent Martyr*. Some of the stories in *The Consolation of Nature* are set in New Orleans, but they were written in Massachusetts. For *The Great Divorce*, I came back to New Orleans to spend time at the zoo and do a little research, but most of the time I was in Massachusetts.

Does the distance allow you to see places more clearly?

I think it does. When you're in a place, you feel like you have to keep up with it. But when you're away from it, it lives in your imagination. For me, this is especially the case with New Orleans, which I know so well.

Human interaction with animals is prominent in much of your fiction, especially in *The Great Divorce* and *The Consolation of Nature.*

I didn't realize how much I was preoccupied by animals until I wrote *The Consolation of Nature.*

So that wasn't a conscious choice?

It wasn't. They were always present, and now I realize that from looking at my earliest stories. New Orleans is full of strange, transforming experiences. Transformation into and out of animals is the basic stuff of myth, and I've always liked those kinds of stories.

There are some excellent writers who write nonfiction about this topic, but I don't see much in fiction. I've always been preoccupied with it, and I'm not exactly sure why. I like animals, but I don't think of animals as being like me. I sometimes think animals know a lot more about us than we know about them. I remember when I was a kid, when there were mosquito trucks that would spray DDT on everything, then all the kids would get on bikes and ride through the spray. It shows how little we knew about insects. By trying to wipe them out, we were on the verge of wiping ourselves out.

Did the story of the Catwoman of St. Francisville, in which a woman turns into a panther (or at least believes she does), in *The Great Divorce* come from an actual legend?

It was totally fabricated. One reviewer referred to it as "a beloved local story." I read a story when I was a kid about a woman who lived on the Mississippi River who supposedly had a centaur living in her house. He would come to New Orleans and go to the opera with her. You couldn't see the horselike part of his body because the opera box hid it. The woman would later be seen disappearing down the alley on the back of a horse.

There is a movie called *Cat People* about a woman who turns into a cat, and there have been two versions of that. One takes place in New Orleans. When I wrote *The Great Divorce*, I hadn't seen the original film. One reviewer claimed that I had stolen from this film and didn't credit it. I had never seen it, so I went and rented the film. My daughter and I watched it. She said, "Oh, Mom, this is creepy. It's so close."

You've said that psychological violence and sex are related. In *A Recent Martyr*, you explore radical differences in the ways people perceive sex and religion. Emma and Pascal are attracted to violence and sex, while Claire feels her greatest trait is her virginity. Is this a way to examine extremes in the novel?

That novel is heavily thematic and schematic, maybe too much so. The challenge for me was to try to make a good character who was somebody I could appreciate. I think it would be difficult to be a saint; it would involve daily struggle. I was trying to give some notion about what that struggle would involve, what the difficult things would be. Of course, for Claire it's that she doesn't like people much. Her desire to be with God is the opposite of what it should be, which is the desire to love. Hers is a desire to withdraw. In the church, those two choices have always existed. Monks withdraw from the world; saints go out to the world: Both are possible. Then, the whole business of religion and sex is potentially a desire to experience transformation: The saint wants to be overpowered by God, and the ordinary lover wants to be overpowered by sex. John Donne wrote a great many poems on this subject several hundred years ago. I wanted to play with those ideas. I like the idea of a book about religion and sex, and so did the Catholic Church, I'm happy to say.

How did the Church react?

I was invited to speak at a conference about religion and writing. It was at Loyola, but I wasn't able to attend. I wrote back and said, "I have to tell you that I'm not Catholic." That didn't bother them. They wanted me to talk about writing on religious experiences. I was flattered and wanted to go, but I was teaching at the time.

One of your most recent books, *Italian Fever*, is in third person, another mock Gothic, as you've called *Alexandra.*

It's much lighter than most of my books. It's about art: what art is, what it does to us if we are or are not artists, how people who are artists feel about people who are not artists and vice versa, and how art itself can ruin your life. Everybody in *Italian Fever*, to some extent, is destroyed by art.

Do you prefer writing novels or stories?

I love to write short stories, but they take longer for me. It takes me twice as long to write a thirty-page short story as it would take me to write thirty pages of a novel. In some ways, I prefer to work on a novel because I feel I'm getting more for my time investment. In other ways, I wish I could have a few years to do nothing but work on stories. When I complete a story, it has that nice, compact feeling, as if you can put it in your wallet and carry it around with you. They are jewel-like, whereas novels are sprawling creatures.

What book of yours are you most proud of?

The Great Divorce. It's my most complex book, though it was not the most difficult to write. That was *Salvation: Scenes From the Life of St. Francis. The Great Divorce* has three separate stories playing against one another, one of which takes place in the deep past of the other two, so I felt that I was doing a balancing act in time and space. It was also an emotionally complex and painful book for me to write, because it forced me to face my own conflicted feelings about the fate of the wild. I had to admit to myself that though I can't bear the thought of a world without tigers, I don't ever want tigers to move in next door.

In the afterword of *Mary Reilly*, the fictional editor of Mary's diary

Valerie Martin on Her Influences

What writers influenced you to write about religion?

Flannery O'Connor [*Everything That Rises Must Converge*] is instructive, especially in her notion of grace that we encounter in moments of extreme pressure and also her notion that to get a character to reveal his makeup, his true ethical identity, you have to really put him under pressure. So in some ways, the plague is there in *A Recent Martyr* because it puts characters under the kind of stress that makes them reveal what kind of people they are.

Which writers do you feel you've learned most from in terms of craft?

One of the big books for me was Camus's *The Stranger*, which made me want to have a simple style and made me see what is possible with a first-person voice. Flaubert provided subject matter that has never left. The question of how a romantic education ill-equips us to live in the world and the conflict between romanticism and realism still is a subject matter for all of literature. Again and again, that is what I write about: the conflict between what we wish the world to be and what it really is, how much we long not to face reality. We still receive a romantic education. We haven't gotten to the point where when we raise a child our greatest hope for that child is that he will be able to see reality. In fact, our greatest hope is usually that the child will be able to escape reality.

This is reflected in *The Great Divorce*, especially in the way Lillian and Celia react to the breakup of their parents' marriage.

I think that's where it started to work. I sat down to write the

continued

book knowing that I wanted to push these ideas, which have always been the background of what I've been doing, as far as I could take them. There are two daughters, and one, Lillian, is squarely and firmly placed in the real world. The other, Celia, is the one who gets into trouble. Celia is the one Emma almost loses, and she has to struggle to restore her daughter to reality. She feels she is successful because Celia becomes interested in the work at the zoo and likes to take X rays. She likes to get a good, clear picture. I wasn't thinking of that when events happened in the book, but now I see why those things happened.

writes: "The sad and disturbing story unfolded for us in the pages of Mary's diaries is now and always was intended to be nothing less serious than a work of fiction." What is your role as a fiction writer?

It's astonishing how many Americans don't understand that fiction is made up. Look at the recent flood of memoirs and the popularity of what people think of as a true story, many of which, if they are true, I'll eat the entire copy. I have received letters from people who believe that Mary Reilly is a real person. I've had students and other readers ask me where I found the diary. That is one level of the readership: those who believe there is no such thing as fiction. Fiction itself has begun to comment so heavily on itself, it has become so obsessed with talking about itself, that it's not any wonder people are confused. But, fortunately, there are still those who understand that when you make up a story, you actually leave your ordinary reality behind and go off in search of a believable fictional world.

laughter at 3 a.m.

ELIZABETH McCRACKEN

Even after distinguishing herself with *The Giant's House*, her National Book Award-nominated novel, Elizabeth McCracken sometimes still prefers to think of herself as a librarian.

McCracken's first book, *Here's Your Hat What's Your Hurry*, a collection of stories, appeared the same year that she completed her library science degree at Drexel University. It contains stories featuring tattoo artists, retired circus performers, a former child prodigy, and a father who abandons his children to strangers.

The Giant's House, in which the main character is a librarian fascinated with an "overly tall" young boy, was named a notable book of the year by the American Library Association in 1996 and also earned McCracken a Barnes and Noble Discovery Award. She has received notable mentions from *The Best American Short Stories* and *The Best American Essays*. In 1996, *Granta* chose her as one of the "Best Young American Novelists."

McCracken, who was born in 1966, has received the Harold Vursell

Award from the American Academy of Arts and Sciences and a fellowship from the Guggenheim Foundation.

A graduate of the Iowa Writers' Workshop, McCracken has taught creative writing workshops at the University of Iowa, Western Michigan University, and the Fine Arts Work Center in Provincetown.

Books by Elizabeth McCracken

Here's Your Hat What's Your Hurry (stories), Turtle Bay Books/Random House, 1993

The Giant's House (novel), The Dial Press, 1996

Niagara Falls All Over Again (novel), The Dial Press, 2001

Beginning as a teenager, you worked at libraries for many years. How has your relationship with books developed through this kind of work?

A lot of writers say that when they first went into a library they were awe-filled around all the books and developed a great respect for books. For me, the experience was the exact opposite. I shelved fiction from the time I was fifteen until I was eighteen, and the main thing I learned was that books are objects. Like all teenage shelvers, the part of the job I hated was the work. You need to be a fairly obsessive-compulsive person to enjoy alphabetizing books. But I loved being in the library. I spent a huge amount of time reading books while on the job—classics, classics that had fallen out of favor and young adult books, which my mother didn't approve of because she feels that teenagers should be reading *The Human Comedy* or Dickens. I lost a lot of respect for books in a healthy way because I looked at the jacket photos and thought, "Practically anybody can write a book." Many people treat their books as sacred objects and put acetate covers on them. I get lipstick on them. I read in the bathtub and while I eat. I don't fold down corners, and I never write in books—there's nothing worse than somebody who writes in books—but I use cocktail napkins or whatever comes in handy to mark my place. Library work gave me the sense that books are nonsacred objects that people can use.

What made you seek a library job when you were that young?

It was either that or waiting tables. No, that's not exactly it. I was not perfect at getting books back to the library on time. There were times when I was in debt to the public library and wasn't allowed to go back. A huge benefit of working in libraries was not having to pay the fines.

I was a clumsy, socially backward teenager. I didn't want to waitress or work in a coffee shop or sell cookies. On my fifteenth birthday, I went into the library in Newton, Massachusetts, asked for a job, and got one. I worked at that same library until just before my twenty-second birthday, which is when I went to Iowa. That library building doesn't exist any more, but it heavily inspired the library in *The Giant's House*. Much more than any person or thing that I've ever written about, there is a direct correlation between that building and the fictional building in the novel.

Did you write during those early years?

I was a kid who always wrote. I didn't write much fiction, but I wrote rhyming verse. Actually, I probably wrote plenty of fiction, but I was better at metered verse, so I've chosen to remember that as what I wrote.

Your parents were academics and editors. Did that help move you toward writing?

I'm sure it did in some way. When I went to Iowa, one of the things that floored me was that there were people whose parents did not think what they were doing was a good thing. People had to fight against their parents, who said, "Why are you going to graduate school in this? For that matter, why did you get an undergraduate degree in English?" My parents never asked those questions. I'm not sure if it was because they were academics or just because they were terribly impractical people. They both came from families with lots of amateur and professional artists. My cousin Elizabeth was a dance teacher. My mother's sister is a sculptor. So writing didn't seem like an unusual thing to do.

Many people treat their books as sacred objects and put acetate covers on them. I get lipstick on them. I read in the bathtub and while I eat.

How do you bring a story to life?

The first thing that comes to me, generally speaking, is the narrator, the main character. Once I come up with some sense of the voice, I have to teach myself how to think like that character. I have to completely give my own imagination over to the character.

I hate hearing myself talk about this because it sounds like I'm mystical in a way that I'm not, or that I attribute writing to something other than the human imagination, which is all that it is.

There's no point in coming up with too much plot before I know a character's voice. But it's important that I have some sense of plot because if I don't, I write in circles. Once I do, I have to be willing to let it change completely with how the character thinks. After I finish a first draft, the second part of rigging up the story is to figure out the pattern so I can get a sense of structure and plot. I know that the character and the thought process will change while I write. I have to rewrite quite a bit to make sense of things, to understand a character.

Ann Patchett, one of my best friends and my best writer-friend, thinks a lot about her work before she begins to write. She wrote her first two books quickly, that is, the actual writing, because she felt that what she had in her head was right. I can sit and think for months, but the minute I start to write, things change completely. I've learned that, for me, thinking too much about what I'm writing is merely a form of procrastination, at which I am a champion. In order to think about writing, I have to be writing.

But when you're involved in a novel, isn't it always on your mind?

My work demands a lot during the hours I'm not writing, but I don't write every day. I binge write. I go through periods where I write every day for hours at a time. But weeks will go by when I don't write. Frankly, when I'm not writing, I don't think about it. I always tell myself, pathetically, that those times are probably valuable for my work because I think about it subconsciously or I allow myself to forget about what I'm working on so that it's fresh when I get back. If I take a month off from a book, I really take a month off from it. When I work, I work eight, twelve, occasionally sixteen hours a day. People always say that writing pays terribly if you work it out to an hourly rate—maybe fifty cents an hour. My rate is higher because I don't work that much.

Most of your work has been in first person. Have all your projects begun that way, or is that one of the things that tends to change?

In "The Goings-On of the World," I had tried to write about Mr. Green, a character based on an actual murderer who worked around the house for my father's parents in Des Moines, but I didn't get any real sense of him in third person. Then, the first-person character came bouncing out. *Niagara Falls All Over Again* began in third person but changed to first person. With the stories in *Here's Your Hat What's Your Hurry*, the voices came first, and the plots came second.

Did "Here's Your Hat What's Your Hurry," the only third-person narrative in the collection, start that way?

Yes, I think, but I have this great ability to forget the process. If you had asked me about *The Giant's House*, I would have said that the first line was always the same, once I'd decided on Peggy Cort as the narrator, but I recently found an early draft, and that's completely untrue. I wrote a prologue that I had completely forgotten about.

How did Peggy take over the narration of *The Giant's House*?

I came up with the idea for *The Giant's House* when I was supposed to be paying attention in rare books class in library science school. I thought about it for a couple months. I had worked some on the novel when I was in school, and then I got a fellowship at the Fine Arts Work Center in Provincetown. I sat down and spent two weeks working on the version that wasn't about Peggy. I had plenty of time to dedicate to the work, so I started to write Peggy's voice just to get a handle on her. In the first version, there had been one throwaway line about her. Then I thought, well, she is going to be a more important part of this book and I'll start to write in her voice. She compelled me in a way that the other characters didn't.

I do a lot of outside writing when I work. I need to write stuff that I know I'll throw away. There are times when I write seven pages to get one very clever line. I believe I'm quoting Ann directly: She would kill herself if she worked the way I do. It's inefficient. I throw out many, many pages, but I do it cheerfully. I take it for granted. Often, I write pages in the voices of characters who I know won't narrate the book just so I can get to know them. One of the dangers of writing a first-person novel is to not pay attention to the other characters. In order to get into the other characters, I need to do something else. And like I said, I can't do it by just wondering, "Well, what does this character think?" I have to discover their voices. In some ways, *The Giant's House* is flawed because an antisocial person tells the story and the other characters are not particularly clear.

So both of your novels started as third-person narratives, but you changed them to first person. What happened?

I guess I'm still dancing around the issue of third person. I always remember Frank Conroy [*Stop-Time*] saying with great authority that first person is more difficult to write than third person. Some people feel more naturally inclined to write in third person, as some are more naturally inclined to first person.

I once had a conversation with Allegra Goodman [*Kaaterskill Falls*], who is a friend of mine, about point of view. She's primarily a third-person writer, but she was starting a new novel in first person. She said, "You were absolutely right. First person is much easier." She could have at least pretended it was a little bit hard! I do think it's easier for some people.

The novel that I worked on during library science school, which I eventually gave up on, was a third-person novel. I was in school, taking two classes a semester, working about fifty hours a week at different jobs. I thought that teaching myself how to write a novel and how to write a third-person narrative at the same time was too much. I couldn't teach myself to do both. I gave it up to write *The Giant's House.* I'm not sure I would ever be all that interested in writing a novel that was third-person limited to one character, although I love to read them. With a few exceptions, like Tremain's *Sacred Country* and, of course, Faulkner, I rarely think that a novel with multiple first-person narrators is a good idea. If I want more than one point of view, I'll use the third person.

***The Giant's House* and many of your first-person stories are written as memoirs. Is that your way of getting into a particular character's voice and of understanding his or her experience?**

One of the things I've always been interested in has to do with the way the story is told, the nature of the characters who tell the story, the time at which they tell it, and the ideas they relate. I rarely ever write something that's narrated in the present tense. It seems logical to me that the reason a character tells the story makes a difference. My stories typically end up being told many years after the fact. I guess I'm interested in—and this is going to make me sound like such a jerk—the nature of memory. What writer is not interested in the nature of memory? But I do play with that formative nature of mind and memory. I have the narrator constantly revise his or her experience.

That's present in *The Giant's House.*

If any of the events in the book ever happened, it's for sure that they never happened even close to the way Peggy says they did.

So she's unreliable?

Oh, extremely. I don't know how to write a reliable narrator because people *are* unreliable. There are few people in the world who could tell you something accurately. Some writers do see a divide between reliable and unreliable narrators. To me, there is no divide. There are just levels of unreliability. You sink yourself into your characters, and you must devote yourself to their thought processes. They will always deviate from the facts in greater or lesser degrees.

You've said that your characters sometimes scandalize you. What is your relationship with them?

I have individual relationships with each character. When I was working on *The Giant's House*, I thought it was autobiographical. After I finished it, I was horrified to think that I'd ever thought that. I read it and realized that I didn't agree with 90 percent of what the narrator says. Sometimes the relationship of a first-person narrator with the author is, I don't know, poltergeist to haunted house. There are certainly characters I've become much fonder of than others. Some remain distanced.

There were conflicting rumors about your novel *Niagara Falls All Over Again* before it was published. Do you know why this came about?

I did a reading several years ago from a book that has a character with Alzheimer's in it. When I ran into someone who had been at the reading, he asked if I had finished the book about the lady with Alzheimer's. And I just stared at him for a few seconds before I realized that he was right, that he hadn't confused me with somebody else. Originally, it was going to take place over a couple of weeks with a woman who had left Des Moines and got forcibly returned when she developed the disease. I needed to write some background about her. And then I was writing this giant book about a Jewish family in Des Moines to incorporate a lot of stories that I had always loved about my mother's family. It was going to be a big, historical family novel. I wrote about two hundred pages of that, and I was having a good time writing in third-person omniscient, switching characters.

Then, two things happened. I wrote an essay called "The Love Interest" about my childhood love for Abbott and Costello and realized that I'd like to write a novel about a comedy team.

The second thing I realized was that there was no discernable plot line in the book I was writing. My friend Wendy said, "So you're going to write two books in a row about Jewish families in Iowa? Can you *do* that?" I said, stubbornly, "Yes, of course I can do that." Then I realized that Wendy was completely right. I couldn't write two books about Jewish families set in Iowa, and I was more interested in the story about the comedy team.

A few years ago, on my way to the Fine Arts Work Center, where I frequently rent a place, I decided that I would abandon the first book and write about the comedy duo. Ann was coming to join me a week later. I spent that week writing about the comedy team so that she wouldn't think that I just got some wild idea to throw out what I'd been working on and start something new to avoid work. I wanted to give her enough to judge, so I wrote seventy-five pages of the book in a week and gave it to her when she arrived. She gave me the go-ahead, so I kept writing.

I also always think I will write something that happens within two weeks in the time that I am writing—late twentieth, early twenty-first century—and that it will be very funny, but I always get waylaid somehow.

Revising and revisiting material is something you've done throughout your work. You've taken subjects that you visited in your stories—physical abnormalities, tattooing, circus performers—and used elements of them in *The Giant's House.*

I read at a high school a couple years after *The Giant's House* came out, and a student said, "It's really interesting that you wrote, essentially, a version of *The Giant's House* in 'It's Bad Luck to Die.' " I had no idea.

I think I go back to the same obsessions over and over again. I'm so frightened to write the same book over and over again. I'm terrified that's all I ever do. Sometimes, I steal lines from myself. I think, "Did I rewrite that enough so that I can use it?"

What role does reading play while you write?

Reading is extremely important to my working process. There are people who won't read anything when they work, but I read a lot. But if I read Grace Paley [*Enormous Changes at the Last Minute*], for instance, I become infected with her and write really bad Grace Paley. I don't read Raymond Chandler or anybody who's really idiosyncratic while I work. There is one paragraph in *The Giant's House* that I wrote when I was reading Carole Maso [*Ghost Dance*]. Every time I read that paragraph, I think, "Oh, my God, that's the Carole Maso paragraph."

I rarely get depressed by reading great books, as some writers do. I read when I work because it makes me excited about all the possibilities. It's absolutely essential to read in order to write fiction. You have to know how people have succeeded in other books.

Who are writers you like to reread, who give you the energy you're talking about?

The two books that I reread a lot are *Lolita*, which is perhaps my favorite novel of all time, and *Sacred Country* by Rose Tremain, who is a wonderful writer. There is something about both of those books that I find deeply moving and inspiring. I have Jeremy Irons reading *Lolita* on tape, and I listen to it like music. There's one line late in the book that I often rewind to. One of the things that I love about the autobiographical nature of certain types of narrators is the direct address of the reader. I probably indulge way too much in that. I just adore it. My favorite line in *Lolita* is a parenthetical aside, "(hi, Rita—wherever you are, drunk or hangoverish, Rita, hi!)." My friend Max says that it's interesting how many of Nabokov's best lines are failed palindromes.

I also love reading Dickens when I write. It depends on what I'm writing. Last year while I was working, I read *Freedomland* by Richard Price, who is a writer I have absolutely nothing in common with. I love books that make me think about things that I don't automatically think about. One of the things that Price is great at and that I'm miserable at is paying attention to how characters stand. The physicality of his characters is amazing, as are his plots—that sense of how you can keep people reading a five-hundred-page novel without being manipulative—which is not one of my strong points. Even the dictionary has a hard time distinguishing between the definition of moving and manipulative. Somehow, there is a line between the two things. But where is it, exactly?

In your *Salon* essay on *Great Expectations*, "A Splendid Invention," you wrote that the simple pleasure of reading serious literature is often overlooked.

A friend and I read *Madame Bovary* at the same time. It was amazing to be able to call or e-mail him and say, "This is my favorite part on this page," or "Did you notice how he does this?" I love to scratch my head and say, "How did that happen? How did he pull that off?"

On the same level, how important is it to find pleasure in what you write?

I've always heard the advice "You have to kill your darlings. You have to cut the lines you really like." I hate that kind of advice. One of the main reasons I write is to break into laughter at three o'clock in the morning. Writing can be salacious fun. The lines I love are never the lines that anybody else loves. When I finished "Some Have Entertained Angels, Unaware," I gave it to a friend. I told her that it contains the funniest line I have ever written. She read the story and came up with six guesses. They were all wrong. Even when I told her which page it was on, she had to give up and ask me. And yet when I wrote that line, it made me so happy that the idea of taking it out . . . I just couldn't.

Do you remember the line?

I do. Isn't that pathetic? There's a character, Kenneth, who has three finches and their names are Sidney, Sidney, and Sidney-Lou. I found that so funny. I don't find it quite as funny as when I wrote it, though.

Aside from the humor, the language of your prose is often fresh and lyrical.

I think that if you scanned my novel, you would find that an amazing amount of it is in iambic pentameter. That's just a theory I have. I love language. It's something I have to be careful about because I can get indulgent and write four lines with heavy alliteration, though the narrator wouldn't talk that way. I get language drunk. I adore those moments when a character says something that floors me. Not that it happens all the time. Like I said, I'm a lazy writer. The worst part of writing for me is the hour before I start to write, when I pace around my chair and say, "I don't want to do it, I don't want to do it, I don't want to do it."

How do you know when a book is finished?

Don't. Never do. Though usually I stop when I despise something so bitterly that I wish never to see it again.

How do you deal with editorial suggestions that you don't agree with?

I don't follow 'em. Happily, I have an editor who doesn't insist—except when she knows she's absolutely right and I'm just being stubborn, in which case she makes me ask my first reader, Ann Patchett, what she thinks. We both know that Ann really gets the final word in such things.

We've talked about the pleasures of reading and writing. Do you write what you would want to read?

If I thought about that, I would never finish anything. I suffer from such huge doubts about the intelligence of any project I've ever embarked on. If I try to imagine myself as a reader of the thing, I'll wash my hands of it entirely.

The worst part of writing for me is the hour before I start to write, when I pace around my chair and say, "I don't want to do it, I don't want to do it, I don't want to do it."

Having been through the Iowa program, what do you think are the benefits of working with other writers?

I had many wonderful teachers at Iowa, and my first one was Allan Gurganus [*Oldest Living Confederate Widow Tells All*]. He was astonishing. He made me realize that you must declare yourself a writer, not a hobbyist. His idea was "Aren't we all lucky to be writers?" Studying under him was absolutely transformative for me. He was always an unbelievably thoughtful and generous reader and extremely smart about fiction. He helps writers to push stories to do what they can actually do. He is obsessed with getting writers to write the best things they can write.

I also got to know my grandmother and my cousin Elizabeth, who lived in Des Moines. They were both quite elderly at the time. I visited them in Des Moines every week and helped my grandmother take care of my great-aunt Blanche, who had Alzheimer's. I connected with my family in a way I had never before. This gave me a sense of the layers of family stories in a much deeper way. I heard some versions from my grandmother and some versions from Elizabeth. And having the time to write was useful. Whenever anybody asks me about writing programs, I say, "Go to the place that will give you the most money and has the least requirements because it is your chance to learn work habits." It's useful to be stuck up to your eyeballs in writing for two years.

What did you learn from the writers there?

Elizabeth McCracken on Research

Does your experience as a librarian make you more apt to get lost in research?

There's nothing better than the microfilm department of a library. I can get in trouble flipping through back issues of *Variety.* I try at a certain point to stop and forget a reasonable percentage of what I've learned so that I can deviate from it. When I began the book that I'm writing now, I panicked and thought, "It's 1932 and I don't know if there was a vaudeville house open in that town at that time." It seemed essential that I be accurate, but at some point, I thought, "Who cares?"

Is it through research and constant reading that you write about even minor characters so distinctly?

God knows that I have an absolute obsession with minor fame. My brother's corollary of Andy Warhol's "Everybody will be famous for fifteen minutes" is that every person is famous in some circle. I love to read in the newspaper about child prodigies and circus performers. This is probably directly tied to being a librarian. I like it when the record of a person is ephemera, when there's only an autographed picture or one newspaper article. Those documents resonate. I see a name on a vaudeville bill and think, "This may be one of the only records of this person." My interest in minor fame is directly traceable to that burst of excitement when I realize that maybe nobody has thought of this person for twenty years.

I did some research at the University of Iowa library, where there is this bizarre, random vaudeville archive. I found a stage manager's notes detailing what he told the performers, including the things they were not allowed to say on stage, the parts of their acts they had to cut. There were things like, "Tell comedian that he must cut the joke about the Ku Klux Klan and the Knights of Columbus playing a softball game," which is a reference that I've put into my novel. I have no idea what that joke was. That's what I like about research, the sense that nobody has figured it out yet. I take the easy way out because I'm not a good researcher. In order to connect the steps, I make them up.

Allan always said that in order to move your readers, to put them through any kind of emotional state, you have to put yourself through ten times that much for it to translate to the page. That's the physics of writing. If you're a good writer, you intensely feel anything you write, but you have to learn not to make it easy on yourself or your characters. I especially feel this way about revision, which is frequently a matter of getting closer to the heart of the matter and at the same time pushing yourself further. The reason you have to revise is because you have to wait until you've forgotten how difficult writing was during that first draft. I am capable of writing a draft that I think is obvious, but when I give it to people to read, they say, "I don't understand what happened." I find that writers sometimes want to steer their characters in a way that is not satisfying in fiction. They want to suggest something instead of actually making the characters do it. They take the reader right up to a confrontation and think they stop at a moment of great possibility, but instead they really stop before the conflict of the story begins.

Is it important for you to be in contact with other writers, to see that other people are spending their time in the same way?

I certainly have a lot of friends who are writers and who are invaluable to my work, but Ann wouldn't be my first reader if I did not adore her as a person. One time we had a phone conversation when we were cleaning out our pantries at the same time. We'd say, "What the hell is this jam?" We both agree that it was one of the most gratifying conversations we've ever had, much more gratifying than talking about our books.

I wouldn't want to be a part of a writers' group at this point. Certainly, one of the great pleasures of publishing a book is meeting other writers. But would I rather go to a cocktail party full of writers or one full of steam pipe fitters? Give me the pipe fitters! With writers, there is a limit to how many conversations you can have that are exactly the same, though it's different one-on-one.

What are some things beginning writers should keep in mind?

That there is no single rule of writing that holds true for all writers. It is important to be vigorous about your work, but it is also important to develop your own sense of fiction. I believe firmly in workshop classes, but it is essential to remember that on a good day only 20 percent of the advice you hear will be useful for what you're working on. I've known good writers—people who seem to be strong-minded—who somehow get screwed up trying to apply to their work every piece of advice that sounds intelligent. One of the things you have to learn is to recognize what works for you. You can't spend energy fretting over things that don't apply.

Also fight the urge to be at all interested in publishing. Put all of your worry, ambition, fear, and energy into writing the best thing you can.

How do you respond to reviews of your books? Many critics called *The Giant's House* "a modern fairy tale."

There are words that get applied to certain kinds of books. I think "fairy tale" is frequently used, and it's actually more often applied to women's books. I can think of two reasons it was labeled as a fairy tale. One is that it contains a giant who lives in a cottage. The other is that it's set in Cape Cod in the 1950s, in a world where nothing outside touches the inhabitants of the town. There's a single mention of Elvis Presley, which is the only current event that has any significance in the book whatsoever. I certainly didn't do that to make it a fairy tale. Just like I was originally worried about being accurate about the vaudeville houses in the new book, I began to panic with *The Giant's House* and think that I should mention the Korean War every single page.

When you interviewed Ralph Fiennes for *Elle* magazine in 1997, you identified yourself as a librarian and made no mention that you are a writer. Do you think of yourself as a writer?

You know, I find library work inherently more interesting than writing. Maybe I've just known too many writers. It was clear that Ralph Fiennes, whose mother, Jennifer Lash, was also a novelist, finds library work more interesting than writing. He's shy and formal, but we connected when I mentioned being a librarian—he knew that I was a writer because the magazine sent him a copy of my book—and he said, "Fascinating being a librarian, isn't it?"

Something I've always been interested in is work. I read *Working* by Studs Terkel all the time. Many people think that writing is not real work. Even my mother says, jokingly, "It must be nice to be unemployed."

You've said there are two aspects of writing: the act of writing and the business of publishing. How have you been able to separate those two sides?

It certainly gets harder and harder. I do think that is one of the reasons it took me a while to write a second novel. My new novel really didn't get off the ground until two years after *The Giant's House* came out. I needed to forget the publication process entirely and not pay attention to any of the other concerns but my own pathetic, petty ones. I had to forget things that readers said to me so that I could write selfishly about the things that I was interested in and get back to the reasons that any writer writes—jealousy, revenge, bitterness, and rage. It may be why, to some extent, I don't like going to writer's cocktail parties. I don't like to have those preoccupations in my head at all. And those are the questions people ask me. It's difficult to talk about that aspect of my work. I have an agent I love and trust. That is another way that I can separate the two things.

I'm inherently not interested in the publication process. I like being published, don't get me wrong. It's not like I'd be just as happy if I sat on a mountain and scribbled in my notebook. I wouldn't be, but I'm not interested in the process it takes to get there.

How did you get your first publishing break?

Well, it depends on how you count it. I do remember getting my first acceptance letter, from Larry Goldstein at the *Michigan Quarterly Review*, which said, "I greet you at the beginning of a wonderful career." And I thought, really? Really? I get a story accepted, *and* I get a career? Nifty!

How many rejection letters did you receive before publishing your first story or book? Were any especially memorable?

A nameless editor at *Harper's Magazine* rejected a story of mine about tattooing, explaining that reading about tattoos was like reading about music or food—pretty soon you want to go out and experience the real thing. I still don't know what that means. He also misspelled "tattoo" all through the letter, so I corrected it in red pen.

How did you find or choose your agent?

It was essentially a blind date. My friend Max Phillips insisted that, when his agent came to visit our graduate program, that I give him work. He insisted that Henry read my work with extra care. That was twelve years ago.

What is the most difficult part of the editing process for you?

The manic swing—loving and then despising what I've written, and not knowing where the truth lies.

Part of the business side of writing is awards. You received a lot of recognition for both *The Giant's House* and *Niagara Falls All Over*

***Again.* Does it feel safer now because there's a market for your books?**

I think there's a good chance that there's not more of a market. With literary fiction, I'm not sure a writer's career is ever made or guaranteed. It's certainly not after one successful book. I deeply despise what I have written when I'm finished with a project. If you had asked me about *The Giant's House* after I finished it, I probably would have said that it's a bad book. Sometimes with first novels, if you're lucky, a certain kind of excitement goes into the publication. Literary taste changes quickly. If I take it seriously when it goes well, I have to take it seriously when it goes badly. I would rather not put myself in that position.

Many people think that writing is not real work. Even my mother says, jokingly, "It must be nice to be unemployed."

When did you realize that you could use that humor in your fiction?

I wrote rhyming, metered verse from the time I was a child until high school. To become a writer, I had to learn to not always go for the easy laugh. The short stories that I wrote in college were flip and jokey. I have learned how to avoid that, but now I wish my work were funnier. I would like to write a comic novel sometime because now I think I could do it. I'd like to write something like *A Confederacy of Dunces*, which is a deeply moving and essentially comic novel.

Has that desire to not be so outwardly funny led you to darker subjects? If you take away the humor, many of your stories contain dark moments: a father abandons his children to strangers; a husband murders his wife.

I don't know why I always end up going toward such horrible subjects. I love horrible family stories that make you say, "Oh, my God, I can't believe that." I always end up killing off people when I don't want to.

Is that what you strive for—a mixture of humor and despair?

One of the pieces of advice Allan Gurganus gave us is that you should try to make your readers laugh and cry on every single page. There are frequently award-winning books in which there is no humor and nothing leavening. I cannot stand those books. They preport to be realistic, but they aren't. With no humor, there is no mirror to life. I think that in all the horrible moments of my life, there has been something absurdly and hysterically funny. One day we were trying to move my great-aunt Blanche, who had Alzheimer's, to the nursing home. We sat down to breakfast with her and she was wearing a red sheer blouse over a black bra, which was on backward. It is a detail that my friends still remember when I mention Blanche. That's the way of the world.

the domestic battlefield

ANTONYA NELSON

With compassion, honesty, and painful truths, Antonya Nelson expertly explores the contemporary American family in all its emotions. Adult siblings gather for their parents' remarriage; brothers seek revenge on their sister's rapist. Her latest novel, *Living to Tell*, begins as a young man returns home after serving a jail sentence for killing his beloved grandmother in a drunk-driving crash.

Beginning with her first collection, *The Expendables*, which won the Flannery O'Connor Award for Short Fiction, Nelson's stories have received acclaim for their deftness and smart observation. Raymond Carver, one of our most influential short story writers, awarded the title story of that collection first prize in *American Short Fiction*. Nelson is also a recipient of the Nelson Algren Award, a PEN Syndicated Fiction Award, and grants from the National Endowment for the Arts.

After publishing two more story collections, Nelson's first novel, *Talking in Bed*, won the *Chicago Tribune*'s Heartland Award for fiction. *Talking in Bed*, along with her second novel, *Nobody's Girl*, which satirizes both the mystery and romance genres, were chosen as *The New York Times* Notable Books.

In 1996, she was short-listed as one of *Granta*'s best young American novelists. *The New Yorker* chose Nelson as one of "Twenty Writers for the Twenty-First Century."

Nelson, who was born on January 6, 1961, in Wichita, Kansas, teaches creative writing at the University of New Mexico and the Warren Wilson M.F.A. program. She divides her time between Las Cruces, New Mexico, and Telluride, Colorado, with her husband, novelist Robert Boswell (*Century's Son*), and their two children.

Books by Antonya Nelson

The Expendables (stories), University of Georgia Press, 1990
In the Land of Men (stories), Morrow, 1992
Family Terrorists (stories), Houghton Mifflin, 1994
Talking in Bed (novel), Houghton Mifflin, 1996
Nobody's Girl (novel), Scribner, 1998
Living to Tell (novel), Scribner, 2000
Female Trouble (stories), Scribner, 2002

You've been called a master of the domestic drama because most of your work focuses on problems anchored in the family: adultery, illness, anxiety. Why have you tended to explore family situations?

Most of what one feels compelled to write stems from a deep, emotional uncertainty. In my life, as is the case with many people I know, the most uncertain things are relationships with those I'm closest to. I have family members in the small, nuclear unit, as well as the larger unit toward whom I have a great deal of affection, and there are others toward whom I have tremendous antipathy. It's typical in family situations to be forced into contact, repeatedly, with people you don't particularly like.

You work out your future social abilities and relationships based on what you learn when you are young. For me, these relationships have always been familial. My father and two of his brothers owned property in Colorado, and we would all go there each summer. During the winter, we lived in Kansas, close to my mother's family. There was a constant, rotating band of family members in and out of my house and life.

I'm not entirely sure why I write about family, but I do know that it hasn't stopped interesting me. You meet and leave other people at different stages of your evolution, whereas family is made up of people who are links in your life, who know you over the course of time and have your complete curriculum vitae in their heads.

How is this related to the family as our main battleground, as you've called it?

Middle-class American writers are always going to look for conflict as a source of tension within the family. People question this subject matter because young workshop writers often write about their families and homes. This is because the family is where they've experienced conflict. They aren't being recruited into guerilla armies at the age of thirteen. In some other countries, drama exists elsewhere, outside the house. Most often in America, the trouble seems to come from within the household. The result is that at certain times, writers are called to defend domestic fiction.

In what way have you been called to defend your work on a specific level—as a woman writer, for instance—that differs from having to defend it regardless of gender?

There are plenty of men who write about family, but when I'm asked to explain what I do, it often seems that there's some implicit understanding that novels or stories that tackle political or societal drama serve more serious masters. It's not necessarily that the treatment of characters in these works is a masculine one. It's just that the terrain outside the home is often considered more important. I don't think it is.

Much of your fiction is written in third person. Of the first-person stories, many are told from a male point of view.

Even in third person, I feel close to a male point of view. Most of the time, the narrator in my first-person-male stories is in a state of confusion about his relationship with a woman. It's not often that I write in the first person, but inhabiting the third-person point of view of a man doesn't seem to me strikingly difficult. People occasionally will say, "That must be quite a challenge, to write from the other gender's point of view." I think there are larger challenges that have to do with class or age. It's not difficult to write about a character who shares your same age or class. Empathy is not as complicated when you have some aspects in common with your character; it's not complicated to know someone who's like you in many ways but different in one. This is true especially if you are a reader. Reading makes you accustomed to inhabiting other lives and sensibilities. If you try to inhabit a person who's different in every single way—who's not your age, class, nationality, gender—writing from that character's point of view is much more difficult.

I'm curious about what makes people do what they do. I think about and study people. I think I make people uneasy sometimes because of this. I find myself thinking about this fairly obsessively, and I can't stop until I've found an answer. It doesn't matter whether it's the correct answer for that person. For me, it has to be an answer that seems to be true; it has to make sense to me.

Your story "Unified Front" comes to mind. The event you write about—the theft of a twin baby—came from a news report. Did you follow that incident closely?

Actually, I needed only one article for that story because what happened in fact became less interesting to me than what I imagined. The woman who kidnapped the twin was nuts, and I'm not interested in writing about characters of that nature. I was much more interested in creating a person who had lived through many years of desperate desire for a child. There are fewer ways to identify with insanity than there are to identify with desire. By the same token, I didn't want to write from her point of view, which seemed to me, since she didn't have a decision to make, fairly straightforward. I situated her at the point of making her decision. Her husband's decision to go along with the kidnapping was a moral quandary that I could tackle. I needed to find a way to place myself in the story. That is, I would never steal a baby, but I certainly could understand someone's desire to do so. That seems to me precisely the husband's position. I had to make it his story. The story didn't necessarily have to be told from the point of view of her husband or a man at all; it simply had to be somebody who is loyal to the person who is making the decision. That probably reflects the entangling nature of family. In the end, gender doesn't matter as much as the engagement one character has to the other who is under stress.

Much of the tension in your fiction comes from what the characters and reader never know or are able to learn.

Omniscience is not a very interesting position. If you already know what everybody is thinking, where is the tension? Most of our conflict in life resides in not knowing. I think that is why a single point of view or a limited point of view can create tension and cause the reader to have some stake in watching the character do the right or wrong thing.

You've also experimented with the mystery genre, especially in *Nobody's Girl*, which, in some ways is an antimystery. There's a great buildup of questions and puzzles that can't be untangled, and we realize, as the character does, that the solution is not the point.

I love mystery novels. One of the critiques I have of a lot of literary fiction is that its writers don't seem to understand the human desire for mystery and suspense that genre fiction has exploited. Genre writers take one thing and make it the focus of the work. Sometimes literary writers completely renounce these things and say, "I don't believe I'll indulge."

I started *Nobody's Girl* out of the desire to write about a particular character. I had two different stories in mind and I decided I would force them together—the story of a teacher, Birdy, who has an affair with a student, and the story of a writer, Mrs. Anthony, who has no writing talent but who does have a great story to tell. The element of mystery and subversion of the genre came to me in the second draft of the book. By then I was also trying to delve into the romance genre, too. Our expectations of these genres are that mysteries will be solved and that the romantic figures will eventually be together. But, of course, by solving one mystery, you open ten others in the process, and one successful romantic quest does not equal a happy life because the more satisfying relationships are often tangential. The shape of the book turned out to be the process of a character who is growing up, but this can't be accomplished by solving a mystery or by having an affair. To grow, she has to be able to see herself as somebody's protector and champion, as opposed to being somebody's lover. That was always the arc I had in mind for the book. I think the reader's expectations in solving a mystery, and even the character's expectations in solving one or having a romance concluded, might be enough, but I wanted to undo these expectations.

I'd probably write that book again if I had a chance. I would have liked the reader to come to the same sort of realization that I did, which is that the true shape of the book is to be able to envision being a parent. This is the huge transitional state for Birdy. Mystery and romance, and many other genres, were fun to play with because Birdy, as an English teacher, has such disdain for bad writing. Even as she's trying to create a more literary story, she finds herself in the middle of several genres.

There's a nice paradox here: Birdy has the knowledge and background to write a literary story, but she says she can't write because she has read too much; and Mrs. Anthony, who has a dramatic story—the mysterious deaths of her daughter and husband—has no writing talent.

I liked being the character Birdy for a while. I liked being in her dark sensibility and being able to have her talk about literature. One of my least favorite things about writing is that I'm not supposed to write about books. Characters aren't allowed to read often or to think about literature in a serious way. As a writer, I'm always looking for analogues in art. It's irritating not to be able to note the influence literature has on a character. Readers often don't have a shared reference. I could write, "He read 'Sonny's Blues' and started weeping," and some readers would be clueless. It is a much more shared experience if I dramatize a situation that generates the same emotion.

You mentioned wanting to rewrite *Nobody's Girl.* Do you often think about rewriting a story or book? Do you keep characters in your mind even though the book is finished?

If the book is finished—published and on the shelf—I don't think of revising it. But if I'm not finished psychologically with characters, they will recur, either as themselves or as new slightly altered manifestations, and their same issues will reappear. It's a matter of the subject and emotional investment and my own obsessive thinking about various issues. Given the opportunity to rewrite a novel or story, I'm afraid I would do more damage than good because I'm not in that space anymore, and I can't get myself worked up to be, for instance, where I was fifteen years ago when I wrote the stories in *The Expendables.* I do revisit whatever issues weren't solved for me in those first stories. It's an unconscious process. To say that a single story is not done isn't quite true. A story can be finished and judged successful or not by somebody else, but if the main issue in that story is not done for me, I can count on its reappearance.

You have written several short stories about one group of people, the Link family, including "Bare Knees," "The Control Group," and the novella *Family Terrorists.* Is there an advantage to using the same characters for stories rather than writing a novel about them?

Well, it gives me the opportunity to bail out pretty quickly. If I write one or two stories, they can claim their place, but it doesn't commit me to the kind of insecurity that a novel does for two, three, or four years. I think story cycles in general are enticing. They also may be more difficult than most people who start out writing them would imagine. You don't want to repeat yourself, and you don't want to have the movement of each new story replicate too closely the movement of the last story. You don't want the stories dependent on each other when you're sending them out for publication, nor do you want them to be mirror images when they're sitting next to each other in a book. I guess, for me, writing a few connected stories seemed to be a nice bridge between writing short stories and writing novels. It also works well because you can present one story in the point of view of one character in a family, then another story from somebody else's point of view. This gives you a position as a writer of wandering through the house and observing everybody's relationships, how they influence, harm, and help each other. It makes sense to me that people write connected stories that have to do with families before they write a novel. It's a more manageable form, even if it's actually more difficult to pull off.

Do you know the full histories of the characters in your story cycles, even though you give us only glimpses of them with gaps in between?

One of the complicated things for me to do would be what Larry McMurtry [*Lonesome Dove*] has done so admirably in his work. He has novels in which primary characters of other novels appear in subordinate roles. He wants a full secondary character who has a whole life that he can immediately call up to make the most temporary appearance on the page convincing. But on the other hand, his characters' histories can be crippling. You can tell their histories sometimes get in his way. A writer can make big mistakes by doing this. You realize, suddenly, that a character couldn't have come back at this time because you wrote another story where he was off in the war or in the asylum at that moment.

I don't know what happens in the gaps between my stories. If I wrote too many stories with the same characters, I would spend an awful lot of time making maps. It's better to erect a new family, which is precisely what I did in *Living to Tell.* There are some basic similarities between the

Mabie family and the Link family, but I didn't want to be bound by the Link family history. The central defining events of that family would start taking on weight that I wouldn't want to deal with in this novel.

You've said that your parents weren't prohibitive with your reading material when you were growing up. Was this from an early age?

Our house was open. My parents taught literature at Wichita State University. They were connected to their graduate students and to the politics of the times. They marched in peace protests. Lots of people, including writers, passed through our house. My father was friends with Allen Ginsberg, who wrote a series of poems set in Wichita. There's one poem, "Wichita Vortex," in which Ginsberg claimed that I am the little four-year-old girl. Our house was always full not just with books but with the notion of writing—not just writing but cutting-edge writing. My parents always allowed me to read anything. I read *Valley of the Dolls* and then *Emma*. I can remember reading *The Naked and the Dead*, and I can also remember finding my father's pornography library. That kind of freedom, that kind of trust, is rare. They permitted their kids to be exposed. Ironically, they didn't have that trust with food. They were a lot more restrictive with that than with my reading diet. My eating habit, I should point out, is horrible, while my reading habit is terrific.

For me, the process of writing is an entertainment. I'm more entertained by interesting language than I am by an interesting story.

Your parents were both teachers in the same department, and now you're married and you teach in the same department as your husband, Robert Boswell. Does it surprise you that your life echoes your parents' this way?

Sometimes people say, "Of course you're a writer. Your parents were English professors." But I have four siblings who don't write. I think I've

Antonya Nelson on Word Play in Writing

You chose the playful name "Mabie" for that family. You write: "Winston Mabie wasn't going to belly flop on the landing strip . . . . . Winston Mabie would survive. Oh, maybe all of this was useful." You've used this kind of word play in several of your books, especially *Nobody's Girl.*

I'm a huge fan of stand-up comedy. I'm not a huge fan of puns, but I do like things well put. Typically, I like a mix of diction in writing. A successful mix can be measured in a person's ability to persuade or entertain, to be able to go high and low in the same sentence or thought, and thereby to create some way of arresting the attention of the reader. When this is done, the reader is never sure what the next word will be.

I've read since I was young and have been captivated by the way things are expressed, almost to the exclusion of *what* is being expressed. Again, the character Birdy in *Nobody's Girl* gave me material I could play with. She's often critical of how Mrs. Anthony writes, and because Birdy focuses on her grammar, Birdy is ignorant of what is being expressed. I can forgive meanness if the person being mean is also being funny. I can treasure the humor and forgive the meanness just to be entertained. I can see how people would criticize this trait in me; I criticize it in myself, via Birdy.

If something doesn't compel me by how it sounds, it is unlikely that it will make the page. For me, the process of writing is an entertainment. I'm more entertained by interesting language than I am by an interesting story. I read aloud. I try to make my prose economical. The writing I find the most tedious to read is the kind where the writer simply conveys information and makes no attempt to entertain or to be good at it.

channeled in this direction because I had a desire to please my parents and because I have an inclination to read and write. I have a brother and sister who are both psychologists, and this comes from the same background and the same type of interest: to sit around and hear stories all day, to be invested in human stories at a high level.

My mother also writes fiction. I think she's proud of me, and I know my parents understand what it means that I'm a writer. Occasionally, it would be nice to have that generic, parental, "I saw your last article. Very nice. Congratulations." Robert's mother is supportive like that. Sometimes it's uncomfortable because my mother knows the difference between William Morrow and Alfred Knopf, while Robert's mother doesn't know Knopf from Knickerbocker. His mother was so funny when *Crooked Hearts* went out of print and was remaindered. She didn't realize what that meant. She was at a Wal-Mart in Arizona and saw a stack of the book marked down for $1.98. She took the whole stack in a cart to the manager, outraged, and said, "This book costs $24.95. How dare you sell it for this price?"

Have your other family members read your work?

I sent my first book to everybody. Every time another book is published, I send it to fewer people. When *The Expendables* came out, my grandmother, who is a Southern Baptist, told my cousins it was smut, although she did display it on her living room table. The most moving responses have been when family members read my stories or novels and understand that, for whatever reason and in whatever way, the person being exposed the most in the books is myself. I think when family members don't see obvious connections with my life it makes them feel, to an extent, better. My latest novel, *Living to Tell*, is set in Wichita, where I grew up, in a house much like the house I grew up in. By a strange set of circumstances, the bound galleys arrived while I was there for Christmas with my family. I had the opportunity of watching my family members sit in chairs all over the house reading the book. Nobody said one word to me about it.

They told Robert they liked it. But nobody said anything to me, which is exactly how family is.

How do you and your husband work together?

Fortunately, we write very differently. He's helpful when he reads my work because he can step away from it and say, objectively, what I'm trying to do in the story. For instance, he'll narrate through the plot and allow me to see that there is not a cause-and-effect relationship between what happens and what the characters experience. For him, I'm much more useful as a line editor. He occasionally has a tendency toward silliness or sentimentality, which are some of his best qualities but maybe not the best qualities of a fiction writer. When he starts straying in those directions, I help bring him in. I probably read ten times as much as he does. This helps me to be able to tell him if something seems familiar, if it sounds like something else I've read recently. I have a superficial way of obtaining information, while he deeply absorbs what he reads. This is related to how we address each other's work.

I think for the most part we are each other's first readers. We don't pull punches with each other. There's no one else I would be as frank with; we already have established a mutual trust and respect, whereas in a workshop situation you have to prove to the people whose work you are addressing that you have their best intentions in mind.

What have you noticed that most beginning writers need help with?

I think shape is one of the issues that new writers feel least comfortable figuring out. They have learned, erroneously, to equate plot with shape. And so when their work isn't going anywhere plot-wise, they think the story is a failure, when in fact all they really need to do is reimagine the terms of the story. The shape then becomes something other than plot. That was an enormous discovery for me, one that made a huge difference in how I write, so it seems important for me to continue to promote that, to think of shape in terms other than plot. I think plot is a minor part of stories.

What is your advice for beginning writers trying to make it in this competitive marketplace?

Acquire—cultivate—a leather ass. Do not attempt to please any reader but yourself. Write as if you were reading, and put down the sentence you yourself would next like to read. In the question posed above, remove the phrase "competitive marketplace" and insert "complex, magical, mysterious world." Then remember to write because you want to make something beautiful and thoughtful for yourself.

What was it like for you, as a young writer, to learn that Raymond Carver had chosen your story "The Expendables" as the first-prize winner in the journal *American Fiction* in 1988?

It was great. I don't know what to say beyond that. By all accounts, he was a generous man who read voraciously and had enthusiasm for other people's work. At that time I had a new baby. I was thrilled, but the award wasn't the biggest thing on my mind. When my first story was accepted by *Mademoiselle*, that seemed to me a huge step. When my first book was taken and when *The New Yorker* accepted a story were watershed moments that resonated. The thing is that I always keep raising my own bar. I have a desire to not just have more but to do more, to do something different. I bore myself if I repeat stories. I wrote *Nobody's Girl* with the notion that there weren't many third-person narrated novels with a single point of view. It seemed to me that is what everybody thought of as the default mode. Most novels are written from first-person or third-person multiple points of view. In creating that project for myself, I was able to up the stakes and have something new happen inside of myself, as well as outside.

How do you decide when a story or novel is finished?

A story feels finished to me when I can read it as if I didn't write it. This necessitates a distance from the material that can be accomplished in a few different ways. One way is to distance myself from the work by

Antonya Nelson on Writing in Different Forms

You've published an almost equal number of novels and collections of stories. Are you more at ease with one form?

When I began writing, I wrote stories because they seemed more manageable than novels. But I also feel that many people are encouraged to write novels when what they have on their hands is a short story. When I made the transition from novella to novel, I was doing so because I needed to for the story. I tried to write a story, but the material wouldn't conform to the boundaries of that form. From there, it became a project that I named a novella for a while, and then when that wasn't sufficient, it became a novel. That is one of the great things about feeling confident in both forms or at least a little confident in both forms. I start with the notion that I'll write a story. My first two novels started as stories but wouldn't stay. *Nobody's Girl* was a story called "Sadness," and I really liked the character, so I blew the story up larger and larger until it was a novel. *Living to Tell* is the exception. I knew that it had to be a novel. As a result, I had a hard time starting out. *The New Yorker* excerpted one of the chapters, but I couldn't have found a contained story in that book myself. The story I'm working on now, which may become a novel, started out as nine pages long and is now twenty-four. I have a lot to insert in it, and I have a feeling that it will grow into a novel.

I'm happy to write a good story. I don't feel like everything I dream up has to be set within the novel form. I always have a few projects going on simultaneously. Whatever hits me, whatever I encounter, I can put somewhere. It's sort of like when you play bingo and have more than one card; a number is called and you see that it's not on one, but it might be on one of the others.

the passage of time: Put it away for a few months, and it won't seem like something I wrote. Another is to hand the work to someone else (my husband, for instance) and ask for editorial remarks. Remaking the piece, based on others' trustworthy (an essential ingredient) instincts and instructions, also creates distance from the original draft and sometimes allows me to read the story as if some other writer wrote it. Finally, I feel finished with a piece when, reading it over, I feel some visceral response to its wholeness, some tiny shiver of recognition of its mysterious completion.

I always keep raising my own bar. I have a desire to not just have more but to do more, to do something different.

What are some things you've learned the hard way about writing?

For years before I actually believed it, I preached to my students and friends that writing—the actual physical act of sitting at the keyboard, composing, thinking, playing (as it were)—had to be its own reward. It is the only part of the writing-publishing business that the writer has full control over. Moreover, I would claim, it is, truly, the most energizing, exciting part of the process. I paid lip service for years to this and finally have come to absolutely believe in it. The best part of the writing biz, the most pleasurable aspect, is the creative act. If you don't like that part, you should quit right now. Everything else involves compromise, disappointment, anticlimax, or a combo plate of the three.

Writing is a solitary act. You go into a room and create worlds through sentences. But then it becomes public. How do you balance these extremes?

I wish it were a bit more public! I have a laptop computer, and I can be alone when I need to. My kids are old enough now that I can tell them to scram when I need to write. If I have an idea, I can tell my husband that I'm going away for a little while. He understands. I also get up in the middle of the night and write. That feels to me like the most private time of the day. No one is going to phone or knock on the door; the mail is not going to come, and the kids are asleep and safe. I can be alone with the computer. That privacy is necessary to me. I like that sense of being in a dark world, where the only source of light is the screen. It's a way of entertaining myself, of having a short conversation with myself. Writing is so private and exclusive; it's nearly masturbatory. I am the only audience, and I am working through something with utter honesty. I don't have to be embarrassed or feel self-conscious. I can evaluate it, manipulate it, and move to the next level. That private moment, that series of moments, over the course of however long it takes, eventually turns it into something I want to show somebody.

The emotional side is messy, but then I can make sure that the technique, form, shape—all of the elements that are craft-related—are in place. The sentences have to sound good. There has to be a balance between characterization, summary, memory, and action. That procedure tends to let me approach the work from some distance so that when it's finally printed and I hand it to Robert, I don't feel like I'm confessing things or writing things I don't want anyone to see. I distance myself in some way. I become bulletproof by employing what I know about craft.

Robert evaluates it, and because he's close to me and I trust him, he permits the next level of modification so that it can go out into the world to another reader and be less of me, less exposing because it has passed through these stages. And then if somebody critiques it, fine; if somebody accepts it, excellent. I remove myself by taking advantage of what I know about craft. The private emotion of a public piece goes through stages, like a naked body being dressed.

the trick of it

ANN PATCHETT

If you ask Ann Patchett about her fiction, she will likely say that she writes only one book: a group of strangers are forced together and must somehow form a family. From her first novel, *The Patron Saint of Liars*, to PEN/Faulkner Award-winning *Bel Canto*, she has explored the ways people relate and respond to each other under duress.

Patchett, born in Los Angeles on December 2, 1963, attended Sarah Lawrence College and later received an M.F.A. from the University of Iowa. She taught at Allegheny College and wrote for various popular magazines, including *Seventeen* and *Vogue*.

The Patron Saint of Liars, which takes place in a home for unwed mothers run by Catholic nuns, was adapted for film by CBS. Her second novel, *Taft*, follows a retired blues drummer turned bar manager in Memphis who becomes an unintentional surrogate father to two directionless teenagers. The main character of *The Magician's Assistant*, a gay magician married to his beautiful, straight assistant, dies in the first sentence, and the assistant is left to reconstruct his life beneath the falsehoods he told her. *Bel Canto*, set during a three-month hostage situation in an unnamed

South American country, won Patchett widespread recognition and major literary awards, including the Orange Prize for Fiction.

She lives in Nashville, Tennessee.

Books by Ann Patchett

The Patron Saint of Liars (novel), Houghton Mifflin, 1992

Taft (novel), Houghton Mifflin, 1994

The Magician's Assistant (novel), Harcourt Brace, 1997

Bel Canto (novel), HarperCollins, 2001

***The Paris Review* published your first story, "All Little Colored Children Should Learn to Play Harmonica," when you were twenty-one. You said you had the courage to write that story because you were young. But as your career has progressed, you've continued to write about many different types of people: a gay, Vietnamese man; a black man; a Japanese translator; Catholic nuns; magicians. What has caused you to explore such a wide range of characters and topics?**

I would have written the story regardless. It is, I think, not problematic. The title showed, perhaps, a little moxie. Now, I call it "The Harmonica Story." I can't really bring myself to say the title at this point in my life.

The secret is that I always write fiction entirely for myself, except possibly sometimes for Elizabeth [McCracken]. I never think about who's going to read it. I pick what's interesting to me or what I'm batting around in my head at the time. I don't ever think about how it will be perceived until I'm finished. I'm not going to talk myself out of writing a novel because I think it might be received a certain way.

Your first novel, *The Patron Saint of Liars*, is told by three first-person narrators. How long did you spend getting to know each of them? When did you know the novel would be structured this way?

I spent a year putting that book together before I started writing it. I was twenty-five. I had been teaching at Allegheny College in Pennsylvania and got divorced. I then moved home to Nashville and got a job at the local T.G.I. Friday's, where one of the tasks each night was to roll a hundred fifty packets of silverware. There were private jobs, where you squirreled into a corner and did repetitive acts, which I enjoyed tremendously. That's when I started putting the book together. My first idea about it was, "What if a woman in a home for unwed mothers secretly gives birth at the home so she can spend time with the baby before it is taken away?" At that time, I was writing short stories for *Seventeen*, and I think I was trying to put that idea together for the magazine. But then I started thinking about the other people who were with the woman, helping her through labor. Where did they come from? What were their stories? I settled on the character Rose, who leaves her husband without telling him that she's pregnant. I think these ideas came to me because I had just gotten divorced and realized that I didn't want to have children and that I was never going to. During that same time, my sister married someone she didn't really know and then was pregnant. I was coming out of a weird marriage, and she was going into a weirder marriage, and we were both making decisions about children.

The last two things I do when I start a book are naming the characters and figuring out the narrative structure. Those are the hardest things for me, so I put them off as long as possible. I think I knew before I started *The Patron Saint of Liars* that it was going to be three first-person narratives. If I didn't know this when I started, I learned it quickly. I didn't know how to write a third-person narrative. Much of my career has been about the quest to write in third person. I got close with *The Magician's Assistant*, which has a limited third person. *Bel Canto* is where I broke into a true omniscient third person. I absolutely didn't know how to do that when I was writing *The Patron Saint of Liars*. I knew that these characters couldn't communicate with one another, and I didn't know how to write an omniscient narrative, so the only thing I could think to do was to have multiple first-person sections. It was born out of weakness and inability.

What goals do you set for yourself when you begin a new novel?

For each new novel, I come up with a trick—a puzzle to solve—that's just for me. In *The Patron Saint of Liars*, the trick was to write a novel, which I didn't know how to do. I feel like the real shortcoming of that book is that it's completely out of time. It has no responsibility to anything—to the calendar, to the clock, to government. There's one moment that tags that book in time: when Rose picks up a hitchhiker who has gone AWOL during the Vietnam War. With *Taft*, I wanted to write a book set in a real city, with real issues, and with real time. In *The Magician's Assistant*, part of the puzzle was to write in third person, although I think that failed because the third-person viewpoint is close to a first-person one. I also wanted to have a book in which the main character dies in the first sentence and yet still maintains his status as the main character with only nominal flashbacks. He is kept alive through conversation and thought. And then with *Bel Canto* it was, "What if the characters don't have a common language? How do you move a book forward without language?" That took me to music.

Is this how the character Roxane Coss, the opera singer, came to you?

It seemed like such an operatic story. Even though I didn't know anything about opera, I knew enough to know operatic when I saw it.

You've said that you were surprised that John Nickel became the narrator of *Taft*. When and how did this happen?

I rewrote the first twenty pages of that book twenty times. First, the mother of Carl and Fay was the narrator. She wasn't even a major character by the end of the book. Fay was the narrator for a long time. Then Carl was the narrator. But they were all too shiftless. They couldn't sustain the narrative. I went through the characters and came to John. It was like the characters threw a ball around, and I watched to see who was most capable of catching it and taking over. I found John to be the most honest and strongest of the characters. People always say it's a big deal to write a book in the first-person voice of a black man, and I think that's ridiculous. Would it be anything more than if he was just a black male character in the book?

The last two things I do when I start a book are naming the characters and figuring out the narrative structure. Those are the hardest things for me, so I put them off as long as possible.

***Bel Canto* is loosely based on the1996 takeover of the Japanese Embassy in Peru. The novel ends the way the takeover did: Soldiers arrive on the scene and kill the terrorists. Did you feel bound by the ending of that event?**

I felt liberated by it. It was a wonderful gift—if you can call the slaughter of all those people a gift—because it gave me a construct. It gave me a time frame to work with as well as the beginning and the end. It took my mind off worrying about it.

How does research fit into your writing?

Research is, for me—as it is for a lot of writers—the La Brea Tar Pits of the novel. It's a great place to sink. For *Bel Canto*, I did a lot of research on opera because I knew nothing about it. I felt like I had to understand and have a passion for it to write this book. And yet, at the same time, I was lying on the couch all day listening to opera and reading libretto. My friend, Karl, would go to work in the morning and say, "What are you going to do today?" and I would say, "Well, I'm going to read the libretto for *Alcina*, and then I'm going to read it while listening to the opera, and then I'm going to listen to it one more time without reading the libretto." When I finished, it was time for dinner.

Many aspects of my job embarrass me, especially in relation to another person who has a job and does important things. Karl's a doctor. He

Ann Patchett on Planning Her Novels

You've talked about thinking through a book before you begin to write it. What does this mean for you?

I don't make notes, and I think if I did I would find so much comfort in them that I wouldn't write the book. As I get older, it gets harder to concentrate. To allow yourself to think about something in a physically passive way can be difficult. I think about my work when I drive or run or wash dishes. I keep the music off and make myself think about it.

I've found the best thing is if I can talk to somebody about my work, especially Elizabeth McCracken. We had two meetings at the Fine Arts Work Center in Provincetown this year, where we were both judging. She picked me up both times I flew in, and we drove to the center and talked about all sorts of things. The trips were three weeks apart. Each time, I wanted desperately to talk to her about a problem I was having with the novel I've started. I sat in the car, thinking, "Ask her! Ask her!" I almost couldn't. Finally, on the last leg of the trip, I said, frantically, "I have to talk to you about something!" The conversation we had changed everything. It gave me clarity and set me on the right track. I don't know why that was hard, why I couldn't cut to that sooner.

My publisher gave me a lovely luncheon a few months ago. At one point, somebody said, "Tell us about the novel you're working on." And the person sitting next to her immediately said, "No self-respecting author would do that!" I would have given anything to say, "Okay. What would you think if this person did this?"

I love the story E.L. Doctorow tells. He didn't have an idea for a book, so he started writing about the wall and then about the window and the garden, and the next thing he knew, he had written

Ragtime. Never in a million years would that happen to me. If I don't know where I'm going when I sit down to write, I don't get anywhere.

Do you know the whole shape of the book when you begin?

I know the whole book in the same way you know how you're going to drive from New Orleans to Nashville. You get a map and figure out how long it will take and which road you will use. You know how many hours it should take, but you don't know where you will stop to eat or get gas or what the weather will be like. All sorts of things will surprise you.

People always say, "Don't the characters take over? Aren't you surprised by them?" And I say, "No. I know that I'm writing a book. I'm taking it where I want it to go." All sorts of things develop on the way. Characters I never imagined come in and have prominence. My favorite example of that is a character that I love in *Taft*, Ruth. I had no idea there was a Ruth. The narrator goes to dinner at his ex-girlfriend's home, and I thought, "What if the ex-girlfriend's sister is there?" Ruth was much spicier than the other people in the book, and I wanted to keep her there. There are those kinds of surprises, but basically I know where I'm going.

doesn't judge me at all, but when we sit down for dinner and he says, "What did you do today?" sometimes all I can say is, "I wrote half a page," and that really is all I did. When I ask about his day, he'll say, "I saw forty patients in the office. Somebody had a heart attack." I spent an entire day coming up with two characters' names, the two adopted kids in my new novel.

You've talked about your friendship with Elizabeth McCracken and how you edit each other's work. You originally wrote a first-person

prologue to *Bel Canto*, told from the translator's point of view. When Elizabeth told you to cut it, you did. How did losing the prologue change your perception of the novel? At what point did you cut it?

The prologue stayed on until I finished the book. Elizabeth wasn't reading every chapter as it came along, the way we worked early in our relationship. Now, we get huge chunks of work done before we share it. We've internalized one another so much that I know what she's going to say before she says it, and it becomes a game for me to find what I think she will want me to fix.

The prologue and the epilogue were narrated by Gen. Elizabeth told me that what I was saying, essentially, is that this looks like an omniscient third-person novel, but it's not. I was giving myself a safety net, which I needed to have in place in order to do this thing that I've been trying to do for all these years. Now that I'd done it, she told me to take the net away.

Originally, the epilogue was Gen sitting in a performance hall watching Roxane rehearse and thinking through what had happened. Elizabeth said to change that to third person, as well. A. Manette Ansay read the book after Elizabeth and said, "No. The epilogue needs to take place in Italy. The characters Simon Thibault and his wife, Edith, have to be there because it's important that Edith comes back in the end. You'll have a scene from Gen and Roxane's wedding day." When Manette said that to me on the phone, I began to cry. I cry once every three years. But this was so incredibly moving because it was absolutely correct, and I never would have come up with it. To see somebody take your work and understand it that way is amazing. The combination of Elizabeth and Manette was great. I had done a similar thing for Manette on *Midnight Champagne*. Then she came right back and returned the favor. She was having a lot of trouble with her eyes then, so I recorded *Bel Canto* for her.

What type of editing experience was that?

I always read my books aloud when I'm finished, and it's always torture.

But there are things you catch when you hear it that you just can't see when reading. While working on *The Magician's Assistant,* I got my dog, Rose. When I finished, I read the novel aloud to my grandmother. Every third metaphor in the book was a dog metaphor: "He stretched out on the floor like a dog"; "Her hair was like a bunch of springer spaniels." Every time I heard the word "dog," it hit me like a gong.

You and Elizabeth McCracken both say the other is indispensable in the writing process, but your styles seem different.

That depends on who you talk to. My parents think we're the same person. Every now and then, somebody will say, "Oh, you're so similar." We certainly think of ourselves as being worlds apart, and yet I can see her all over my work, as I can see myself all over her work. We push each other. For me, it's Elizabeth saying, "Write more. Expand this section." I'm always telling her to cut something out. I'm always pulling her in, and she's pushing me out. She'll write three hundred pages and cut them all. And I write everything too short. I once had a teacher who said I wrote like condensed orange juice and I needed some water.

Have you learned anything the hard way about writing?

The better the editor, the fewer the edits. This is something that I come up against in my magazine work. If you have young and inexperienced editors, they will make you rewrite every sentence and change things at will, just to make it their sentences and not yours. If you're working with a senior editor, that never happens. This is not to say that the better editor realizes that I'm a better writer, but most people know to just leave things alone. I've learned a lot from magazine writing, how to roll with things and when to pick your battles.

What do you do when you have comments from an editor that you don't agree with?

As far as my four books are concerned, I didn't have comments. My editor for the first two novels never made so much as a pencil mark on the books. My second editor did some copyediting on the book. After Elizabeth McCracken and A. Manette Ansay read *Bel Canto*, I sent it to Christopher Potter, who is my editor in the United Kingdom and the biggest opera buff I've ever met. He did some wonderful, important work on the book in terms of changing operas. I had some sentimental, florid language about music, and he took it out. Originally, Roxane's signature aria was from *La Wally*, which he said I couldn't use because of *Diva*, a French pop film. He said that anybody who knows about opera would know that *La Wally* belongs to *Diva*. I asked what the aria should be, and he said, "Let it be *Rusalka*."

I always read my books aloud when I'm finished, and it's always torture. But there are things you catch when you hear it that you just can't see when reading.

How did you get your first publication?

I sent "All Little Colored Children Should Learn to Play Harmonica" to Tom Jenks at *Esquire*, who then sent it to *The Paris Review*, where Mona Simpson was the fiction editor. She called me and said that she wanted to have lunch, but she didn't say whether she would publish the story. When I got to *The Paris Review* office, someone said, "Who are you?" I said, "I'm Ann Patchett. I'm here for lunch." And I could see all their faces melt. This cloud of disappointment came over the room. I didn't realize it right away, but I came to understand that they had invited me to see if I was black. Mona and the managing editor took me to lunch. They were very disappointed. At the end, I finally said, "So, are you going to take the story?" And she said, "Yeah, I guess so."

How and when did you find an agent?

I got an agent, Binky Urban, when "All Little Colored Children Should

Learn to Play Harmonica" was published. She was the novelist Allan Gurganus's agent, and he is my hero in life. Binky said, "When you've got a collection or a novel, call me. I want to be your agent." She was my agent for years, and I had no contact with her. Then she called and said that she was being promoted to the head of fiction at ICM, and I would be handed over to her assistant, Lisa Bankoff, who turned out to be one of the true loves of my life. I may switch publishing houses, I may switch editors, but as long as Lisa is an agent, she is my agent.

Among your novels, *Bel Canto* has the widest range of characters. Did you think about each of them—what their nationalities would be, what their back stories were—before you started writing? Did you know all of the characters well?

I don't know some of the minor characters as well as the main ones. I wanted to structure that book as an opera, to give it several tiers so that there are main, mezzo, then chorus characters. I had a list of names that I kept by my computer while writing the book—one, because I couldn't remember all the names, and two, because I checked it all the time to see when a character should walk by and when another one needed to come in. I had countries and blocks of character names from each country so that I could say, "Now there needs to be a scene where somebody from Denmark comes in." I could then look up that country and bring the character in.

I knew the main characters, not just the four man characters, but also the generals and a couple of the terrorists. I knew how Cesar and Ishmael would turn out. I knew how the Russian, Fyodorov, would turn out. Initially, I thought there would be a whole leitmotiv in that book, like the scene when Fyodorov, through the translator Gen, expresses his love for Roxane. After I wrote the scene with Fyodorov, I realized that it implies that this keeps happening to her. I would have been happy to write twenty more like it, but I didn't need them. The same is true of the dream sequences in *The Magician's Assistant.* I could have written those scenes all day long. It took every bit of restraint I had not to pack the book full of them.

You've mentioned Thomas Mann's *The Magic Mountain* as an influence. Are there other books that have served as models for your writing?

The Magic Mountain influences me over and over again. That's the story I write. I read it first in high school, then again in college. There are many similarities among my novels. A bunch of people get stuck in a house for a limited period of time. It's about internment and what happens to people in a confined environment.

There are many books that I've loved that I wish had influenced me. I wish that I had been profoundly influenced by *Lolita, One Hundred Years of Solitude,* and *The Optimist's Daughter*, but there is nothing of those books in my work. I think it's all about books that you connect with in some way. Something in you says, "Yes, there it is. There's a good model for me."

What role does reading play when you're involved in writing a novel?

When I wrote *The Patron Saint of Liars,* I didn't let myself read fiction, especially not contemporary fiction. Since I've gotten older, other people's fiction doesn't influence me as much, and if it does, it's in a good way.

I feel that my life is now divided into two lives: the person who writes and the industry of Ann Patchett. My attention span gets smaller and smaller. The phone rings all day long. I'm always shuffling through plane tickets. Newspapers send me e-mail messages that say, "If you would just answer these ten questions." Answering "these ten questions" is what I do most. My reading becomes fragmented. When my life begins to quiet down, which it has now that I've gone back into writing, I can sit down and read for three or four hours without getting up. I associate that with writing, just the act of being still, the act of concentrating and being quiet.

Ann Patchett on Magical Realism and Issues of Race

There is a magical element present in your books, even though they're realistic.

When I got reviews, both good and bad, for the first three books, they all talked about magic—fairy tales, fantasy—and I would think, "I'm writing such realistic books. So now I'm going to write a book that is magical and fantastical." *Bel Canto* is a lot more allegorical than my other books, but it's also the only one based on a true story.

Being a Catholic makes things seem totally normal to me that appear magical to other people. I grew up reading *Lives of the Saints* and going to Mass and believing that, yes, Saint Lucy's eyes were in her head and on the plate, all four of them looking at you at the same time. That didn't seem like magic to me. That's just the story. Gabriel Garcia Marquez does the same thing. He says, I knew a beautiful girl in our town, and she went up to heaven with the sheets. Everybody saw her float to heaven. That's not magical realism. It happened. I think it has to do with your point of reference.

Elements of Catholicism are present in each of your books. *The Patron Saint of Liars* is about signs from God and takes place in a home for unwed mothers run by nuns. The characters in *Taft* go to church. The priest, Father Arguedas, plays a large role in *Bel Canto.* Religion plays a natural part in the narrative.

If you have religion, it has to be about religion. Religion is part of my life, but my life isn't about religion. It's there. I'm a Catholic, and I believe in God. It's a backdrop, and it seems logical to put that in books. I want to write books about black people and white

continued

people that are not racial books. I live in the South. We're white and we're black. We're with each other every day. But we're not thinking, "I wonder how you feel about the oppression of your people." You just live your life with people. I never see that in books. If you have two races, it has to be about race.

What were some of the first books you read, authors who helped you realize you wanted to write?

Humboldt's Gift by Saul Bellow. I read it six times when I was in junior high. I read what my mother and stepfather read. People say that it's not whether your parents read to you but whether you see your parents reading serious literature that makes the difference. I have no memory of anyone reading anything to me as a child, but I remember my parents, of which I have many, engaged in serious reading all the time. Bellow, John Updike, and Philip Roth were the three people I read at home before I went away to college. Bellow's bare and straightforward approach probably did more than any other writer to influence my writing.

Do you ever complete a book or prepare for it to be published and then worry about how it might be perceived?

There are times when I feel sort of exhausted with myself and think, "Why are you doing this?" The book that I'm just starting is about a white family who adopts two black sons. The adopted mother dies early on. So there's a white father and a white son of natural origins and then two black adopted sons. The black mother comes back and the white brother falls in love with her. I'm thinking, "Christ, give yourself a break. Why are you doing this?" And I don't know. It's just again and again what's interesting to me: family and origin issues; how families are constructed; issues of race. Again and again, these are the things that I find compelling.

welcoming the bears

MELANIE RAE THON

Melanie Rae Thon writes to understand. She invents people and situations that disturb and confuse her in order to more fully comprehend the lives of people she faces every day. She writes, she says, to become the person she knows she should be.

Born August 23, 1957, in Kalispell, Montana, Thon has, with three novels and two collections of stories, created a diverse body of work. A sharp divide—in theme, language, narrative style, and subject matter—exists between her first three books and her most recent work. *Meteors in August*, *Girls in the Grass*, and *Iona Moon* explore issues of family, origins, dependence, and sexuality in straightforward stories. These books often focus on young characters who seek ways to escape their circumstances. Thon created a new voice and style for herself in *First, Body*, her second collection of short stories, and *Sweet Hearts*, her most recent novel, which contain dark tales of homelessness and violence. The story collection and novel are peopled with desperate, lonely men, women, and children who see no easy escape from their sufferings but who continue to believe in the possibility of love and who often experience grace through their own acts of mercy.

Named one of *Granta*'s "Best Young American Novelists" in 1996, Thon has been awarded grants by the Ohio Arts Council, New York Foundation for the Arts, Massachusetts Artists Foundation, and the National Endowment for the Arts. She received a Whiting Writers' Award in 1997. A devoted writing instructor, Thon has taught creative writing and literature at Harvard University, Emerson College, Syracuse University, and Ohio State University.

She lives in Salt Lake City, where she teaches at the University of Utah.

Books by Melanie Rae Thon

Meteors in August (novel), Random House, 1990
Girls in the Grass (stories), Random House, 1991
Iona Moon (novel), Poseidon Press, 1993
First, Body (stories), Houghton Mifflin, 1997
Sweet Hearts (novel), Houghton Mifflin, 2001

What was the experience of spending eight years writing your first story?

Eight years, and it's only acceptable failure, which is what I believe I achieve with any piece. I was eighteen when I started "Repentance," and I thought it was the one story I had to tell. In time, I would discover many stories, but I couldn't see them yet because I was too afraid of the territory I needed to explore. As I tried to understand the girl in "Repentance," I felt bound by factual truth, and this didn't allow me to expose what writer Tim O'Brien so wondrously calls the "story truth." Facts snared me. Many years later I was able to go back to that tale as a stranger, unburdened by events as I remembered them.

Is this because you felt bound by the truth but didn't want to reveal the facts?

Part of that conflict comes from the desire for privacy and the wish to keep some distance between story and autobiography, and part of it comes from my belief that there is a failure of truth. "Repentance" is the tale of a young girl who feels responsible for her grandmother's death. As I tried to sort through the details of what had actually happened the night my own grandmother fell, I discovered there were endless gaps. The guilt that I took on about her fall may or may not have been realistic. It was interesting to find out that my sister also felt responsible. In this way, facts are inadequate and finally unknowable.

Is that why you use multiple points of view in several of your stories?

It usually takes five, six, seven, or eight perspectives to tell a story well. It's difficult to manage that many perspectives in a single story or even in a novel, but in life, as well as in fiction, I think we must keep readjusting our perspectives in order to seek a complex vision of "truth." As different ideas converge, we may begin to make sense of what might be possible.

The first two scenes in *Meteors in August* portray violence juxtaposed with religion. What relationship do you see between the two?

I think that violence and grace often illuminate each other. Flannery O'Connor [*Everything That Rises Must Converge*] talks about that mystery in the most eloquent ways. Our country has flourished through violence and, because of that, I have a sense we are still caught in a state of upheaval. Wars define the history of the United States: Without the Revolutionary War, we would still be a colony; without the Civil War, we might be two countries instead of one. The Indian wars allowed for vast expansion, and the two world wars defined our international mission. We began by fighting to have a country; then we launched into a conquest of native peoples in order to make it larger. I think that violence and the myth of "regeneration through violence," as writer Richard Slotkin calls it, are very much parts of our national character and our mythic vision of ourselves. At the same time, many immigrants came to America because they wished to worship with freedom. The fusion of religion and violence, worship and conquest is, I think, quintessentially American.

Melanie Rae Thon on Her Writing Process

What is your writing method?

It's different with every piece. My work almost always begins with an intimate question: Why does the orderly try to lift the 326-pound dead woman alone? Did the slave murder her master's son? Why is the girl lying in the abandoned refrigerator, burning in the Florida sun? Later, I move between doing research and writing fictional explorations. Sometimes I have to stop doing research because it limits my imagination and keeps me at a distance from my people. But I love research! As I write, I study photographs of lizards whose tails regenerate and buffalo that once traveled in herds twenty-five miles wide and fifty miles long. I learn about glacial movement, silver mining, tuberculosis, polio, diabetes, hurricanes, Haitian immigrants, the murder of Emmett Till, ivory carvings made by the Inuit, the battles of Song Be and Dalat, the lives of vireos, the appetites of coyotes. I've witnessed an autopsy and climbed in the Absaroka Mountains. Whatever my characters remember or experience, I too must understand.

How do you handle all the material when it's time to edit?

That's the desperate part. Many times I realize I've made the process so complicated for myself that I can hardly work through it. Sometimes I put aside all those notes for a while and try to remember the most important pieces. I try to see my people in time and place. I try to imagine what's most important to them, what each one would notice, how each person's memory would spin between past and present. Then I try to write a rough draft before going back to my notes to see whether anything else is usable. I cut the story "Little White Sister" from two hundred pages to twenty. I made four hundred pages of notes before I began writing "Necessary Angels." So much can be discarded in the end; but for me, exploration is an essential part of the process. I don't write to publish; I write to understand.

What comes first in a story or novel?

My stories almost always begin with an image that leads to a mystery I must pursue. "Necessary Angels" came to me as a vision of a young girl living in an abandoned refrigerator in a field. I had to discover who she was and why she was there. I wanted to see her safely home. The novel *Sweet Hearts* began with the image of a deaf woman standing silhouetted at a window, *signing* a story that no one wanted to hear out loud. It took two more years for me to begin to understand the tale she needed to tell.

A black man watches a white woman running barefoot in the snow—a boy catches a lizard by the tail, and the tail breaks off in his hand—a hospital worker tries to lift a 326-pound dead woman—this is how stories come to me! Something startles my senses, and I start asking questions.

You said you had never worked with such intensity for as long as you did with *Sweet Hearts* and that it took you one year to write the first forty-five pages. How do you know when it's time to step back and begin to edit?

I've discovered there is a point where I begin changing the work without making it stronger. That's when it's time to let go, to move on to new challenges so that I can continue to grow as a writer and a person.

***Girls in the Grass* contains two stories, "Iona Moon" and "Snake River," about the protagonist of your novel *Iona Moon.* How did you**

take those existing stories and build a novel?

Those pieces were polished and complete, so it was difficult to break them open again and integrate them into the novel. I hadn't planned or intended to write a novel when I started working on "Iona Moon."

When did you realize these stories and characters were part of something larger?

I had written four stories before I accepted the idea that I might be writing a novel. But the people in "Iona Moon" gripped me immediately. Until I wrote that piece, I had always worked in a basically linear way. The story that led me to the character Iona Moon changed my process of writing. Late one night, a friend told me he had been attacked by a seventeen-year-old girl when he was fifteen. That seemed phenomenal to me because he was a great big Montana man, six foot two, with a full beard and broad shoulders. I couldn't imagine anybody trying to molest him, especially a teenage girl. He told me this story twenty years after he'd been jumped, and he still burned.

The girl took him out for ice cream but wouldn't bring him home. She parked her truck down by the river, grabbed his belt, and kissed him hard. She told him she knew he wanted it. When he got away from her, he started walking home. He hadn't gone far before he heard tires spinning in the mud. He could have left her there, five miles from town—he was angry enough—but he turned, walked back down to the river, and helped push his attacker out of the rut. I thought his story was amazing. I didn't know anything about the girl. I just felt that I wanted to see inside this boy. I needed to understand the gap between his kindness and his rage. As soon as I started working on the story, I realized there was no way that I could get those two people to the river together unless I knew who Iona Moon was. I couldn't tell a complicated tale from a single point of view. Somehow, I needed to discover Iona in my imagination.

I started doing explorations. I tried to *see* Iona. I followed her home in my mind. I needed to meet her family and walk on their farm. I imagined

Iona milking the cows and thought, "Why does she have to milk the cows if she has three brothers?" Every small detail became a new mystery, and I ended up with forty scenes: some of them from Jay's point of view, some from Willy's perspective, and some from Iona's experience. This was the first time I'd had to grapple with multiple sensibilities. I still thought this was just a story, that I was done, but Iona had seized me. She was hungry and hurt. I'd learned that her mother was very sick. At the end of the story, Iona realizes she has forgotten to buy chocolate for Hannah, and she's crushed by her own failure. Months after I wrote that scene, I began to understand that Iona's mother was dying, that when she asks for chocolate and tells Iona, "I've got to have some pleasure," the simple words are dense with passion. When I glimpsed this part of the story, I knew I was writing a novel and that I had to stay with Iona.

You seem to know each character in *Iona Moon* as well as you know Iona. Did you go through that process of exploration with all of them?

I thought about every *one* and every *thing* in the novel. I watched cows. I meditated on potatoes. Every time I picked one up, I pondered its weight and heat and shape and texture. I tried to understand every aspect of my people's lives. My process exploded. During the years that I worked on the novel, I also wrote five thousand pages in my journals. I wasn't trying to translate my own experience into the novel, but I was learning patterns of thought, the way the mind leaps between memories. I'd been very sick, and everything in my life was suddenly heightened. Memories resurfaced with startling clarity and in endless combinations. Each new memory challenged my vision of the truth and compelled me to reimagine what I thought I knew. I realized Iona's life was as complicated as mine, that every person in the novel must have a web of memories as intricate and specific as hers. Memory is alive, not static. You can't simply figure out your past and be done with it. Each new experience, each recovered memory, illuminates and alters the narrative you tell yourself about your past and who you are.

How did the characters change throughout this process?

I thought I felt the most compassion toward Willy when I started the novel. He was the boy who had been attacked by the river, but his judgment of Iona and his cruelty toward her made me feel judgmental of him! It took me a long time to find that boy again and feel tenderness and sympathy.

You talk about all the pages of exploration, but the story flows smoothly. The reader feels like he could drive those back roads, find Iona's house, and visit her because she's real.

I'll show you the road! She is real to me now. She's still teaching me. I'm glad to hear that the prose seems smooth. Most days, I feel incredibly stupid and slow because I see all the mud and snow I've dug out in order to find my stories.

The sparse, cutting prose of *First, Body* and *Sweet Hearts* is different from your earlier work. Are these recent books conscious efforts to experiment with the boundaries of language?

I'm not interested in language simply for its own sake. But I'm interested in what language can evoke through the beauty of rhythm and tone. I don't think you can reach meaning without paying attention to sound. There is something that happens on a subconscious level with sound that can't be defined or explained by the meaning of the words that are being said. I'm interested in this subconscious force underneath language. My approach to the stories in *First, Body* emerged from the lives and voices of the characters. These people are not in possession of their stories in the same way that Lizzie Macon is in possession of *Meteors in August.* Lizzie is making a deliberate effort to tell her story coherently: She has an investment in trying to move chronologically. It's a way for her to control her family history—or to imagine she can contain and understand her sister's disappearance. The characters in *First, Body* don't know or experience their own histories in that way. Their memories erupt; the past splinters the present. In "Little White Sister," Jimmy's memories are cyclical. By the time I finished that story, I was sitting in a room by myself in Vermont chanting the story backward and forward. I worked in eighteen-hour stretches. The story has internal logic, an organic movement, but Jimmy spins through many memories in order to explain to himself why he fails to help a woman in trouble. In our memories, some brief events become vast and timeless while entire years of our lives shrink to seconds; events that happened five months in the past fuse with those that happened two decades ago because there is some mysterious connection through image or sensation or emotion.

How did you know your cycle of stories about Nadine ("Nobody's Daughters") wasn't another novel?

I couldn't find any way out of Nadine's sorrow. I feel that there is a vision of redemption in her stories because of Nadine's faith, because of her capacity to love her sister and her friend Emile, because of her desire to live a decent life and to experience tenderness. But I don't feel hopeful about what will happen to her on the streets. Some savior might appear. She could be that lucky kid who finds a job and a place to live, who gets a stranger's help. But those solutions felt artificial, and I didn't want to impose them on the story. I wanted to see her experience honestly, yet I didn't want to inflict that ultimate grief upon the reader. So her story stayed short, as I think her life is short.

Were the stories in *First, Body* written with a common tone in mind?

I wrote the stories in *Girls in the Grass* over a period of thirteen years, and I spent about four years on *First, Body.* I didn't begin with a plan for a collection, but the stories emerged from the idea that there are moments in people's lives that change them completely. Some people reach a line and step across it—or are catapulted across it. After that, nothing is ever the same again. I became interested in those moments and the people who survive them. The first story that I explored was "Little White Sister." A fifty-four-year-old black man sees a white woman in trouble and decides he can't help her. When she dies, he knows he'll feel the weight of that decision for the rest of his life. This is not the kind of experience that makes you think, "I feel wretched today, and I'm going to feel badly for a year." This is a moment where a person's entire life is realigned, where he must reimagine everything that has ever happened to him in light of what he has chosen *not* to do on this particular night. I kept coming across amazing tales, ones that inspired me but that I didn't even try to fictionalize.

I read about a man who may have killed his own son. He went into a blackout—he was drunk—and the child was dead when he woke the next day. He probably killed the child, but he can't ever be sure. Perhaps he failed to protect his son from an intruder. Either way, he believes he's responsible for the child's death. Now he's in prison for life in Alaska, trying to live a decent life and educate other people. I kept wondering how a person finds the courage and strength to live past a catastrophe. How do we remake ourselves after we are shattered?

So the stories in *First, Body* rose out of that central mystery: Who do we become on the other side? If you're responsible for another person's suffering or death, how do you learn to see yourself with any kind of compassion? For Jimmy, the narrator of "Little White Sister," mercy comes from his recognition that he is bound to the woman who dies. Through his sympathy for her, through his capacity to begin to imagine how they are alike, he realizes their grief has made them equals. This is Jimmy's moment of grace.

I kept wondering how a person finds the courage and strength to live past a catastrophe. How do we remake ourselves after we are shattered?

The deaf narrator of *Sweet Hearts* says (or signs), "If you want to understand, you'll have to watch. You'll have to learn my language."

She relates her family's story in a disjointed language that relies heavily on images rather than a linear narrative structure. How did you create this language to fit your story about a misguided and destructive brother and sister?

The brilliant Russian psychologist L.S. Vygotsky believed that dialogue launches language but that we come to know ourselves and our world through "inner speech," a private language almost without words, a ceaseless stream of images and associations that approach pure meaning. Through this inner speech, a child discovers and creates her own identity and vision of the world. Marie, my narrator, loses her hearing at the age of nine, so she knows the spoken and written word, but, in time, she loses her desire to use her voice, and she comes to depend on sign because it is closer to her inner speech: flexible and cinematic, passionate and quick. She can literally say two things at one time: With the left hand she describes her nephew Flint as brutal, while with the right she exposes his tenderness and vulnerability. In sign, there is no need to reconcile contradictions, no need to construct artificial hierarchy or order. Marie can reveal detail then panorama, moving swiftly between perspectives. Signed languages depend on intimate engagement, on the "listener's" attention to the flight of the hands, the expression of the face, the gesture of the body. There is no such thing as "overhearing" a sign or catching it in passing. If you avert your gaze, you've lost it.

I loved the possibilities of sign, the challenge of trying to render a new and complicated language within the limits of my own language. It is impossible to translate sign into written English, but I have tried to capture the intensity of Marie's sensations and memories. Images erupt. Because she's been deprived of her hearing, every other sense is heightened.

In *Sweet Hearts*, there's no clear hero or villain, and we're never sure how to feel about the young criminals and the hopelessness of their lives. What do you intend your readers to experience through this book?

I hoped to re-create some of my own struggle and confusion. When I first began working on the novel, my friend Jan told me about a man whose hand was so badly burned that the doctors sewed it inside his chest, hoping his body might heal him. I didn't understand what the image meant, but I realized I had to keep moving toward it, that this was the fire guiding my journey. Five years later, I finally began to see: We do not heal ourselves by severing our damaged limbs or by turning our hurt and troubled children into exiles and outcasts. We heal ourselves by taking the wounded inside, bringing them as close to our hearts as we can bear to hold them.

Aren't most of us afraid to live this way?

Yes! Myself included. We long to believe in our own "goodness," and one of the ways we do this is to imagine "evil" lurking outside us—in the woods, in wolves or serpents, in other people's children.

During the fall of 1998, I lived alone in a cabin at the edge of a lake in Montana, a lake deep enough for sturgeons, wild as a sea during storms and deceptively calm at sunset. One day, sitting at my computer five hours before daybreak, I heard someone knocking on my window. I looked out and met only my own reflection. The visitor tried the doors, front and back, rattling the handles, then banged again at another window. I was living without a phone, half a mile from my closest neighbor. There was no one to hear me scream at this hour—except perhaps the one outside, the one circling and hammering.

When I turned off the lights, I saw the long nose and furred back of an auburn bear. Like most other bears in Montana that year, she was hungry. The huckleberry crop had been unusually sparse, and now, facing winter without enough fat to keep them alive through months of hibernation, the bears were desperate.

I had plenty of food in my cabin. I made weekly treks to Polson or Bigfork and had stocked my cupboards and refrigerator with soup and fish and vegetables. We could have shared. But I am no saint. I am not one of those monks in the desert who befriends beasts and tames their wild spirits. I had enough food but not enough faith to feed us. And I saw that the bear had come to teach me about the boy in my story, about his hunger and my fear, about my willingness to let children like him starve in body and in spirit, about my need to make him an exile so that I might live with the illusion of safety. I saw the limits of my compassion and the failure of my courage.

Like everyone in Flint's family, I refused to love him. I needed to meet the bear in order to understand the people in my story. It is always my wish that the work will change me, that I will become braver in how I choose to live, less quick to judge, less fearful.

Your narrator, Marie, keeps going through permutations of the Catholic catechism. What is your understanding of her process?

Marie has endured enormous loss in her life: When she was eleven, her mother drowned, and she is still trying to understand this tragedy. Now her sister's young children have become outlaws. How do we make sense of our sorrow and misfortune? Do we think we "deserve" punishment? For Marie, that's a dangerous and destructive philosophy. She is a person of deep faith who is not afraid to question God, but she also hopes in God. She believes redemption is possible for every human being. Even in the face of the most extreme act of violence, she seeks evidence of grace, a vision of mercy that will allow Flint to feel compassion for his victims.

Marie enters the rigid catechism again and again in order to break it apart and find her own answers. The Word of God is not a final, static statement of law in Marie's mind: It is the Living Word, ever changing. She believes we must rediscover our own moral conscience in each individual circumstance. Human law does not allow this. Perhaps her deafness, her isolation, has given her freedom of thought. Almost all her speech is the inner speech Vygotsky describes.

By imagining the life and death of Lucie Robideau, Marie glimpses a

God who is both incomprehensible and tender, a God who comes not to judge or punish, but to share our pain and suffer with us.

You've tackled these kinds of questions in both novels and short stories. Do you work on both forms simultaneously?

I tend to immerse myself in one project at a time. It's misleading because *Girls in the Grass* was published one year after *Meteors in August.* It looks as if I'm much more productive than I am! But the stories in *Girls in the Grass* emerged slowly, from 1976 to 1989. I did write another story during that time, and this became the seed for *Meteors in August.* I was never satisfied with it as a story. I sent it to the wonderful George Garrett, who had been my teacher for a single semester. It took him a whole year to write back to me, but when he did, it was at great length—forty pages of widely spaced, handwritten notes. It was a huge and generous response. He helped me to see my own story. The most important thing he told me was that it could be bigger, that the people and the place were more surprising than I realized. It was a gift to have somebody say, "This is extraordinary material." Strangely enough, I needed to be reminded how unusual Montana is, how different my internal and external landscapes might be. He gave my people and my place back to me and challenged me to see it as a stranger would, or as one who comes home after a long absence. By then, I'd lived in Ann Arbor for six years and Boston for three. I *was* a stranger! Montana startled me, and my life there became mysterious and interesting.

When I was growing up in Montana, I was oblivious to the racism. It's a deceptively homogenous environment—just about everybody you see is white—so the underlying racism is often hidden and denied. I lived very close to two Indian reservations in Montana. Indians who live outside the reservations are often completely assimilated. The kind of racism you witness every day within a city isn't always immediately visible. It took me a long time to appreciate the depth and seriousness and sorrow of our history. I had seen it many times but failed to grapple with the trauma it inflicts on both the Indian and white communities. I failed to see it in a critical way because it had been my place. I feel embarrassed to think about how oblivious I was. I saw the extreme poverty on the reservations, but I didn't ask myself difficult questions about it. I had to live in Boston—an incredibly segregated city—before I could begin to see the racial boundaries in Montana. In Boston, you can walk across a street and under a bridge and be in another country. That is still amazing to me. What I had experienced as a child and what I was experiencing as an adult converged and cast a brilliant light on each other.

You didn't explore a main character with Native American roots until *Sweet Hearts.* Is this something you've always felt compelled to write about?

Yes, I was compelled—but I didn't know it! My ancestors were among the first white settlers in Montana, and I grew up swirling in the mythic tales of their conquests. My great-great-grandfather died trying to stop Chief Joseph from reaching Canada. He thought he was doing the right thing, for his God and his country. In every tale I ever heard, he was a hero. Imagine! But I love Montana. It is my true home. I am grateful to have been born there. Do you see? This makes me part of the crimes still being perpetrated against native peoples. I cannot condemn my forefathers for what they did if I am also forever thankful.

So what do I do with this impossible contradiction?

I write. I try to uncover histories that have been lost or buried. I try to imagine the other side of every story through the unique lives of the people in my stories. I speak only for them, the ones I invent. I make no claims on any "greater message." Every human life is mysterious at the center, unknowable. But the journey—the desire to see all that I can, the belief that I might move into the space between myself and another person—is important. I am not trying to resolve my vision of the past; I am trying to complicate it through the power of research and memory, language and imagination.

You often take from past images and themes from your work and explore them in different ways. The metaphor of grass—playing in grass, discovery of sexuality in grass—runs throughout your books. In the first three books, it's the state of innocence on the verge of experience. In *First, Body*, it becomes something darker.

I think you are right to see that movement. I haven't looked back at old work and consciously tried to revisit old material. But it's also true that there are certain images that recur. I'm obsessive. There's no escape from sorrow. We would have to lose our memories to experience true catharsis. Sensual images resurface, too. The soft Montana grass becomes the dangerous sawgrass of Florida. There is a failure of language; "grass" can be one thing or quite another, depending on where you are. When Dora grabs the grass in "Necessary Angels," it cuts her hand.

I try to uncover histories that have been lost or buried. I try to imagine the other side of every story through the unique lives of the people in my stories.

You said that reading wasn't a large part of your life when you were young. Did it surprise your family when you began to write?

They were surprised. I wrote dreadful poetry when I was in high school and a few short stories. My mother thought I was going to be a lawyer or maybe a judge or even an artist like my older sister, but she was the one who helped me find *Wuthering Heights* and *Anna Karenina.* It's not a bad beginning, really—Tolstoy and Emily Brontë and *The Ghost of Dibble Hollow*, which is a book I want to recommend to everybody. As soon as I started college, I told people I *was* a writer. I was incredibly naive. I had no idea what it would mean to live as a writer or what it would cost me.

How did you find your agent? And how do you advise writers looking for an agent?

My wonderful agent (Irene Skolnick) found me! She read the short story "Iona Moon" in *The Hudson Review* and was intrigued enough to call. But we didn't sign a contract until I'd finished my first novel, *Meteors in August.* We both wanted to be sure her response to the longer work was as strong as her connection to the story.

My advice? Don't look for an agent too soon! Wait until you have a significant body of polished, accomplished work to show. Try to meet any prospective agent. Can you imagine having a relationship with this person for the next ten, twenty, forty years? It's an important commitment! Does the agent speak of your work with passion and insight? Does he or she grasp your vision? Could you trust this person to put your manuscript in the hands of the right editors?

Do you show your work-in-progress to anyone before sending it to your agent?

I rarely *show* my work-in-progress to anyone. If the story is ready to show my friends, it's also ready to send to my agent. But I have several extraordinarily kind, generous, indulgent friends who will let me read excerpts to them as a story grows. This helps me hear how the language is working (or not working), and their encouragement gives me confidence and energy for the long, lonely journey. Some of my stories have taken several years to complete, so it's important for me to surface from the privacy of the fictional world once in a while and reveal pieces of it to friends I trust.

What do you think critics have missed about your work?

There is something about a writer's work that is often invisible. Writing is a practice to me, a way of expanding my intimate experience. I hope to learn how to live more generously. If I were brave enough to share my food with hungry bears, if I could embrace those I fear, I would not need to be a writer. My wise friend Mark Robbins told me that writing is like prayer, "the dedicated concentration of your being on that which will help you become the person you know you should be."

When I was working on the novel, I heard about a seventy-year-old man in Montana who pulled another man from a burning car. The savior had only one leg and had suffered a massive heart attack the year before. But he didn't hesitate. He looked at his prosthesis and said to his leg, "You're going down there whether you want to or not." Clarence Purdy dared to conceive a preposterous strength and stability within his own body.

Every act of courage requires great imagination. If I could be certain I could live this way—boldly, with absolute faith and unshakable conviction—I could give up writing. But until that day, I need the daily ritual and devotion of storytelling to keep me awake, to help me pay attention, to prepare me so that when I am called to act, I will be ready.

The lives of the characters in *First, Body* and *Sweet Hearts* are dark and often devastating to follow. Early in *Sweet Hearts*, the narrator says, "There's no safe place in this story." It's often uncomfortable to read what your characters experience.

There is a wonderful essay in Andre Dubus's last collection, *Meditations From a Movable Chair.* He talks about an experience he had before he lost one leg and the use of the other one. He once helped push a man in a wheelchair up a hill. In his essay, he writes about his *failure to imagine* that person's life. He was doing his good deed. And he truly *thought* he was imagining this man's struggle. But it was not until Andre Dubus was in a wheelchair himself that he realized he did not have the "courage for compassion." He was not brave enough to think about every moment of that man's life. He didn't envision him using the toilet or taking a shower or making love. He couldn't begin to fathom how this man saw and touched and dreamed his own body. Until Andre was in that situation himself, he had not been compelled to do the work of the fiction writer; he had not tried to enter the other man's private experience.

I didn't *choose* my people. I didn't decide that I *wanted* to write about a homeless girl in Boston. But Nadine wouldn't be ignored. During the entire time I lived in Boston, I couldn't turn a corner without being among the homeless; I couldn't walk four blocks without seeing runaway and throwaway kids. It is hard to live in this world and look away. It takes a huge amount of energy to keep averting your thoughts and gaze. In Boston, there is astonishing wealth. In Harvard Square, you walk past a woman and her daughter who are wearing matching fur coats. Then you walk past all the homeless kids in torn jackets and muddy jeans. I kept wondering how the rich and the rejected saw each other. I had to confront my own fear and privilege. When I write something, I'm not thinking that other people want to know what I see. I'm not thinking, I want to publish a story. I'm thinking, I need to understand this. If I'm going to live in the world, I need to understand.

Index